The Second World War

Fact and Quiz Book

The Second World War

Fact and Quiz Book

WILLIAM E. SCOTT

Darby Press, Springfield, Pennsylvania

Copyright © 2024 William E. Scott
All rights reserved. No part of this book may be used or reproduced by any means, graphic, electronic, including photocopying, recording, taping, or by any information storage retrieval system without the permission of the author except in the case of brief quotations embodied in critical articles and reviews.

Because of the dynamic nature of the Internet, any web addresses or links contained in this book may have changed since publication and may no longer be valid.

Library of Congress Control Number: 2024907337

ISBN: 979-8-218-38894-2 (paperback)/979-8-218-38893-5 (hardback) Darby Press

Cover photograph by Major Robert Jacquot, U.S. Navy

In memory of
"The Squad"

Vic Morrow
"Sergeant Saunders"
(1929–1983)

Dick Peabody
"Littlejohn"
(1925–1999)

Rick Jason
"Lieutenant Hanley"
(1923–2000)

Pierre Jalbert
"Caje"
(1925–2014)

Jack Hogan
"Kirby"
(1929–2023)

and

my father-in-law

George E. Parsons Jr.
(1938–2024)

"We jumped into the little tractor boat and quickly settled on the deck. 'Oh, God, I'm scared,' said the little Marine, a telephone operator, who sat next to me forward in the boat. I gritted my teeth and tried to force a smile that would not come and tried to stop quivering all over (now I was shaking from fear). I said, in an effort to be reassuring, 'I'm scared, too.' I never made a more truthful statement in all my life......"

—*Robert Sherrod*, war correspondent
Tarawa Atoll
November 20, 1943

"We're deafened by the airplanes, which make a never-ending round, very low; obviously what I thought were German airplanes are quite simply English ones, protecting the landing. Coming from the sea, a dense artificial cloud; it's ominous and begins to be alarming; the first hiss over our heads. I feel cold; I'm agitated. I go home, dress more warmly, close the doors; I get Bernice (a neighbor) to get into the trench, a quick bowl of milk, and we run—just in time! The shells hiss and explode continually......"

—*Marie Louise Osmont*, wife of a Norman doctor
Normandy, France
June 6, 1944

"When daylight came we began to get ourselves organized into a group and the leaders began to come out. When first light came we had between three and four hundred men in our group. I would guess that probably seven or eight hundred men made it out of the ship. I began to find the wounded and dead. The only way I could tell they were dead was to put my finger in their eye. If their pupils were dilated and they didn't blink I assumed they were dead. We would then laboriously take off their life jacket and give it to men who didn't have jackets. In the beginning I took off their dog tags, said The Lord's Prayer, and let them go. Eventually, I got such an armful of dog tags I couldn't hold them any longer......"

—*Dr. Lewis Haynes*, chief medical officer
USS *Indianapolis* (C-35)
July 31, 1945

Contents

Introduction		xi
Chapter One:	Adolf Hitler and the Holocaust	1
	Answers	23
Chapter Two:	Generals and Admirals	27
	Answers	52
Chapter Three:	Battles and Campaigns	55
	Answers	77
Chapter Four:	Weapons	81
	Answers	104
Chapter Five:	Conferences and Code Names	109
	Answers	131
Chapter Six:	Complete the Quotation	143
	Answers	167
Chapter Seven:	G.I. Jargon	171
	Answers	189
Chapter Eight:	Hollywood Goes to War	193
	Answers	214

Chapter Nine:	The Living Room War	217
	Answers	237
Chapter Ten:	The Way We Were: 1939–1945	241
	Answers	263
Appendix: Did You Know?		267
Abbreviations and Acronyms		275
Acknowledgements		277
Endnotes		295
Bibliography		305
About the Author		323

Introduction

On June 6, 2024, the nations of the "Free World" commemorated the 80th anniversary of D-Day, the largest and most complex seaborne invasion in military history. Attending the official ceremonies in Normandy, France were heads of state, foreign dignitaries, and an ever-dwindling number of veterans who participated in the assault. While the surviving heroes who made the world safe for democracy are now diminished by time, the images of that bloody and harrowing day remain their constant companions.

In the early morning hours of June 6, 1944, after five long and arduous years of total war, an armada of 6,000 Allied warships and lesser craft transported 156,000 American, British, and Canadian troops, as well as soldiers and sailors from Australia, Belgium, Czechoslovakia, Denmark, France, Greece, the Netherlands, New Zealand, Norway, and Poland across the English Channel to five pre-determined landing zones along the Normandy coast. Their objective: to free Europe from the tyranny of Nazi domination.

Although meticulously planned down to the last detail, Operation OVERLORD, like most military ventures, was not without its problems. Coalition forces, racked by sea-sickness and unrelenting fear, were forced to contend with inclement weather, malfunctioning equipment, miscommunication, and the intimidating defenses of Germany's *Atlantikwall* (Atlantic Wall), a system of concrete and steel bunkers and fortifications augmented with artillery, machine guns, mortars, and an array of beach obstacles including belts of barbed wire, pressure and radio-controlled mines, and "Rommel's Asparagus" (sharp wooden poles with explosive tips). The prospects of success, especially on OMAHA Beach, were anything but guaranteed and failure was a distinct possibility.

Yet through it all, the grit, determination, and courage exhibited by the "citizen soldier" carried the day. By D+1, the Allies had gained control of the designated sectors; securing a precious, yet precarious foothold on the continent.

By the late summer of 1944, American, British, Canadian, and Free French forces were making slow, but steady progress toward the German frontier, and it seemed that a *Wehrmacht* collapse was inevitable, if not imminent. Some in the Allied high command even predicted that the war would end before the onset of winter. This sentiment, however, was not shared by Adolf Hitler.

Believing that the Anglo-American alliance was fragile and would collapse when faced with a powerful offensive, Hitler proposed an ambitious plan to stave off an Allied invasion of the Fatherland. His aim was to reach the Belgian port of Antwerp thereby driving a wedge between American and British forces. With the western Allies defeated, Germany could then concentrate its remaining assets in a total effort to repel the Soviet juggernaut on the Eastern Front.

On December 16, 1944, what became known as the Battle of the Bulge commenced when three German armies comprised of more than 200,000 troops (with 800,000 in reserve) and over 1,000 tanks, tank destroyers, self-propelled guns, and artillery pieces attacked a seventy-five-mile front along the Franco-Belgium border. The focal point of the operation was the Ardennes Forest, a densely wooded and hilly region defended by inexperienced and battle-worn troops from three United States (US) infantry divisions.

Hoping to replicate the success they achieved in 1940, German forces, aided by frigid and snowy conditions, the worst Europe had experienced in sixty years, drove the dazed and disorganized American soldiers backwards, creating the 'bulge' that gave the battle its legendary name. These initial gains were, however, short-lived. A break in the weather two days before Christmas, allowed Allied aircraft to pound enemy positions while counterattacks from Field Marshal Bernard Montgomery's 21st Army Group in the north and General George S. Patton's Third Army in the south slowed the offensive. Ultimately, Hitler's gamble failed to meet its operational objectives, but more importantly, it squandered valuable resources needed to defend the homeland.

As the Allies converged on Germany from all sides, they uncovered the embodiment of man's inhumanity to man: the Nazi death camps. In all, hundreds of camps were liberated, but not before six million Jews had been murdered while in captivity. If the ordinary foot soldier questioned why he was fighting, he need look no further than the "killing centers" at Auschwitz-Birkenau, Belzec, Chelmno, Majdanek, and Treblinka where human depravity and barbarism knew no bounds.

With the last vestiges of the once invincible German Army collapsing around him, Hitler, in a final act of defiance or cowardice, committed suicide in his Berlin bunker on April 30, 1945.

Germany's final humiliation came eight-days later, when in a little red schoolhouse in the historic city of Reims, France, *Generaloberst* Alfred Jodl, representing the German high command, signed the unconditional surrender of all Axis forces. At 23:01 (CET), some 2,077 days after the invasion of Poland, the guns fell silent in Europe.

For America, the taste of victory was short-lived as another war continued to rage in the Pacific. Beginning with "the unprovoked and dastardly attack by Japan"[1] on December 7, 1941, Japanese naval and land forces scored victory after victory until the tide began to shift in favor of the US at the Battle of Midway in June of 1942. For the next three years American forces moved methodically from island chain to island chain with the heaviest fighting taking place in February and April of 1945 on the islands of Iwo Jima and Okinawa.

With Japan's warlords giving no indication of their willingness to surrender, the Allies prepared for a ground assault on the Japanese home islands, a massive effort that some analysts estimated would result in one million casualties and a prolongation of the war by at least a year. However, there was an alternative.

When President Harry Truman took office following the sudden death of President Franklin D. Roosevelt (FDR) on April 12, 1945, he was briefed on the Manhattan Project, a three-year scientific program to create a weapon of enormous destructive power: the atomic bomb. Given the options of a costly ground invasion, continuing the conventional bombing of Japanese cities or using a new, but as yet unproven weapon, Truman made the difficult decision and chose the atomic bomb.

At 8:15 a.m. on the morning of August 6, 1945, a B-29 *Superfortress* piloted by Colonel Paul W. Tibbets, dropped the first uranium-based weapon on the industrial city of Hiroshima. Three days later, a plutonium-fueled implosion device, the equivalent of 21,000 tons of TNT, was dropped on the port city of Nagasaki. Within forty-eight hours, the Japanese surrendered.

WILLIAM E. SCOTT

On September 2, 1945, six years and one day after World War II began, a contingent of diplomatic and military dignitaries of the Empire of Japan stood solemnly on the teak wood decks of the 57,000-ton battleship USS *Missouri* (BB-63) and signed the Instrument of Surrender. At the conclusion of the twenty-three-minute ceremony, General Douglas MacArthur offered the benediction: "Let us pray that peace be now restored to the world and that God will preserve it always. These proceedings are closed."[2] And with those words, the most cataclysmic of all wars came to an end.

For the "Greatest Generation," who fought in the teeming jungles of Guadalcanal and New Guinea, on the beaches of Normandy, and in the skies over Berlin and Tokyo, World War II was a seminal moment. For the rest of their lives, the valor and sacrifice they exhibited defined who they were and what they represented to their families, friends, and to the world.

Having taught social studies for nearly thirty years, I understand the relevance of history and the lessons it teaches. History not only illuminates the past, it also provides a foundation for understanding the present and is a roadmap to the future.

In a 1965 *Ebony Magazine* article, the American writer and civil rights activist James Baldwin spoke eloquently about the importance of remembering the past. "History, as nearly no one seems to know, is not merely something to be read. And it does not refer merely, or even principally, to the past. On the contrary, the great force of history comes from the fact that we carry it within us, are unconsciously controlled by it in many ways, and history is present in all that we do."[3]

With first-hand accounts of World War II becoming increasingly scarce, due to the dwindling numbers of veterans worldwide, it is crucial that we continue to remember the people, places, and events that shaped the second half of the 20th century and beyond.

Published by Darby Press, *The Second World War Fact and Quiz Book* offers the casual student of history, as well as the experienced military enthusiast, a unique perspective on mankind's deadliest of all conflicts. Comprised of 1,000 thought-provoking questions (and answers, if required), *The Second World War Fact and Quiz Book* contains chapters filled with information on Adolf Hitler and the Holocaust, generals and admirals, battles and campaigns, weapons, conferences and codenames, famous quotes, G.I. Jargon, films, TV programs, America's home front, and an intriguing section entitled "Did You Know?" While many of the questions will be easy to answer, others may prove more challenging. For example:

- How many German generals were taken prisoner at Stalingrad?
- Which US general was also a field marshal in the Philippine Army?
- During what battle did the Japanese launch the first kamikaze attacks?
- Who is the only German soldier buried in Arlington National Cemetery?
- How many American airmen died in training accidents during World War II?
- What was the first American film to depict a simulated Nazi concentration camp?
- How many gallons of oil continue to leak from the USS *Arizona* (BB-63) each day?
- Who was the correspondent who gave the B-17 *Flying Fortress* its iconic nickname?
- On the ABC war drama *The Rat Patrol*, which word was included in the title of every episode?
- Which alumnus of the Ringling Bros. and Barnum & Bailey Clown College impersonated the voice of FDR in the motion picture *Darkest Hour*?

Whatever your level of interest or expertise, you will find *The Second World War Fact and Quiz Book* both enlightening and informative. I hope it will encourage you to read, study, and explore more deeply mankind's most senseless and destructive war.

CHAPTER ONE

Adolf Hitler and The Holocaust

1. Adolf Hitler was born on April 20, 1889 in the Austrian town of _____.
   A. Hallein
   B. Lustenau
   C. Stockerau
   D. Braunau am Inn

2. The fourth of six children born to Alois Hitler and his third wife, Klara Pölzl, Adolf Hitler was baptized into the Christian faith but was never a practicing _____.
   A. Baptist
   B. Catholic
   C. Lutheran
   D. Methodist

3. A sensitive child, Hitler was deeply affected by the death of his brother Edmund in 1900. From which of the following did he die?
   A. Measles
   B. Pneumonia
   C. Scarlet fever
   D. Tuberculosis

4. Hitler's relationship with his father could best be described as _____.
   A. nurturing
   B. supportive
   C. contentious
   D. overprotective

5. Alois's wish was to have his son pursue which of these careers?
   A. Politics
   B. Finance
   C. Teaching
   D. Civil service

6. With the death of his father in 1903, Hitler was free to follow his dream of becoming a(n) _____.
   A. artist
   B. sculptor
   C. architect
   D. musician

7. In 1908, Hitler suffered his greatest loss when his beloved mother succumbed to _____.
   A. meningitis
   B. tuberculosis
   C. heart disease
   D. breast cancer

8. After his mother's passing, Hitler moved to Vienna, Austria where he made a living by _____.
   A. playing the violin
   B. working in a bank
   C. painting and selling postcards
   D. dancing and singing in a bistro

9. During his time in Vienna, Hitler applied to and was twice rejected by this school.
   A. Vienna Conservatory
   B. Academy of Fine Arts
   C. Industrial Arts Institute
   D. Royal Academy of Music

10. Name the two political figures who influenced Hitler's early political views.
    A. Martin Kirschner and Karl Daub
    B. Adolf Wermuth and Julius Bahsen
    C. Georg von Schönerer and Karl Lueger
    D. Wilhelm Dilthey and Arthur Hobrecht

11. Prior to the outbreak of World War I, Hitler voluntarily enlisted in the Bavarian Army. To which unit was he assigned?
    A. 4th Reserve Cavalry Platoon
    B. 8th Reserve Mortar Regiment
    C. 11th Reserve Artillery Brigade
    D. 16th Reserve Infantry Regiment

12. According to historian Brendan Simms, who did Hitler believe posed the greatest threat to Germany?[4]
    A. Russia
    B. France
    C. America
    D. Great Britain

13. Why did Hitler call December 2, 1914, "the happiest day of my life"?[5]
    A. He killed his first French soldier.
    B. He shot down an English patrol plane.
    C. He was promoted to the rank of sergeant.
    D. He received the Iron Cross (Second Class).

14. During the Battle of the Somme in 1916, Hitler was wounded while serving as a(n) _____.
    A. tank driver
    B. artillery spotter
    C. dispatch runner
    D. ambulance driver

15. On August 4, 1918, Hitler received one of Germany's highest decorations. Can you name it?
    A. Cross of Honor
    B. War Merit Cross
    C. Iron Cross (First Class)
    D. Star of the Grand Cross

16. Less than one month before the end of World War I, Hitler was transported to a field hospital. Why?
    A. He was suffering from trench foot.
    B. He had received a shrapnel wound.
    C. He had been blinded in a gas attack.
    D. He had attempted to commit suicide.

17. After learning of Germany's surrender on November 11, 1918, Hitler reportedly said it was _____
    A. "the loneliest day of my life."
    B. "the end of Teutonic civilization."
    C. "the greatest villainy of the century."
    D. "the final chapter of German history."[6]

18. What did Hitler call those who negotiated the armistice that sealed Germany's fate?
    A. "The Son's of Evil"
    B. "The Elders of Zion"
    C. "The Devils of Death"
    D. "The November Criminals"[7]

19. According to Syracuse University Professor Emeritus David H. Bennett, the First World War left a lasting imprint on European society because _____

    A. "It resulted in…another revolution in Germany, which brought Hitler to power."
    B. "It led to the Russian Revolution, the collapse of the German Empire, and the collapse of the Hapsburg Monarchy …"
    C. "It led to the restructuring of the political order in Europe and in other parts of the world, particularly in the Middle East."[8]
    D. All of the above

20. In what way(s) did the Versailles Treaty make it difficult for Germany's new government, the Weimar Republic, to succeed?
    A. Germany had to reduce the size of its army to fifty thousand men.
    B. Germany had to pay reparations to compensate the victorious powers.
    C. Germany had to accept guilt for starting the war and for all the damage it caused.
    D. B and C

21. Following the war, Hitler returned to Munich and found work as a(n) _____.
    A. waiter at the Hirschgarten Beer Hall
    B. tour guide at the Nymphenburg Palace
    C. lecturer at the Bavarian Academy of Fine Arts
    D. intelligence officer for the *Reichswehr* (German armed forces)

22. On September 12, 1919, Hitler attended a meeting of the German Worker's Party (DAP). Who was the honorary chairman and founder of the DAP?
    A. Anton Drexler
    B. Gustav Drexler
    C. Wilhelm Drexler
    D. Frederick Drexler

23. Impressed by Hitler's oratorical skills, Drexler encouraged him to read his anti-Semitic and anti-Marxist pamphlet entitled _____.
    A. "How Fascism Works"
    B. "My Political Awakening"
    C. "The Anatomy of Revolution"
    D. "Emerging From the Darkness"

24. When Hitler joined the DAP, his membership number was _____.
    A. 333
    B. 444
    C. 555
    D. 666

25. In April 1920, the DAP became the National Socialist German Workers Party (NSDAP) or Nazi Party with Hitler as its leader. What is the English translation of the NSDAP slogan, *Ein Volk, Ein Reich, Ein Führer?*
    A. "One Hand, One Heart, One Leader"
    B. "One People, One Realm, One Leader"
    C. "One Nation, One People, One Leader"
    D. "One Voice, One Country, One Leader"

26. The cornerstone of the NSDAP was Hitler's 25 Point Program. It included the following demands *except* _____
    A. "land and territory for the sustenance of our people."
    B. "membership and an equal vote in the League of Nations."
    C. "abolition of the mercenary troops and formation of a national army."
    D. "equality of rights for the German people in respect to the other nations."[9]

27. Hitler's power and authority increased significantly when the NSDAP incorporated the *Sturmabteilung (SA)*, a paramilitary organization, into its ranks. The *SA*'s more recognizable name was the _____.
    A. "Hitlerians"
    B. "Brownshirts"
    C. "Grey Wolves"
    D. "Aryan Guards"

28. What function did the *SA* perform?
    A. Distribute anti-Semitic literature
    B. Fight other paramilitary groups
    C. Provide protection for Nazi officials
    D. All the above

29. On November 8–9, 1923, Hitler and his followers attempted a government takeover in what became known as the _____.
    A. National Socialist *Putsch*
    B. Communist Party *Putsch*
    C. Weimar Republic *Putsch*
    D. Munich Beer Hall *Putsch*

30. Who was the well-respected German general who participated in the failed coup d'état?
    A. Erich Ludendorff
    B. Wilhelm Groener
    C. Max von Bahrfeldt
    D. Karl von Fasbender

31. Convicted of high treason for his role in the *Putsch,* Hitler received a _____ sentence in Landsberg Prison.
    A. one-year
    B. five-year
    C. eight-year
    D. twelve-year

32. While incarcerated, Hitler dictated his now infamous autobiography *Mein Kampf* to which fellow inmate?
    A. Karl Fiehler
    B. Rudolf Hess
    C. Herbert Backe
    D. Franz Breithaupt

33. A rambling diatribe, *Mein Kampf* included all of the following anti-Semitic accusations *except* _____.
    A. "he [the Jew] intentionally and cunningly misrepresents himself by infecting the masses with the vile and disgusting rhetoric of the Bolshevik hordes."
    B. "he has found the weapon which lets him dispense with democracy and in its stead allows him to subjugate and govern the peoples with a dictatorial and brutal fist."
    C. "he contaminates art, literature, the theater, makes a mockery of natural feeling, overthrows all concepts of beauty and sublimity, of the noble and the good, and instead drags men down into the sphere of his own base nature."

D. "he refuses the state the means for its self-preservation, destroys the foundations of all national self-maintenance and defense, destroys faith in the leadership, scoffs at its history and past, and drags everything that is truly great into the gutter."[10]

34. What was the original title of *Mein Kampf*?
    A. *Why Germany Lost the Great War*
    B. *My Role in Bringing Stability to a Failed Regime*
    C. *The Struggle to Save the West from the Mongrel Hoards in Russia*
    D. *Four and a Half Years of Struggle Against Lies, Stupidity, and Cowardice*

35. Name the political figure who found *Mein Kampf* both superficial and tedious.
    A. Joseph Stalin
    B. Edvard Beneš
    C. Benito Mussolini
    D. Francisco Franco

36. Released from prison after serving only eight months, Hitler sought to reestablish his control of the Nazi Party. In 1925, he counterbalanced the burgeoning authority of the *SA* by creating his own personal bodyguard unit, the _____.
    A. *Schutzstaffel (SS)*
    B. *Geheimpolizei (GP)*
    C. *Soldatenjungen (SJ)*
    D. *Feuerwehrmann (FE)*

37. In which of the following years did the Nazis first stand candidates for the German legislature (*Reichstag*)?
    A. 1926
    B. 1927
    C. 1928
    D. 1929

38. Until the rise of the Nazis in the early 1930s, this left-wing party had the largest representation in the *Reichstag*.
    A. German People's Party
    B. Social Democratic Party
    C. Bavarian Libertarian Party
    D. Communist Workers' Party

39. Hitler realized that using violence to take control of the government would not work. He instead sought to gain power through legal means. What event allowed Hitler to re-enter the political arena in 1929?
    A. Hamburg trade union riots
    B. America's Wall Street Crash
    C. French occupation of the Ruhr
    D. Increased crime in German cities

40. To increase their popularity with the German people, the Nazis promised all of the following *except* _____.
    A. employment and wages would increase
    B. Jews would be protected by the government
    C. all German-speaking people would be united in one country and there would be special laws for foreigners
    D. farmers would be given their land, pensions would improve, and public industries such as electricity and water would be owned by the state

41. In the 1932 German presidential election, Hitler ran against and lost to President Paul von Hindenburg. What was Hitler's campaign slogan?
    A. "The Time is Now"
    B. "Blood and Wealth"
    C. "Food and Prosperity"
    D. "Hitler Over Germany"

42. Despite losing the presidency, the Nazi Party won this percentage of the seats in the *Reichstag*.
    A. 31%
    B. 34%
    C. 37%
    D. 39%

43. After meeting Hitler for the first time, Hindenburg said that he was only qualified to _____.
    A. work in a bank
    B. collect garbage
    C. run a post office
    D. manage a brothel

44. Following a succession of three ineffective chancellors, Hindenburg reluctantly named Hitler to the post on _____.
    A. March 30, 1932
    B. August 15, 1932
    C. January 30, 1933
    D. February 25, 1933

45. Which political figure lobbied for Hitler's appointment as chancellor believing that he could be controlled?
    A. Erich Kessler
    B. Franz von Papen
    C. Alfred Hildebrandt
    D. Gustav Stresemann

46. Including Hitler, how many Nazi Party members held seats in the first *Reich* cabinet in 1933?
    A. One
    B. Three
    C. Seven
    D. Eight

47. On February 27, 1933, arson destroyed the 19th century *Reichstag* building. Who was the twenty-four-year-old Dutch communist who was arrested and later executed for the crime?
   A. Frans van Hall
   B. Jan van der Geest
   C. Christiaan van Eeghen
   D. Marinus van der Lubbe

48. In the wake of the Reichstag fire, Hindenburg issued the "Decree for the Protection of People and the *Reich*." Popularly known as the *Reichstag* Fire Decree, it gave government officials the power to _____.
   A. suppress publications
   B. abolish political organizations
   C. suspended due process rights
   D. All of the above

49. On March 23, 1933, the passage of the Enabling Act laid the foundation for the Nazi dictatorship. Officially the "Law to Remedy the Distress of the People and the *Reich*," it _____.
   A. banned all non-Aryans from owning property
   B. prohibited the sale of all Jewish publications in Germany
   C. called for the removal of President Hindenburg from office
   D. allowed the government to issue laws without the consent of Germany's legislature

50. In April 1933, the first significant anti-Jewish legislation was passed by the German government. What was it called?
   A. "Law for the Protection of German Industry"
   B. "Law for the Security of all Aryan Citizens of *Reich*"
   C. "Law for the Restoration of the Professional Civil Service"
   D. "Law for the of the Confinement of the Mentally Challenged"

51. During this period, the Nazis enacted hundreds of anti-Semitic decrees and directives including the Nuremberg Race Laws which prohibited _____.
    A. marriages between Jews and citizens of Germany
    B. Jewish couples from conceiving more than two children
    C. relations outside of marriage between Jews and citizens of Germany
    D. A and C

52. With whom did the Nazis sign a concordat or agreement, in July 1933?
    A. Switzerland
    B. Great Britain
    C. Catholic Church
    D. League of Nations

53. The murder of German diplomat Ernst vom Rath, by a seventeen-year-old Polish Jew on November 9, 1938, led to forty-eight hours of violence including the destruction of thousands of synagogues, homes, businesses, and cemeteries. It was the event that marked a turning point in the lives of Germany's Jewish population.
    A. *Todesnacht* (Night of Death)
    B. *Scheckensnacht* (Night of Terror)
    C. *Dunkelheitnacht* (Night of Darkness)
    D. *Kristallnacht* (Night of Broken Glass)

54. On May 13, 1939, a passenger liner sailed from Hamburg, Germany carrying 900 Jews attempting to flee Nazi persecution. "Abandoned by the world,"[11] the majority of refugees were turned away by the US, Cuba, and Canada before the ship eventually returned to Germany. What was the name of the ill-fated ship?
    A. MS *St. Louis*
    B. MS *St. Charles*
    C. MS *St. Augustine*
    D. MS *St. Petersburg*

55. Seen as a threat to Hitler and the German Army, the *SA* hierarchy, including its leader Ernst Röhm, was arrested and executed between June 30 and July 2, 1934. This three-day orgy of violence was known as the _____.
    A. "Night of the Iguanas"
    B. "Night of the Generals"
    C. "Night of the Long Knives"
    D. "Night of the Hummingbirds"

56. Following the death of President Paul von Hindenburg on August 2, 1934, Hitler declared himself *Führer*, the unquestioned leader of Nazi Germany. Which factor contributed to his meteoric rise?
    A. He restored pride in the nation after its stinging defeat in World War I.
    B. He was portrayed as a messiah who was sent to save the German people.
    C. He introduced a new style of politics e.g., mega-rallies and public meetings.
    D. All of the above

57. Scholars agree that the genocide of European Jews occurred between 1933 and 1945. Hatred toward the Jewish people was based on a pseudo-scientific field of study popular in the late 19th and early 20th centuries known as _____.
    A. Eugenics
    B. Diuretics
    C. Bubonics
    D. Heuristics

58. During the 1920s, German Jewish families _____.
    A. rejected German culture
    B. were well-established in German society
    C. maintained their own dietary, dress, and linguistic traditions
    D. B and C

59. Why did the Germans people accept Hitler's hatred of the Jews?
    A. He was a persuasive speaker.
    B. They were caught up in the Nazi hysteria.
    C. His arguments were based on fact-based information.
    D. A and B

60. The Holocaust was different from other genocides in that _____.
    A. it was government sanctioned
    B. it took place in the 20th century
    C. it was aimed at an entire population
    D. All of the above

61. Nothing symbolized the inhumanity of the Nazi regime more than the incarceration and treatment of Germany's "perceived" enemies. Established in March 1933, and situated on the grounds of a vacant World War I munitions plant in southwest Germany, it became the first Nazi concentration camp for political prisoners.
    A. Dachau
    B. Treblinka
    C. Kaiserwald
    D. Esterwegen

62. In 1934, which *SS* unit was given control over the concentration camp system?
    A. "Mountain"
    B. "Grenadier"
    C. "Death's Head"
    D. "Urban Assault"

63. Created in 1937, _____ was one of the largest facilities constructed in Nazi Germany.
    A. Arbeitsdorf
    B. Buchenwald
    C. Ochstumsand
    D. Herzogenbusch

64. How were most Jews transported to the camps?
    A. Ship
    B. Train
    C. Airplane
    D. Horse and wagon

All concentration camp inmates would ultimately be required to wear on their uniforms a colored badge to show the nature of their "crimes." Match the color with the group it represented.

65. _____ Red   A. Gypsie
66. _____ Blue   B. Anarchists
67. _____ Pink   C. Emigrants
68. _____ Brown   D. Homosexuals
69. _____ Purple   E. Jehovah's Witnesses

70. If not executed by the Nazis, inmates generally died as a result of _____.
    A. malnutrition
    B. overcrowding
    C. harsh working conditions
    D. All of the above

71. What type of punishment could inmates expect from their Nazi captors if they did *not* follow orders?
    A. Physical abuse
    B. Food rationing
    C. Solitary confinement
    D. All of the above

72. The life expectancy of a concentration camp inmate was an estimated _____.
    A. seventeen days
    B. thirty-one days
    C. forty-two days
    D. sixty-eight days

List in chronological order, the events that put Germany on the path to war.

73. _____ A. Hitler remilitarizes the Rhineland
74. _____ B. Germany and Italy sign the Pact of Steel
75. _____ C. Austria is annexed by Germany (*Anschluss*)
76. _____ D. *Luftwaffe* units take part in the Spanish Civil War
77. _____ E. Germany occupies and annexes Bohemia and Moravia-Silesia
78. _____ F. Munich Agreement allows Germany to annex Czechoslovakia

79. On September 1, 1939, the Second World War began with Germany's incursion into Poland. In order to isolate the Jewish population, the Nazis created "ghettos." Where were the majority of ghettos located?
    A. Poland
    B. Romania
    C. Hungary
    D. Germany

80. There were three types of ghettos. What were they?
    A. Female / Labor / Transit
    B. Political / Medical / Labor
    C. Labor / Destruction / Male
    D. Open / Closed / Destruction

81. Approximately how many ghettos were located in Nazi-occupied territories?
    A. 1,140
    B. 1,359
    C. 1,683
    D. 1,975

82. On June 22, 1941, German forces invaded the Soviet Union. Following Hitler's troops into the newly occupied territories were *Einsatzgruppen* or "special operation units." Their primary function was to _____.
    A. identify potential German opposition
    B. distribute food and clothing to the peasant population
    C. conduct public executions aimed at annihilating entire Jewish communities
    D. A and C

83. The first documented massacre perpetrated by the *Einsatzgruppen* occurred in the Ukraine. Where did the executions take place and how many Jews were murdered?
    A. Izyum / 18,564
    B. Odessa / 26,403
    C. Babi Yar / 33,771
    D. Avdiivka / 41,362

84. Which Nazi official issued orders in the summer of 1941 calling for a plan to address the systematic liquidation of Europe's Jewish population?
    A. Adolf Hitler
    B. Karl Kauffmann
    C. Hermann Göring
    D. Wilhelm Klagges

85. On October 20, 1942, high-ranking Nazi and government officials convened in this suburb of Berlin to coordinate the "Final Solution of the Jewish Question."[12]
    A. Hagen
    B. Aachen
    C. Wannsee
    D. Mannheim

86. Who was the SS officer charged with creating the blueprint for the extermination of European Jewry?
    A. Theodor Daluege
    B. Heinrich Himmler
    C. Kurt Eichenbacher
    D. Reinhard Heydrich

87. From the German point of view, the "Final Solution" required _____.
    A. blind fanaticism
    B. careful planning and efficiency
    C. indifference to the plight of the Jews
    D. All of the above

88. Of the estimated 44,000 camps created by Nazis Germany and its allies, which ones were designated as "killing centers"?
    A. Dachau, Kaiserwald, Plaszow, Belzec, Slavonska-Pozega, and Zemun
    B. Edineti, Bisingen, Dautmergen, Treblinka, Chelmno, and Dortmettingen
    C. Belzec, Chelmno, Sobibór, Treblinka, Auschwitz II-Birkenau, and Majdanek
    D. Rawa-Russkaja, Jastrebarsko, Stara-Gradiska, Salapils, Buchenwald, and Westerbork

89. According to official documents, _____ were normally selected for execution.
    A. Young children
    B. Pregnant women
    C. Intellectually disabled
    D. All of the above

90. The decision as to which individuals would be put to death was generally determined by whom?
    A. Guards
    B. Inmates
    C. Commandant
    D. Medical personnel

91. One of the many misconceptions surrounding the Holocaust is that the Jews did not resist or fight back against the Nazis. On the contrary, Jews conducted acts of resistance in every German-occupied country and in the territories of Germany's Axis partners. The Jews were however, hampered by _____.
    A. an inability to obtain weapons
    B. the overwhelming power of the Nazis
    C. fear of retribution against family members
    D. All of the above

92. Where *did* the Jews rebel against their Nazi captors?
    A. Bisingen, Edineti, Treblinka, Chelmno, and Salapils
    B. Treblinka, Babi Yar, Sobibór, Janówska, and Auschwitz
    C. Buchenwald, Majdanek, Gross-Rosen, Stutthuf, and Vaivara
    D. Osthofen, Sachsenhausen, Dachau, Kauen, and Arbeitsdorf

93. In August 1945, with the war still raging in the Pacific, the Allied nations created the _____ to punish Nazi war criminals.
    A. European Court of Inquiry
    B. International Military Tribunal
    C. Allied Council for Social Justice
    D. National War Crimes Commission

94. Following Germany's defeat, the Nuremberg trials were held from November 20, 1945 to October 1, 1946 to try Nazi defendants for invading sovereign countries and committing atrocities against the population. How many leading Nazis were charged?
    A. Twenty-two
    B. Twenty-four
    C. Twenty-seven
    D. Twenty-eight

95. What charge was made against them?
    A. Conspiracy to commit war crimes
    B. Conspiracy to commit crimes against peace
    C. Conspiracy to commit crimes against humanity
    D. All of the above

96. How many Nazis were ultimately sentenced to death?
    A. Eight
    B. Twelve
    C. Fourteen
    D. Seventeen

97. What could have been done to aid the Jews?
    A. Imprisonment of Germans and Italians in Allied countries
    B. Permission for temporary admission of refugees to a host nation
    C. Frequent warnings to the Nazi government and citizenry that those participating in the annihilation of the Jews would be held strictly accountable
    D. B and C

98. This was the only country that permitted large-scale Jewish immigration during World War II.
    A. Portugal
    B. El Salvador
    C. Mozambique
    D. Dominican Republic

99. Which title was given to people who assisted Jews during World War II?
    A. Children of Israel
    B. Prophets of Judah
    C. Soldiers of Virtue
    D. Righteous Gentiles

100. Name the national holiday in Israel that commemorates those who lost their lives during the Holocaust.
    A. Tisha B'Av
    B. Yom HaShoah
    C. Rosh Hashanah
    D. Yom Hazikaron

Chapter One Answers

1. D. Braunau am Inn
2. B. Catholic
3. A. Measles
4. C. contentious
5. D. Civil service
6. A. artist
7. D. breast cancer
8. C. painting and selling postcards
9. B. Academy of Fine Arts
10. C. Georg von Schönerer and Karl Lueger
11. D. 16th Reserve Infantry Regiment
12. D. Great Britain
13. D. He received the Iron Cross (Second Class).
14. C. dispatch runner
15. C. Iron Cross (First Class)
16. C. He had been blinded in a gas attack.
17. A. "the loneliest day of my life."
18. D. "The November Criminals"
19. D. All of the above
20. D. B and C
21. D. intelligence officer for the *Reichswehr* (German armed forces)
22. A. Anton Drexler
23. B. "My Political Awakening"
24. C. 555
25. B. "One People, One Realm, One Leader"
26. B. "membership and an equal vote in the League of Nations."
27. B. "Brownshirts"
28. D. All of the above
29. D. Munich Beer Hall *Putsch*
30. A. Erich Ludendorff
31. B. five-years

32. B. Rudolf Hess
33. A. "he [the Jew] intentionally and cunningly misrepresents himself by infecting the masses with the vile and disgusting rhetoric of the Bolshevik hordes."
34. D. *Four and a Half Years of Struggle Against Lies, Stupidity, and Cowardice*
35. C. Benito Mussolini
36. A. *Schutzstaffel (SS)*
37. C. 1928
38. B. Social Democratic Party
39. B. America's Wall Street Crash
40. B. Jews would be protected by the government
41. D. "Hitler Over Germany"
42. C. 37%
43. C. run a post office
44. C. January 30, 1933
45. B. Franz von Papen
46. B. Three
47. D. Marinus van der Lubbe
48. D. All of the above
49. D. allowed the government to issue laws without the consent of Germany's legislature
50. C. "Law for the Restoration of the Professional Civil Service"
51. D. A and C
52. C. Catholic Church
53. D. *Kristallnacht* (Night of Broken Glass)
54. A. MS *St. Louis*
55. C. "Night of the Long Knives"
56. D. All of the above
57. A. Eugenics
58. D. B and C
59. D. A and B
60. D. All of the above
61. A. Dachau
62. C. "Death's Head"

THE SECOND WORLD WAR FACT AND QUIZ BOOK

63. B. Buchenwald
64. B. Train
65. B. Anarchists
66. C. Emigrants
67. D. Homosexuals
68. A. Gypsies
69. E. Jehovah's Witnesses
70. D. All of the above
71. D. All of the above
72. C. forty-two days
73. A. Hitler remilitarizes the Rhineland
74. D. *Luftwaffe* units take part in the Spanish Civil War
75. C. Austria is annexed by Germany (*Anschluss*)
76. F. Munich Agreement allows Germany to annex Czechoslovakia
77. E. Germany occupies and annexes Bohemia and Moravia-Silesia
78. B. Germany and Italy sign the Pact of Steel
79. A. Poland
80. D. Open / Closed / Destruction
81. A. 1,140
82. D. A and C
83. C. Babi Yar / 33,771
84. C. Hermann Göring
85. C. Wannsee
86. D. Reinhard Heydrich
87. D. All of the above
88. C. Belzec, Chelmno, Sobibór, Treblinka, Auschwitz II-Birkenau, and Majdanek
89. D. All of the above
90. D. Medical personnel
91. D. All of the above
92. B. Treblinka, Babi Yar, Sobibór, Janówska, and Auschwitz
93. B. International Military Tribunal
94. B. Twenty-four
95. D. All of the above

96. B. Twelve
97. D. B and C
98. D. Dominican Republic
99. D. Righteous Gentiles
100. B. Yom HaShoah

CHAPTER TWO
Generals And Admirals

1. Who was the only US general to command a division, a corps, and an army during World War II?
   A. LeRoy Irwin
   B. Manton Eddy
   C. Lucian Truscott
   D. Geoffrey Keyes

2. A senior British admiral, _____ coordinated the evacuation of Dunkirk and later directed Allied naval forces for the invasion of France.
   A. James Curtis
   B. Dudley Pound
   C. Bertram Ramsey
   D. Arthur Cunningham

3. On June 13, 1943, this great-grandson of a Civil War hero was the first American general killed in action in the European Theater of Operations (ETO).
   A. Ulysses S. Grant III
   B. Stonewall Jackson III
   C. William T. Sherman III
   D. Nathan Bedford Forrest III

4. An artillery officer during the First World War, he held the distinction of commanding both *Luftwaffe* and *Wehrmacht* forces during the Second World War.
   A. Hugo Sperrle
   B. Albert Kesselring
   C. Reinhard Richter
   D. Gerd von Rundstedt

5. What did the phrase "Old Blood and Guts" mean to General George Patton's troops?
   A. "His guts, our blood"
   B. "Our guts, his blood"
   C. "His blood, our guts"
   D. "Our blood, his guts"[13]

6. Name the Imperial Japanese Army (IJA) officer who presided at the surrender of US and Filipino forces on the island of Corregidor.
   A. Seizo Arisue
   B. Hiroshi Akita
   C. Saburo Hayashi
   D. Masaharu Homma

7. Prior to his appointment as commanding general, ETO, Dwight Eisenhower was ____.
   A. military aide to FDR
   B. chief of the War Plans Division
   C. acting superintendent of West Point
   D. chief of staff to General Douglas MacArthur

8. Written in 1925 by British journalist Hector Bywater, it *may* have inspired Admiral Isoroku Yamamoto to attack Pearl Harbor.
   A. *Conflict in Asia*
   B. *Navies and Nations*
   C. *The Great Pacific War*
   D. *Sea Power in the Pacific*

9. The youngest US major general to command a division, ____ would go on to serve in the Kennedy administration as ambassador to France.
   A. James Gavin
   B. Leland Hobbs
   C. Ernest Dawley
   D. Myron Shimkus

10. An expert in jungle warfare, "The Tiger of Malaya" was executed on February 23, 1946, for war crimes relating to the Bataan Death March.
    A. Senjuro Hayashi
    B. Torashira Matsui
    C. Hajime Kuribayashi
    D. Tomoyuki Yamashita

11. One of America's architects of victory in World War II, _____ ironically, never led troops in battle.
    A. John Hines
    B. Thomas Handy
    C. George Marshall
    D. Joseph McNarney

12. Germany's last living field marshal died on July 2, 1973, at the age of eighty-one. Who was he?
    A. Ernst Busch
    B. Walter Model
    C. Gunther von Kluge
    D. Ferdinand Schörner

13. An outspoken proponent of fighter aircraft, _____ commanded the famed "Flying Tigers" and later the US Fourteenth Air Force in the China-Burma-India Theater.
    A. Billy Mitchell
    B. George Kenney
    C. Claire Chennault
    D. Willis Bridesberg

14. On June 22, 1940, which French general signed an armistice with Germany in a railroad car?
    A. Ferdinand Foch
    B. Henri Demarche
    C. Maurice Gamelin
    D. Charles Huntziger

15. His failure to act decisively following the Allied landing at Anzio resulted in his removal as commander of the US VI Corps.
    A. John Lucas
    B. George Bell
    C. Ernest Dawley
    D. Peter Luckenbill

16. A graduate of the Imperial Japanese Naval Academy (Class of 1908), he led the Pearl Harbor Strike group.
    A. Seiichi Ito
    B. Chuichi Nagumo
    C. Shigeyoshi Inoue
    D. Isoroku Yamamoto

17. Who was the US brigadier general, and son of a former president, who was posthumously awarded the Medal of Honor for his leadership on D-Day?
    A. Grover Cleveland Jr.
    B. Benjamin Harrison Jr.
    C. William McKinley Jr.
    D. Theodore Roosevelt Jr.

18. The chief of the *Oberkommando der Wehrmacht*, _____ signed the unconditional surrender document at Reims, France on May 7, 1945.
    A. Alfred Jodl
    B. Karl Uberlitz
    C. Gerhard Kittleman
    D. Walther von Brauchitsch

19. A skilled administrator and logistician, this West Point graduate served as military governor of the American sector of occupied Germany from 1947 to 1949.
    A. Lucius Clay
    B. Edwin Kelly
    C. Norman Cota
    D. Clarence Huebner

20. Educated at Saint-Cyr, a military academy in Paris, _____ replaced General Maurice Gamelin as commander-in-chief of French forces during the Battle of France.
    A. Henri Bouchot
    B. Philippe Leclerc
    C. Alphonse Georges
    D. Maxime Weygand

21. One of only nine US Marines to receive the Distinguished Service Cross and the Navy Cross during World War I, his US 4th Marine Division took part in the Battle of Iwo Jima.
    A. Clifton Cates
    B. Keller Rockey
    C. Graves Erskine
    D. Douglas LeBrock

22. A vice admiral in the Imperial Japanese Navy (IJN) and "Father of the Kamikaze," _____, committed ritualistic suicide (*hara-kiri*) following the unconditional surrender of Japan.
    A. Seiji Sato
    B. Takijiro Onishi
    C. Akira Nakayama
    D. Naoto Kawamura

23. On March 30, 1945, he became the highest-ranking US general killed in the ETO.
    A. Frank Mahin
    B. Maurice Rose
    C. William Upshur
    D. Clarence Tinker

24. Adolf Hitler's former chauffeur and bodyguard, _____, led the Sixth *Panzer* Army during the Battle of the Ardennes.
    A. Kurt Meyer
    B. Paul Hausser
    C. Felix Steiner
    D. Sepp Dietrich

25. One of General George Patton's most aggressive subordinates, he commanded the US Eighth Army during the Korean War until his untimely death in December 1950.
    A. Hugh Gaffey
    B. Edwin Patrick
    C. Walton Walker
    D. Clarence Huebner

26. The son of a Prussian Army officer and a World War I veteran, his ideas helped to revolutionize modern tank warfare.
    A. Josef Nehring
    B. Heinz Guderian
    C. Reinhard Moltke
    D. Ernst Volckheim

27. Which USN rear admirals were killed in action during the Naval Battle of Guadalcanal on November 13, 1942?
    A. Frank Akers and Charles Cecil
    B. Donald Moon and Robert English
    C. Henry Mullinnix and John Wilcox
    D. Daniel Callaghan and Norman Scott

28. A serving officer in the British Army, he held commands in the Middle East, Norway, and India, and led the 8th Army prior to General Bernard Montgomery.
    A. Neil Ritchie
    B. Alan Cunningham
    C. Richard McCreery
    D. Claude Auchinleck

29. Name the US three-star general and four-star admiral who were relieved of duty following the Pearl Harbor disaster.
    A. Richard Lee and William F. Halsey
    B. Geoffrey Keyes and Charles McMorris
    C. Walter Short and Husband E. Kimmel
    D. Jonathan Wainwright and Robert Miller

30. The recipient of the *Pour le Mérite* for valor during the First World War, _____ achieved fame commanding Germany's "Ghost Division" during the Battle of France.
    A. Ludwig Halder
    B. Erwin Rommel
    C. Hermann Balck
    D. Otto Eberhardt

31. A graduate of the Massachusetts Institute of Technology, with a doctorate in aeronautical engineering, he led the first US air raid on Tokyo.
    A. Chuck Yeager
    B. Elwood Quesada
    C. Millard Harmon
    D. Jimmy Doolittle

32. Chief of the RAF Fighter Command during the Battle of Britain, _____ was instrumental in establishing the first radar-based air defense system.
    A. Charles Portal
    B. Arthur Tedder
    C. Hugh Dowding
    D. Edward Ellington

33. Posthumously promoted to brigadier general in 1945, he organized and trained the US 1st Ranger Battalion for the invasion of North Africa.
    A. James Walker
    B. Lawrence Belford
    C. William O. Darby
    D. Mitchell Sutherland

34. Who became commander-in-chief of the Japanese Combined Fleet after the death of Admiral Isoroku Yamamoto?
    A. Jinichi Kusaka
    B. Mineichi Koga
    C. Gunichi Mikawa
    D. Toshihira Inoguchi

35. In his wartime memoir *Crusade in Europe*, General Dwight Eisenhower referred to this US general as someone who "shunned the limelight and was so modest and retiring that the public probably never became fully cognizant of his value."[14]
    A. Carl Spaatz
    B. Barton Yount
    C. Harold Huglin
    D. Frederick Castle

36. Twice decorated Hero of the Soviet Union, his forces took part in the capture of Berlin in April 1945.
    A. Ivan Konev
    B. Aleksei Brusilov
    C. Rodion Malinovshy
    D. Valentine Korabelnikov

37. The commanding general of the US Fifth Army in Italy, he subsequently served as US High Commissioner of Austria and president of The Citadel, The Military College of South Carolina.
    A. Mark Clark
    B. Oliver Leese
    C. Vyvyan Pope
    D. Louis Dubail

38. During the Battle of Midway, this Japanese rear admiral and veteran of the Pearl Harbor operation was killed in action aboard the aircraft carrier *Hiryu*.
    A. Dewa Shigeto
    B. Kojuro Nozaki
    C. Chiaki Matsuda
    D. Tamon Yamaguchi

39. Recognized for his easygoing manner, he earned the moniker the "G.I.'s General."
    A. Ralph Eaton
    B. Omar Bradley
    C. Lawton Collins
    D. Thomas Waverly

40. The chief architect of Great Britain's strategic bombing campaign against Germany, he was "the sort of commander who emerges in a crisis, one for which his knowledge and experience happen to have particularly prepared him."[15]
   A. Arthur Harris
   B. Roderick Carr
   C. William Sholto Douglas
   D. Robert Brooke-Popham

41. Following the Axis victory at the Battle of Kasserine Pass, who replaced Major General Lloyd Fredendall as the commanding officer of the US II Corps?
   A. Terry Allen
   B. James Chaney
   C. George Patton
   D. Joseph Webber

42. This high-ranking SS officer and brother-in-law to Eva Braun was executed for desertion in April 1945.
   A. Otto Kumm
   B. Georg Keppler
   C. Wilhelm Mohnke
   D. Hermann Fegelein

43. How many US generals were taken prisoners of war (POW) following the fall of the Philippines?
   A. Eleven
   B. Thirteen
   C. Eighteen
   D. Nineteen

44. Known as "Lawrence of Manchuria" for his military exploits in China, _____ was executed for war crimes on December 23, 1948.
    A. Isamu Cho
    B. Ando Teibi
    C. Sadao Araki
    D. Kenji Doihara

45. The United States Military Academy (USMA) class of 1915 ("The Class the Stars Fell On") graduated 164 second lieutenants. How many became generals by the end of World War II?
    A. Twenty
    B. Fifty-nine
    C. Sixty-seven
    D. Eighty-eight

46. A rear admiral in the IJN and a brilliant naval tactician, _____ reinforced and resupplied Japanese troops during the Guadalcanal campaign via the "Tokyo Express."
    A. Raizo Tanaka
    B. Fushimi Yoshika
    C. Chuichi Nagumo
    D. Nobutake Kondo

47. The commanding general of USA Ground Forces, he was killed by "friendly fire" on July 25, 1944, near Saint-Lô, France.
    A. Jacob Devers
    B. Martin Smith
    C. Leslie McNair
    D. Warren Jeffries

48. Which British Army officer formed the special operations unit known as the "Chindits"?
    A. Orde Wingate
    B. Michael Barker
    C. Walter Lentaigen
    D. Archibald Wavell

49. Educated at the United States Naval Academy (USNA) and a recipient of the Medal of Honor, _____ was tactical commander of US naval forces at the Battle of the Coral Sea.
    A. John McCain
    B. Frank Fletcher
    C. Bernard Austin
    D. George Mitchell

50. Chief of the General Staff of the *Luftwaffe*, he died from injuries sustained in the July 20, 1944 assassination attempt on Adolf Hitler.
    A. Heinz Mueller
    B. Gunther Korten
    C. Hans Jeschonnek
    D. Ritter von Brandt

51. An implacable commander, _____ began the war with the 305th Bombardment Group in the ETO and later served in the Pacific Theater of Operations (PTO) where he developed and executed the air offensive against Japan.
    A. Richard Ellis
    B. Curtis LeMay
    C. Donald Dawson
    D. Ellard Michelsen

52. Who was the only high-ranking German officer ever awarded the Grand Cross of the Iron Cross?
    A. Werner Kreipe
    B. Hermann Göring
    C. Josef Kammhuber
    D. Gerd von Rundstedt

53. The first Native-American to graduate from the USNA (Class of 1917), _____ commanded Task Group Three during the Battle of the Philippine Sea.
    A. Joseph Clark
    B. Arthur Bristol
    C. Robert Carney
    D. Arthur Radford

54. Called "General Offensive," he was mortally wounded by Ukrainian guerrilla fighters in 1944.
    A. Igor Grechko
    B. Nikolai Vatutin
    C. Fyodor Tolbukhin
    D. Andrey Yeryomenko

55. This veteran of the Spanish-American War and World War I became the only US admiral to simultaneously hold the combined titles of commander-in-chief, US Fleet, and chief of Naval Operations.
    A. Ernest King
    B. Elmo Zumwalt
    C. Thomas Moorer
    D. Forrest Sherman

56. A member of Baron Manfred von Richthofen "Flying Circus," _____ went on to serve as head of procurement for the *Luftwaffe* before committing suicide in 1941.
    A. Ernst Udet
    B. Alfred Sturm
    C. Erhard Milch
    D. Werner Anton

57. FDR's chief of staff from 1942 to 1945, Admiral William Leahy held several titles during his fifty-two years of government service including chief of Naval Operations, governor of Puerto Rico, and this post.
    A. Secretary of the Navy
    B. Ambassador to France
    C. Special Envoy to Spain
    D. Proconsul in Australia

58. Nicknamed "The Fox," his Soviet 1st Guard's Cavalry Corps led the initial counterattack against German forces at the Battle of Moscow.
    A. Ivan Konev
    B. Pavel Belov
    C. Josef Vatutin
    D. Dimitri Gorchakov

59. The commanding general of the 101st Airborne Division from 1944 to 1945, he later served as US ambassador to South Vietnam in the Johnson administration.
    A. Edward Miles
    B. Maxwell Taylor
    C. William Schmidt
    D. Lyman Lemnitzer

60. Considered a master of defensive warfare, _____ found more honor in suicide than surrender when he committed *hara-kiri* during the Battle of Okinawa.
    A. Takeo Obato
    B. Keiji Shibazaki
    C. Yoshitsugu Saito
    D. Mitsuru Ushijima

61. One of only four men to achieve the rank of US fleet admiral, he became an aviator at the age of fifty-two. Naval historian Thomas Alexander Hughes described him as the "Patton of the Pacific."[16]
    A. John Towers
    B. Mark Mitscher
    C. Chester Nimitz
    D. William F. Halsey

62. A British major general and military engineer, _____ was responsible for developing many of the specialized armored vehicles used during and after D-Day.
    A. Percy Hobart
    B. Lionel Jeffries
    C. Reginald Beck
    D. Colin Colander

63. Recipient of the Distinguished Service Medal and the Navy Cross, he commanded the US Marine Fifth Amphibious Corps during the Battle of Tinian.
    A. Ralph Keyser
    B. Harry Schmidt
    C. Matthew Brice
    D. William Clement

64. The Chief of the Imperial General Staff from 1941 to 1944, _____ is the only British field marshal buried in Arlington National Cemetery.
    A. Sir John Dill
    B. Sir Alan Brooke
    C. Sir John Vereker
    D. Sir Edmund Ironside

65. Name the US naval hero referenced in a 1971 Paul McCartney song.
    A. Arleigh Burke
    B. Marc Mitscher
    C. Frank Sampson
    D. William F. Halsey

66. An admiral in the French Navy and the commander-in-chief of Vichy military forces, _____ was assassinated by monarchist Fernand Bonnier de La Chapelle on Christmas Eve 1942.
    A. Maurice Martin
    B. François Darlan
    C. Gaston-Henri Billotte
    D. Émile René Lemonnier

67. The commanding general of the Services of Supply in the ETO, his biographer called him "an outspoken advocate of equal opportunity for black soldiers" and the man who "kept the Allied troops fed, their guns loaded, and their tanks gassed up."[17]
    A. John Lee
    B. Walter Taylor
    C. Thomas Handy
    D. Clifton Monroe

68. A Dutch naval officer, _____ followed maritime tradition and went down with his ship at the Battle of the Java Sea.
    A. Johan Evertsen
    B. Karel Doorman
    C. Gerard Callenburgh
    D. Lodewiji van Bylandt

69. In 1935, which future US five-star general was appointed military advisor to Philippine President Manuel Quezon with the rank of field marshal?
    A. Omar Bradley
    B. Henry Arnold
    C. Matthew Ridgway
    D. Douglas MacArthur

70. The acknowledged "Father of the U-boat," _____ served as president of Germany during the final days of the Third Reich.
    A. Karl Dönitz
    B. Erich Raeder
    C. Heinz Stuffel
    D. Peter Bracker

71. Commander-in-chief of the US Pacific Fleet from 1940 to 1941, he warned of possible Japanese aggression against American naval and military forces preceding the attack on Pearl Harbor.
    A. William Pratt
    B. Joseph Reeves
    C. Frank Schofield
    D. James Richardson

72. Known as the Soviet Union's "Marshal of Victory," _____ was admired by General Dwight Eisenhower and feared by Joseph Stalin.
    A. Georgy Zhukov
    B. Nikita Khruschev
    C. Vasily Sokolovsky
    D. Boris Rokossovsky

73. The first African American to achieve the rank of brigadier general, he served in the Office of the Inspector General from 1941 to 1944.
    A. Ronald Bailey
    B. Vincent Brooks
    C. Jacob Washington
    D. Benjamin O. Davis Sr.

74. A graduate of the Royal Military Academy at Sandhurst and a thrice wounded veteran of World War I, _____ rose to become supreme commander of Allied forces in the Mediterranean in 1944.
    A. Daniel Beak
    B. Keith Franklin
    C. Brian Horrocks
    D. Harold Alexander

75. Who was the first commanding officer of the US Eighth Air Force and an early pioneer in the field of strategic bombing?
    A. Ira Eaker
    B. John Cannon
    C. Frederick Bissell
    D. Samuel Anderson

76. This future Japanese admiral lost two fingers on his left hand during the Battle of Tsushima in 1905.
    A. Saigo Judo
    B. Kato Tomosaburo
    C. Akiyama Saneyuki
    D. Isoroku Yamamoto

77. Born in Indianapolis, Indiana in 1895, he served as chief of staff of Supreme Headquarters Allied Expeditionary Force and later as ambassador to the Soviet Union and director of the Central Intelligence Agency.
    A. Harry Butcher
    B. Jeremiah Hawley
    C. William Donovan
    D. Walter Bedell Smith

78. An outspoken *Luftwaffe* fighter ace with over one hundred confirmed kills, _____ became Germany's youngest general at the age of thirty.
    A. Ernst Buffa
    B. Adolf Galland
    C. Erwin Erdmann
    D. Walter Boenicke

79. The first Filipino graduate of the USMA (Class of 1914), he served as the commanding officer of the 41st Infantry Division during the Battle of Bataan. In 1944, he was captured by Japanese forces and executed.
    A. Vincente Lim
    B. Sergio Mabini
    C. Amterio Ricarte
    D. Emilio Aguinaldo

80. On January 31, 1943, outnumbered and surrounded, _____ surrendered the remnants of the German Sixth Army to Soviet forces at Stalingrad.
    A. Kurt Student
    B. Wilhelm List
    C. Friedrich Paulus
    D. Joachim Berthold

81. Name the USMC general who is referred to as the "Father of Modern Amphibious Operations."
    A. George Ellis
    B. Holland Smith
    C. Edward Craig
    D. Oliver Windell

82. A Marshal of the Soviet Union, he commanded the Western Front during the Battle of Kursk.
    A. Markian Popov
    B. Leonid Govorov
    C. Kirill Meretskov
    D. Vasily Sokolovsky

83. Recognized for his keen intellect and grasp of naval tactics, _____ led carrier forces during the Battle of Midway and the Battle of the Philippine Sea.
    A. Donald "Razor Sharp" Duncan
    B. Frederick "Egg Head" Sherman
    C. Paul "The Answer Man" Talbot
    D. Raymond "Electric Brain" Spruance

84. One of the ugliest officers in the IJN, "The Gargoyle" rose to the rank of vice admiral before serving as the last commander-in-chief of the Combined Fleet.
    A. Kiyoshi Imai
    B. Okitsugi Arao
    C. Jisaburo Ozawa
    D. Nobuyoshi Muto

85. A graduate of the USNA (Class of 1917) and a decorated aviator, he helped plan the Doolittle Raid on Tokyo.
    A. John Hoover
    B. Winston James
    C. Donald Duncan
    D. Arthur Radford

86. The military governor of Nazi-occupied Paris, _____, allegedly ignored Adolf Hitler's order to destroy the city.
    A. Hugo Feldmann
    B. Gustav von Clausen
    C. Erwin Bovenschulte
    D. Dietrich von Choltitz

87. Who was the only US four-star general to witness all three German and Japanese surrender ceremonies?
    A. Carl Spaatz
    B. William Simpson
    C. Courtney Hodges
    D. Alfred Gruenther

88. A respected hero of the Great War, the "Lion of Verdun" served as chief of state for the Vichy government from 1940 to 1944.
    A. Robert Nivelle
    B. Philippe Pétain
    C. Charles de Gaulle
    D. Maxime Weygand

89. Known as the "Father of the American Airborne," _____ helped devise the blueprint for air operations on D-Day.
    A. Charles B. Hall
    B. William C. Lee
    C. Aaron P. Daniels
    D. William R. Schmidt

90. Chief of the Army General Staff, he signed the Japanese Instrument of Surrender aboard the USS *Missouri* (BB-63) on September 2, 1945.
    A. Saigo Judo
    B. Heltaro Kimura
    C. Yoshijiro Umezu
    D. Kabayama Sukenari

91. A posthumous Medal of Honor recipient, _____ was killed aboard his flagship the USS *Arizona* (BB-39) during the attack on Pearl Harbor.
    A. Isaac Kidd
    B. Trevor Morris
    C. Robert Davidson
    D. Warren Chapman

92. How many German generals were taken prisoner at Stalingrad?
    A. Eleven
    B. Fifteen
    C. Eighteen
    D. Twenty-four

93. A USNA graduate (Class of 1899), _____ was commandant of the 14th Naval District in Hawaii on December 7, 1941.
    A. Claude Bloch
    B. Richard Leigh
    C. Samuel Robison
    D. Herman Fredericks

94. This highly decorated field marshal led the British Expeditionary Force during the Battle of France.
    A. Allan Adair
    B. Daniel Beak
    C. John Vereker
    D. Victor Fortune

95. Educated at the USMA (Class of 1909), _____ became the first person of Hawaiian ethnicity to attain the rank of brigadier general.
    A. Augustus Lu
    B. Neil Richards
    C. Albert Lyman
    D. Henry Kamano

96. Who led the Japanese Fourth Fleet at the Battle of the Coral Sea?
    A. Yukio Seki
    B. Aritomo Goto
    C. Shigeyoshi Inoue
    D. Kiyohide Ozawa

97. During the Battle of the Ardennes, what was Brigadier General Anthony McAuliffe's response when asked to surrender the besieged city of Bastogne?
    A. "Nuts!"
    B. "Dammed if we will!"
    C. "You must be joking!"
    D. "Hell no, we won't go!"[18]

98. Name the soldier-statesman who led the Polish government-in-exile before his untimely death in 1943.
    A. Wladyslaw Sikorski
    B. Henryk Domrzalski
    C. Stanislaw Bojanowski
    D. Leopold Komorowski

99. Financier Bernard Baruch described him as "one of the few Americans who really understands total war." A USMA graduate (Class of 1914), _____ oversaw the construction of USA training facilities and supply of all American military forces during World War II.[19]
    A. Maxwell Murray
    B. Edmund Gregory
    C. Brehon Somervell
    D. Robert Hasbrouck

100. Which high-ranking Nazi war criminal cheated the hangman by ingesting a potassium cyanide capsule shortly before his scheduled execution?
A. Alfred Jodl
B. Erich Raeder
C. Wilhelm Keitel
D. Hermann Göring

Chapter Two Answers

1. C. Lucian Truscott
2. C. Bertram Ramsey
3. D. Nathan Bedford Forrest III
4. B. Albert Kesselring
5. D. "Our blood, his guts"
6. D. Masaharu Homma
7. B. chief of the War Plans Division
8. C. *The Great Pacific War*
9. A. James Gavin
10. D. Tomoyuki Yamashita
11. C. George Marshall
12. D. Ferdinand Schörner
13. C. Claire Chennault
14. D. Charles Huntziger
15. A. John Lucas
16. B. Chuichi Nagumo
17. D. Theodore Roosevelt Jr.
18. A. Alfred Jodl
19. A. Lucius Clay
20. D. Maxime Weygand
21. A. Clifton Cates
22. B. Takijiro Onishi
23. B. Maurice Rose
24. D. Sepp Dietrich
25. C. Walton Walker
26. B. Heinz Guderian
27. D. Daniel Callaghan and Norman Scott
28. D. Claude Auchinleck
29. C. Walter Short and Husband E. Kimmel
30. B. Erwin Rommel
31. D. Jimmy Doolittle

32. C. Hugh Dowding
33. C. William O. Darby
34. B. Mineichi Koga
35. A. Carl Spaatz
36. A. Ivan Konev
37. A. Mark Clark
38. D. Tamon Yamaguchi
39. B. Omar Bradley
40. A. Arthur Harris
41. C. George Patton
42. D. Hermann Fegelein
43. C. Eighteen
44. D. Kenji Doihara
45. B. Fifty-nine
46. A. Raizo Tanaka
47. C. Leslie McNair
48. A. Orde Wingate
49. B. Frank Fletcher
50. B. Gunther Korten
51. B. Curtis LeMay
52. B. Hermann Göring
53. A. Joseph Clark
54. B. Nikolai Vatutin
55. A. Ernest King
56. A. Ernst Udet
57. B. Ambassador to France
58. B. Pavel Belov
59. B. Maxwell Taylor
60. D. Mitsuru Ushijima
61. D. William F. Halsey
62. A. Percy Hobart
63. B. Harry Schmidt
64. A. Sir John Dill
65. D. William F. Halsey

66. B. François Darlan
67. A. John Lee
68. B. Karel Doorman
69. D. Douglas MacArthur
70. A. Karl Dönitz
71. D. James Richardson
72. A. Georgy Zhukov
73. D. Benjamin O. Davis Sr.
74. D. Harold Alexander
75. A. Ira Eaker
76. D. Isoroku Yamamoto
77. D. Walter Bedell Smith
78. B. Adolf Galland
79. A. Vincent Lim
80. C. Friedrich Paulus
81. B. Holland Smith
82. D. Vasily Sokolovsky
83. D. Raymond "Electric Brain" Spruance
84. C. Jisaburo Ozawa
85. C. Donald Duncan
86. D. Dietrich von Choltitz
87. A. Carl Spaatz
88. B. Philippe Pétain
89. B. William C. Lee
90. C. Yoshijiro Umezu
91. A. Isaac Kidd
92. D. Twenty-four
93. A. Claude Bloch
94. C. John Vereker
95. C. Albert Lyman
96. C. Shigeyoshi Inoue
97. A. "Nuts!"
98. A. Wladyslaw Sikorski
99. C. Brehon Somervell
100. D. Hermann Göring

CHAPTER THREE
BATTLES AND CAMPAIGNS

1. During this battle, eleven African American soldiers from the 333rd Artillery Battalion were tortured and killed by German SS troops in what became known as the Wereth 11 Massacre.
   A. Salerno
   B. Ardennes
   C. Carentan
   D. Heilbronn

2. Military historian John Keegan called it "the most stunning and decisive blow in the history of naval warfare."[20]
   A. Battle of Jutland
   B. Battle of Midway
   C. Battle of Leyte Gulf
   D. Battle of the Java Sea

3. A strategy proposed by Air Marshal Trafford Leigh-Mallory during the Battle of Britain, it called for multiple RAF fighter squadrons to attack incoming *Luftwaffe* aircraft in one large formation.
   A. Big Wing
   B. Twin Wing
   C. Large Wing
   D. Double Wing

4. Part of the Aleutian Islands campaign, the _____ was the first land engagement fought on American soil since the War of 1812.
   A. Battle of Jitra
   B. Battle of Attu
   C. Battle of Kiska
   D. Battle of Endau

5. According to American journalist and author Adam Hochschild, the initial battle of World War II was the _____.[21]
   A. Spanish Civil War of 1936
   B. Saudi-Yemeni War of 1934
   C. Sino-Japanese War of 1937
   D. Soviet-Finnish War of 1939

6. Between 1943 and 1945, Admiral William F. Halsey's US Third Fleet took part in all of the following operations *except* _____.
   A. Formosa
   B. Okinawa
   C. Guadalcanal
   D. Sunda Strait

7. Which US division suffered the heaviest casualties during the Battle of the Hürtgen Forest?
   A. 20th Infantry
   B. 23rd Infantry
   C. 28th Infantry
   D. 29th Infantry

8. After defeating a small but courageous band of American defenders, the Japanese controlled this atoll until September 4, 1945.
   A. Ducie Island
   B. Wake Island
   C. Enoki Island
   D. Tench Island

9. Where did the so-called "Champagne Campaign" take place?
   A. Northern Italy
   B. Southern France
   C. Northern Portugal
   D. Southern Germany

10. Including troops from Finland, Hungary, Italy, and Slovakia, how many divisions did Germany amass for the invasion of the Soviet Union?
    A. 122
    B. 174
    C. 187
    D. 198

11. The home of present-day Kadena Air Base, it was the site of the last major battle of World War II.
    A. Tinian
    B. Kyushu
    C. Shikoku
    D. Okinawa

12. During the Battle of Iwo Jima, who photographed the raising of the American flag on Mount Suribachi?
    A. Robert Capa
    B. Joe Rosenthal
    C. Dickey Chapelle
    D. W. Eugene Smith

13. Air power played a decisive role in which surface action?
    A. Battle of the Coral Sea
    B. Battle of the North Cape
    C. Battle of the Cabot Strait
    D. Battle of the Denmark Strait

14. The controversial destruction of the Benedictine monastery at _____ occurred during the _____ campaign.
    A. Monte Cassino / Italian
    B. Monte Bianco / Borneo
    C. Monte Filippo / Aleutian
    D. Monte Selja / Norwegian

15. Name the Pacific showdown that included the classic naval tactic "Capping the T."
    A. Battle of Gababutu
    B. Battle of Mobile Bay
    C. Battle of Surigao Strait
    D. Battle of Cam Ranh Bay

16. Germany's operational objective during the Battle of the Ardennes was to capture the Belgium city of _____.
    A. Ghent
    B. Brussels
    C. Antwerp
    D. Mechelen

17. After the fall of Berlin, approximately how many German females were brutally assaulted by Soviet troops?
    A. One million
    B. Two million
    C. Four million
    D. Eight million

18. On the anniversary of the Battle of Britain, August 18, 1940, is remembered as "The Hardest Day" because of the _____.
    A. *Luftwaffe* bombing of the Palace of Westminster
    B. sinking of the HMS *Endeavor* in the English Channel
    C. German invasion of Great Britain's Channel Islands
    D. heavy losses sustained by both the RAF and *Luftwaffe*

19. All of the following were part of the New Guinea campaign *except* _____.
    A. Battle of Biak
    B. Battle of Wau
    C. Battle of Morotai
    D. Battle of Rottnest

20. The Battle of Brody, the largest German-Soviet tank battle of 1941, was fought in the triangle of three Ukrainian towns. What were they?
    A. Brody, Dubno, and Lutsk
    B. Bakhmut, Abenaki, and Brody
    C. Pavlohrad, Brody, and Luhansk
    D. Brody, Zaporizhzhia, and Donetsk

21. Originally built as an underground hospital, it served as General Douglas MacArthur's headquarters during the Battle of Corregidor.
    A. Halcon Tunnel
    B. Malinta Tunnel
    C. Canlaon Tunnel
    D. Banahaw Tunnel

22. Between October 1941 and August 1943, much of this Ukrainian city was destroyed in four separate battles.
    A. Odessa
    B. Donetsk
    C. Kharkov
    D. Mykolaiv

23. The _____ resulted in more US casualties than Japanese casualties.
    A. Battle of Peleliu
    B. Battle of Formosa
    C. Battle of Iwo Jima
    D. Battle of Wake Island

24. Which engagement was *not* part of the Battle of the Netherlands?
    A. Rotterdam
    B. Karlskrona
    C. Afsluitdijk
    D. Grebbeberg

25. Made famous by the reality TV series *Deadliest Catch*, _____ in the Aleutians was the site of a Japanese carrier strike on US forces on June 3–4, 1942.
    A. Dutch Harbor
    B. Kodiak Harbor
    C. Pelican Harbor
    D. Skagway Harbor

26. How long did the siege of Leningrad, also called the "900-day siege," actually last?
    A. 841 days
    B. 864 days
    C. 872 days
    D. 887 days

27. The Landing Vehicle, Tracked (LVT) or "Amtrac" was first used for amphibious operations during this Pacific battle.
    A. Inchon
    B. Tarawa
    C. Iwo Jima
    D. Khe Sanh

28. Name the only country to face Germany with a fully mechanized army during the invasion of France.
    A. Canada
    B. Sweden
    C. Belgium
    D. Great Britain

29. Where did the Battle of Edison's Ridge take place?
    A. Eniwetok
    B. Guadalcanal
    C. New Britain
    D. Makin Island

30. Name the titanic clash between German and Soviet armor that began on July 5, 1943.
    A. Battle of Arras
    B. Battle of Kursk
    C. Battle of Arracourt
    D. Battle of 73 Easting

31. Which battle featured a killing field known as "Hacksaw Ridge"?
    A. Saipan
    B. Temor
    C. Okinawa
    D. Guadalcanal

32. During the _____, Germany's U-boats sank roughly 3,500 Allied merchant ships.
    A. Battle of the Barents Sea
    B. Battle of the Mediterranean
    C. Battle of the Glomma River
    D. Battle of the North Atlantic

33. Which of the following was *not* an American objective at the outset of the Battle of Manila?
    A. Seize the Filipino Congress
    B. Reclaim the Malacanan Palace
    C. Evacuate civilians held at the University of Santo Tomas
    D. Liberate the one thousand POWs held captive in the San Juan de Dios Hospital

34. Fought between April 9 and June 8, 1940, the _____ involved fighting on land and sea.
    A. Battle of Narvik
    B. Battle of Kiruna
    C. Battle of Bergen
    D. Battle of Skagen

35. What celebrated Hollywood director was wounded while filming the Battle of Midway?
    A. John Ford
    B. George Cukor
    C. Howard Hawks
    D. Fred Zinnemann

36. Recognized as the last naval duel between German and British battleships, it took place on December 26, 1943.
    A. Battle of Cape Burnas
    B. Battle of Audierne Bay
    C. Battle of the River Plate
    D. Battle of the North Cape

37. In the wartime memoir *With the Old Breed*, author E. B. Sledge chronicled his experiences during the battles of _____.
    A. Saipan and Guam
    B. Peleliu and Okinawa
    C. Iwo Jima and Borneo
    D. Kwajalein and Shikoku

38. The Battle of Leros was part of which campaign?
    A. Po Valley
    B. East Indies
    C. Dodecanese
    D. Central Burma

39. A two-term governor from South Dakota and the first commissioner of the American Football League, USMC Captain Joe Foss received the Medal of Honor for exceptional bravery during the _____.
    A. Battle of Pleiku
    B. Battle of Leyte Gulf
    C. Battle of Guadalcanal
    D. Battle of Komar Straits

40. It was Italy's only tank victory of the Second World War.
    A. Hadi bu
    B. Bir el Gubi
    C. Qalansiyah
    D. Sidi Bou Jid

41. Of the following US divisions, which one participated in the Battle of Buna-Gona?
    A. 12th Cavalry
    B. 32nd Infantry
    C. 18th Cavalry
    D. 25th Infantry

42. Germany's failure to defeat the Soviet Union was due to all of the following reasons *except* (the) _____.
    A. poor strategic planning
    B. superiority of Soviet tanks
    C. inability to replenish manpower and equipment
    D. Russian troops were better trained than German troops

43. What was the largest carrier vs. carrier engagement of the Pacific War?
    A. Battle of the Coral Sea
    B. Battle of the Bismarck Sea
    C. Battle of the Philippine Sea
    D. Battle of the East China Sea

44. Despite its concrete and steel fortifications, gun emplacements, and underground facilities, the _____ proved virtually ineffective against German mechanized forces during the Battle of France.
    A. Voltaire Line
    B. Maginot Line
    C. Bonaparte Line
    D. Joan of Arc Line

45. Where did the first organized *kamikaze* attacks take place?
    A. Battle of Makin
    B. Battle of Leyte Gulf
    C. Battle of Macassar Strait
    D. Battle of Cape Esperance

46. Great Britain's earliest ground victory against German forces came at _____.
    A. Rabat
    B. Bardia
    C. Mechili
    D. El Alamein

47. The first example of urban warfare in the PTO occurred during the _____.
    A. Battle of Truk
    B. Battle of Pusan
    C. Battle of Tinian
    D. Battle of Manila

48. Which of Hitler's strategic decisions contributed to Germany's defeat in World War II?
    A. Creating a two-front war by invading the Soviet Union
    B. Failing to destroy the British Expeditionary Force at Dunkirk
    C. Deciding *not* to declare war on the US following the attack on Pearl Harbor
    D. A and B

49. During this naval battle, USN Lieutenant Commander Robert Dixon uttered the now famous phrase "Scratch one flattop!"[22]
    A. Midway
    B. Coral Sea
    C. Lucas Bend
    D. Samar Island

50. As a result of its role in the North African campaign, the American military _____.

   A. produced battle-hardened troops that would be needed in future operations
   B. gained valuable experience in amphibious, desert, mountain, and urban warfare
   C. learned what it was like to be bombed, and machine-gunned and to keep fighting
   D. All of the above

51. Can you name the two US divisions that took part in the Battle of Peleliu?
   A. 3rd Marine and 1st Infantry
   B. 6th Marine and 2nd Cavalry
   C. 1st Marine and 81st Infantry
   D. 4th Marine and 20th Armored

52. The invasion of _____ was also known as the "September Campaign."
   A. France
   B. Poland
   C. Belgium
   D. Holland

53. An epic thirty-five-day struggle, it featured fighting on Hill 362 and Hill 382.
   A. Battle of Tarawa
   B. Battle of Honshu
   C. Battle of Iwo Jima
   D. Battle of Kwajalein

54. Where and when did the first major tank engagement of the Second World War take place?
   A. Hannut / May 12, 1940
   B. Wroclaw / August 18, 1941
   C. Bytom / September 1, 1940
   D. Libourne / October 28, 1941

55. During this naval action the USS *Lexington* (CV-16) was scuttled.
    A. Battle of Karavia
    B. Battle of the Coral Sea
    C. Battle of Christmas Island
    D. Battle of Blackett Straight

56. Only one of the following statements about the Battle of Britain is accurate.
    A. It was only fought at night.
    B. There were virtually no civilian casualties.
    C. Pilots from four different nations took part.
    D. It was the first battle fought entirely in the air.

57. The American defeat at the Battle of Bataan led to the largest surrender of US forces since (the) _____.
    A. Queen Anne's War
    B. Revolutionary War
    C. First Seminole War
    D. American Civil War

58. What was the ultimate outcome of the Allied landings at Anzio?
    A. the liberation of Rome
    B. a seaborne assault on Naples
    C. an airborne invasion of Taranto
    D. the surrender of all German forces in Italy

59. Military historian and author Harold Goldberg called it "D-Day in the Pacific."[23]
    A. Battle of Saipan
    B. Battle of Eniwetok
    C. Battle of Kula Gulf
    D. Battle of Mindanao

60. This iconic structure survived the Battle of Britain and became a source of inspiration to the English people.
    A. Buckingham Palace
    B. St. Paul's Cathedral
    C. Inner Temple Library
    D. Great Synagogue of London

61. For exhibiting uncommon valor during the attack on Pearl Harbor, he became the first American to receive the Medal of Honor during World War II.
    A. Private Harold Agerholm
    B. Corporal Hershel Williams
    C. Lieutenant Jack Montgomery
    D. Chief Petty Officer John Finn

62. According to Field Marshal Albert Kesselring, the heavy loss of German aircraft during the one-day Battle of The Hague contributed to the *Luftwaffe's* defeat at the _____.
    A. Battle of Crete
    B. Battle of Britain
    C. Battle of Dunkirk
    D. Battle of Smolensk

63. These are the four Japanese carriers that were sunk during the Battle of Midway.
    A. *Akagi*, *Kaga*, *Soryu*, and *Hiryu*
    B. *Kaga*, *Unyo*, *Taiyo*, and *Shokaku*
    C. *Hosho*, *Kaiyo*, *Hiryu*, and *Zuikaku*
    D. *Katsuragi*, *Hiryu*, *Amagi*, and *Kaga*

64. Fortified with barbed wire, pillboxes, machine gun emplacements, minefields, and fifteen German divisions, the _____ was designed to thwart the Allied advance in Italy.
    A. Gustav Line
    B. Tuscan Line
    C. Augustus Line
    D. Mussolini Line

65. The lessons learned from the _____ prepared the Allies for future operations in the Central Pacific.
    A. Battle of Guam
    B. Battle of Saipan
    C. Battle of Tarawa
    D. Battle of Kapyong

66. Approximately how many Allied troops took part in the invasion of Sicily?
    A. 100,000
    B. 125,000
    C. 150,000
    D. 180,000

67. Which three-day battle occurred during the Dutch East Indies campaign?
    A. Trikei
    B. Romar
    C. Dunado
    D. Balikpapan

68. The pride of the British Royal Navy, _____, was sunk by the *Bismarck* during the Battle of the Denmark Strait on May 24, 1941.
    A. HMS *Hood*
    B. HMS *Defiant*
    C. HMS *Victory*
    D. HMS *Suffolk*

69. Implemented in 1943, this strategy was designed to isolate heavily fortified Japanese-held positions, reduce Allied casualties, and maximize military resources.
    A. "Hit and Run"
    B. "Island Hopping"
    C. "Pacific Vaulting"
    D. "Fire and Movement"

70. What was the major difference between combat in World War I and World War II?
    A. During World War I, battles were fought largely by troops in opposing trenches. By World War II, fighting was no longer limited to the traditional battlefield. Unrestricted warfare occurred on land, in the air, and on and under the high seas.
    B. In World War I, troops had at their disposal a limited number of weapons, including machine guns and poison gas. Technological advancements between the wars meant that a variety of more sophisticated and powerful weapons were available during World War II.
    C. During World War I, over eight million soldiers died as a result of wounds and/or disease before receiving adequate medical attention. By World War II, advancements in the field of medical science, including the development of plasma and antibiotics, and the close proximity of aid stations and field hospitals increased the likelihood that the wounded would survive.
    D. All of the above

71. Of the estimated 400,000 British and French troops that took part in the Battle of Dunkirk, how many were evacuated?
    A. 145,000
    B. 296,000
    C. 338,000
    D. 783,000

72. List the following Pacific campaigns in chronological order.
    1. Solomon Islands
    2. Mariana Islands
    3. Volcano and Ryukyu Islands
    4. Gilbert and Marshall Islands
    A. 4., 3., 1., 2.
    B. 1., 4., 2., 3.
    C. 3., 2., 4., 1.
    D. 2., 1., 3., 4.

73. According to official sources, approximately _____ Soviet civilians were killed during the Battle of Stalingrad?
    A. 20,000
    B. 35,000
    C. 40,000
    D. 55,000

74. Considered a relatively easy objective, the _____ cost the USMC over 3,000 casualties in a period of seventy-two hours.
    A. Battle of Majuro
    B. Battle of Tarawa
    C. Battle of Eniwetok
    D. Battle of Gavabutu

75. Situated between UTAH and OMAHA beaches, it was the promontory that US Rangers scaled on D-Day.
    A. Pointe du Hoc
    B. Pointe du Mere
    C. Pointe du Sagres
    D. Pointe du Etretat

76. Where did the Battle of Kolombangara take place?
    A. Mariana Islands
    B. Aleutian Islands
    C. Marshall Islands
    D. Solomon Islands

77. Of the following Allied operations, which one signaled the beginning of the Italian campaign?
    A. Bombing of Naples
    B. Amphibious landings at Salerno
    C. British airborne assault on Sorento
    D. Sinking of the Italian battleship *Enzo*

78. The Battle of Kwajalein taught the Japanese that (a) _____.
    A. poison gas was necessary
    B. American troops were inferior
    C. they could not defeat the Allies
    D. beachline defense was ineffective

79. Who said "What General [Maxime] Weygand called the Battle of France is over. I expect the Battle of Britain is about to begin?"[24]
    A. Adolf Hitler
    B. Francisco Franco
    C. Benito Mussolini
    D. Winston Churchill

80. The first American naval engagement since the Spanish-American War, the _____ took place on January 24, 1942.
    A. Battle of Shilshole Bay
    B. Battle of Balikpapan Bay
    C. Battle of East Matagorda Bay
    D. Battle of Passamaquoddy Bay

81. Because of heavy losses and significant opposition from the civilian population, Adolf Hitler vowed that it was the last time an airborne assault would be conducted by the *Fallschirmjäger* (German paratroopers). Which battle was Hitler referring to?
    A. Crete
    B. Malta
    C. Corsica
    D. Gibraltar

82. Fought between October 25 and 27, 1942, the Battle of the Santa Cruz Islands resulted in the loss of the American aircraft carrier _____.
    A. USS *Hornet* (CV-8)
    B. USS *Andover* (CV-10)
    C. USS *Princeton* (CVL-23)
    D. USS *Saginaw Bay* (CVE-82)

83. Name the bridge that was a pivotal objective for Allied forces during the Battle of Arnhem.
    A. Rhine
    B. Moses
    C. Hovenring
    D. Eilandbrug

84. When did the Japanese air, land, and sea assault on Wake Island begin?
    A. December 8, 1941
    B. December 11, 1941
    C. December 21, 1941
    D. December 30, 1941

85. A war correspondent for United Press International, he first coined the term "bulge" when writing about the Battle of the Ardennes.[25]
    A. Hank Gorrell
    B. James Aldridge
    C. Larry Newman
    D. Walter Cronkite

86. What made the island of Okinawa strategically important to the Allies?
    A. It was a major source of crude oil.
    B. It provided anchorage for US warships.
    C. It could be used as an airfield for B-29s.
    D. B and C

87. The _____ was *not* part of the Dutch East Indies campaign.
    A. Battle of Dubio
    B. Battle of Ambon
    C. Battle of Manado
    D. Battle of Tarakan

88. At the Battle off Samar, which US naval task group faced a formidable Japanese force led by the super battleship *Yamato*?
    A. "Taffy 1"
    B. "Taffy 2"
    C. "Taffy 3"
    D. "Taffy 4"

89. Where and when did American and German troops fight on the same side?
    A. Battle of Badgastein / June 1, 1942
    B. Battle of Castle Itter / May 5, 1945
    C. Battle of Schlossberg / July 9, 1944
    D. Battle of Amstetten / April 8, 1943

90. The primary objective of the Solomons campaign was to _____.
    A. protect the air and sea route to Australia
    B. cut off Japan's air and naval base at Rabaul
    C. secure a US staging area for the invasion of Iwo Jima
    D. establish a supply link with US forces on Guadalcanal

91. In which North African country was the Battle of Hill 609 fought?
    A. Sudan
    B. Tunisia
    C. Algeria
    D. Morocco

92. Approximately how many non-combat casualties did the US Sixth Army suffer in the Battle of Luzon?
    A. 57,000
    B. 63,000
    C. 84,000
    D. 93,000

93. Built in 1935, it was the site of the first glider assault by German troops in May 1940.
    A. Fort Golubac
    B. Fort Delamont
    C. Fort Eben-Emael
    D. Fort San Sebastian

94. The largest *banzai* charge of the Pacific War occurred during the _____.
    A. Battle of Guam
    B. Battle of Tinian
    C. Battle of Saipan
    D. Battle of Honshu

95. Why was the Battle of Stalingrad significant?
    A. It was Germany's first major defeat.
    B. It was the decisive battle on the Eastern Front.
    C. It was Germany's first victory against Soviet forces.
    D. It was the only time a German field marshal committed suicide.

96. Military planners expected the fighting on Iwo Jima to last for seventy-two hours. In fact, the Japanese held out for _____.
    A. eleven days
    B. fifteen days
    C. nineteen days
    D. thirty-seven days

97. Germany lost the Battle of Britain for all of the following reasons *except* _____.
    A. The RAF possessed superior numbers of aircraft.
    B. Germany's strategy shifted from military to civilian targets.
    C. Downed RAF pilots were rescued, and *Luftwaffe* pilots were not.
    D. British radar allowed for early detection of incoming enemy aircraft.

98. The invasion of Eniwetok was significant because _____.
    A. the atoll became a US military base
    B. US forces suffered relatively few casualties
    C. it became a launch site for future operations
    D. All of the above

99. Where did the only tank duel of the Winter War take place?
    A. Jyvaskyla
    B. Camelina
    C. Honkaniemi
    D. Lappeenranta

100. The _____ on October 8, 1944, led to the fall of Aachen, the first German city to be captured by the Allies.
    A. Battle of Dove Hill
    B. Battle of Crucifix Hill
    C. Battle of Seminary Hill
    D. Battle of Cross Keys Hill

Chapter Three Answers

1. B. Ardennes
2. B. Battle of Midway
3. A. Big Wing
4. B. Battle of Attu
5. A. Spanish Civil War of 1936
6. D. Sunda Strait
7. C. 28th Division
8. B. Wake Island
9. B. Southern France
10. B. 174
11. D. Okinawa
12. B. Joe Rosenthal
13. A. Battle of the Coral Sea
14. A. Monte Cassino / Italian
15. C. Battle of Surigao Strait
16. C. Antwerp
17. B. Two million
18. D. heavy losses sustained by both the RAF and *Luftwaffe*
19. D. Battle of Rottenest
20. A. Brody, Dubno, and Lutsk
21. B. Malinta Tunnel
22. C. Kharkov
23. C. Battle of Iwo Jima
24. B. Karlskrona
25. A. Dutch Harbor
26. C. 872 days
27. B. Tarawa
28. D. Great Britain
29. B. Guadalcanal
30. B. Battle of Kursk

31. C. Okinawa
32. D. Battle of the North Atlantic
33. D. Liberate the one thousand POWs held captive in the San Juan de Dios Hospital
34. A. Battle of Narvik
35. A. John Ford
36. D. Battle of the North Cape
37. B. Peleliu and Okinawa
38. C. Dodecanese
39. C. Battle of Guadalcanal
40. B. Bir el Gubi
41. B. 32nd Infantry
42. D. Russian troops were better trained than German troops
43. C. Battle of the Philippine Sea
44. B. Maginot Line
45. B. Battle of Leyte Gulf
46. D. El Alamein
47. D. Battle of Manila
48. D. A and B
49. B. Coral Sea
50. D. All of the above
51. C. 1st Marine and 81st Infantry
52. B. Poland
53. C. Battle of Iwo Jima
54. A. Hannut / May 12, 1940
55. B. Battle of the Coral Sea
56. D. It was the first battle fought entirely in the air.
57. D. American Civil War
58. A. the liberation of Rome
59. A. Battle of Saipan
60. B. St. Paul's Cathedral
61. D. Chief Petty Officer John Finn
62. B. Battle of Britain

THE SECOND WORLD WAR FACT AND QUIZ BOOK

63. A. *Akagi*, *Kaga*, *Soryu*, and *Hiryu*
64. A. Gustav Line
65. C. Battle of Tarawa
66. C. 150,000
67. D. Balikpapan
68. A. HMS *Hood*
69. B. "Island Hopping"
70. D. All of the above
71. C. 338,000
72. B. 1., 4., 2., 3.
73. C. 40,000
74. B. Battle of Tarawa
75. A. Pointe du Hoc
76. D. Solomon Islands
77. B. Landings at Salerno
78. D. beachline defense was ineffective
79. D. Winston Churchill
80. B. Battle of Balikpapan Bay
81. A. Crete
82. A. USS *Hornet* (CV-8)
83. A. Rhine
84. A. December 8, 1941
85. C. Larry Newman
86. D. B and C
87. A. Battle of Dubio
88. C. "Taffy 3"
89. B. Battle of Castle Itter / May 5, 1945
90. B. cut off Japan's air and naval base at Rabaul
91. B. Tunisia
92. D. 93,000
93. C. Fort Eben-Emael
94. C. Battle of Saipan
95. A. It was Germany's first major defeat.

96. D. thirty-seven days
97. A. The RAF possessed superior numbers of aircraft.
98. D. All of the above
99. C. Honkaniemi
100. B. Battle of Crucifix Hill

CHAPTER FOUR

WEAPONS

1. Which *Seattle Times* correspondent dubbed the Boeing B-17 the "Flying Fortress"?[26]
   A. Lewis Kamb
   B. Michael Baker
   C. Drew Middleton
   D. Richard L. Williams

2. The main armament on a *Panzerkampfwagen Tiger Ausf. E* was the _____ tank gun.
   A. 60 mm
   B. 75 mm
   C. 88 mm
   D. 90 mm

3. How many Allied aircraft were lost during "Big Week" (February 20 to 25, 1944)?
   A. 197
   B. 246
   C. 385
   D. 477

4. What was the crew capacity of a Japanese Mitsubishi Ki-213 twin-engine bomber?
   A. Two
   B. Five
   C. Seven
   D. Eight

5. US industrialist and founder of Kaiser Aluminum Henry Kaiser is best remembered for building which of the following naval craft?
   A. Destroyers
   B. Liberty ships
   C. Minesweepers
   D. Torpedo boats

6. These heavy steel obstacles were originally designed by the French to defend roads and bridges, but the Germans used them to prevent landing craft and vehicles from approaching the beaches on D-Day.
   A. Belgian Gates
   B. Grim Reapers
   C. Jodl's Brass Bombers
   D. Hitler's Grasshoppers

7. Equipped with four .50 caliber machine guns, this US anti-aircraft half-track was fittingly nicknamed the _____.
   A. "Meat Mincer"
   B. "Meat Cleaver"
   C. "Meat Grinder"
   D. "Meat Chopper"

8. Built as a catapult-launched reconnaissance float plane, the Japanese Mitsubishi F1M or _____ took on a number of roles including convoy escort and anti-submarine duty.
   A. "Pete"
   B. "Tracy"
   C. "Stephen"
   D. "Kimberly"

9. A giant in the automotive industry, his Willow Run Plant in Ypsilanti, Michigan mass-produced the Consolidated B-24 *Liberator* from 1942 to 1945.
   A. Henry Ford
   B. John Welch
   C. Horace Dodge
   D. Walter Chrysler

10. This version of the Lee-Enfield rifle became the standard issue weapon of the British Army in 1941.
    A. BK 5
    B. ZB 26
    C. No. 4 MK I
    D. No. 6 MK II

11. Which USN *Iowa*-class battleships were never completed?
    A. USS *Alaska* (BB-46) and USS *Indiana* (BB-47)
    B. USS *Colorado* (BB-52) and USS *Kansas* (BB-53)
    C. USS *Illinois* (BB-65) and USS *Kentucky* (BB-66)
    D. USS *Vermont* (BB-70) and USS *Virginia* (BB-71)

12. A German behemoth at 188 tons, it was the largest tank ever built and the biggest waste of time, manpower, and resources.
    A. *Jagdpanther* (Sd. Kfz.173)
    B. *Sturmgeschütz* III *Ausf.* C–G
    C. *Panzerkampfwagen* VIII *Maus*
    D. *Kreuzer Panzerkampfwagen* MK IV

13. The First American Volunteer Group or "Flying Tigers" were organized into three squadrons. Name them.
    A. "Sharks" and "Romans" and "Swordfish"
    B. "Cheetahs" and "Barracudas" and "King Cobras"
    C. "Pythons" and "Bengal Tigers" and "Timberwolves"
    D. "Adam and Eves" and "Panda Bears" and "Hell's Angels"

14. One of the Soviet Union's deadliest weapons, "Stalin's Organ" made its debut during the Battle of Smolensk on July 14, 1941.
    A. Rimouski machine gun
    B. Chikaskia hand grenade
    C. Katyusha rocket launcher
    D. Dubyusha infantry mortar

15. Manufactured by the Lockheed Corporation, the _____ was the most expensive US fighter-bomber produced during the Second World War.
    A. P-51 *Mustang*
    B. P-38 *Lightning*
    C. P-63 *Kingcobra*
    D. P-47 *Thunderbolt*

16. The Japanese tried unsuccessfully to attack the US mainland with this "weapon" in 1945.
    A. Killer bees
    B. Laughing gas
    C. Balloon bombs
    D. Exploding rodents

17. In the words of General George Patton the _____ was "the greatest battle implement ever devised."[27]
    A. M1 Garand rifle
    B. M1917 Browning machine gun
    C. M1918 Smith & Wesson revolver
    D. M1941 Johnson light machine gun

18. Of the following aircraft, which one did *not* take part in the Battle of Britain?
    A. *Buffalo* MK I
    B. *Spitfire* MK I
    C. *Tempest* MK II
    D. A and C

19. These were the most effective weapons used against Japanese fortifications on Iwo Jima.
    A. Flamethrowers, M-1 rifles, and artillery
    B. Anti-tank guns, poison gas, and stun grenades
    C. Hand grenades, flamethrowers, and satchel charges
    D. Bangalore torpedoes, satchel charges, and trench knives

20. A *South Dakota*-class battleship, "Big Mamie" first saw action during the invasion of North Africa. Later assigned to the Pacific, she fired the final salvo of World War II.
    A. USS *Indiana* (BB-58)
    B. USS *Minnesota* (BB-60)
    C. USS *South Dakota* (BB-57)
    D. USS *Massachusetts* (BB-59)

21. Developed during the First World War, the German stick grenade or _____ was one of the most recognizable weapons in the *Wehrmacht* arsenal.
    A. "Firecracker"
    B. "Banana Peel"
    C. "Carrot Stick"
    D. "Potato Masher"

22. Adolf Hitler referred to American entrepreneur Andrew Jackson Higgins as the "New Noah."[28] What did he invent?
    A. Landing Ship, Tank (LST)
    B. Landing Craft, Assault (LCA)
    C. Landing Ship, Flotilla Flagship (LSFF)
    D. Landing Craft, Vehicle, Personnel (LCVP)

23. The main armament on a British Hawker *Hurricane* MK I was _____ and _____.
    A. three x 0.5 machine guns / one x 250 lb. To 1,000 lb. bomb
    B. six x .50 caliber machine guns / one x 100 lb. to 500 lb. bomb
    C. four x 20 mm Hispano Mk II cannons / two x 250 lb. or 500 lb. bombs
    D. eight x .50 caliber machine guns / ten x 5 in. HVAR unguided rockets

24. Also known as "jeep carriers" or "baby flattops," USN *Bogue*-class carriers deployed approximately how many aircraft?
    A. Twelve
    B. Eighteen
    C. Nineteen
    D. Twenty-four

25. Considered the most powerful cannon ever produced, the "Gustav" railway gun could fire a projectile an estimated _____ miles.
    A. five
    B. thirty
    C. fifty-five
    D. sixty-one

26. There were eight battleships anchored at Pearl Harbor on December 7, 1941. Which two remain there today?
    A. USS *Utah* (BB-31) and USS *Arizona* (BB-39)
    B. USS *Arizona* (BB-39) and USS *Nevada* (BB-36)
    C. USS *Oklahoma* (BB-37) and USS *Arizona* (BB-39)
    D. USS *Arizona* (BB-39) and USS *California* (BB-44)

27. A shoulder-held device, the *Panzerfaust* was used primarily against enemy _____.
    A. tanks
    B. aircraft
    C. infantry
    D. artillery

28. Douglas Aircraft's SBD *Dauntless* dive bomber was instrumental in securing America's victory at the Battle of Midway. What was the USAAF version of the *Dauntless*?
    A. A-20 *Havoc*
    B. A-22 *Specter*
    C. A-24 *Banshee*
    D. A-27 *Phantom*

29. This Soviet-made PPSh-41 submachine gun's unusual appearance and peculiar nickname belied its deadly impact on the battlefield.
    A. "Fizz Gun"
    B. "Burp Gun"
    C. "Sizzle Gun"
    D. "Crack Gun"

30. American troops sarcastically referred to it as the "Purple Heart Box."[29]
    A. M3 half-track
    B. T17 armored car
    C. M36 tank destroyer
    D. T82 motor carriage

31. Initially used by the *Luftwaffe* during the Spanish Civil War, it later proved equally effective in Poland, France, and the Low Countries.
    A. Arado Ar 197
    B. Junkers Ju 87
    C. Fieseler Fi 167
    D. Dornier Do 15

32. Because of its record number of accidents, the Martin B-26 *Marauder* was nicknamed the _____.
    A. "Death Trap"
    B. "Crew Killer"
    C. "Flying Coffin"
    D. "Widow Maker"

33. Designed during World War I, the French _____ light tank saw action in the Spanish Civil War and against Axis forces in the initial stages of World War II.
   A. Somua S35
   B. Renault FT
   C. Toulon B28
   D. Hotchkiss H35

34. Who said, "the four keys to victory for the Allies" were "the atomic bomb, the jeep, the bazooka, and the C-47 transport?"[30]
   A. Hideki Tojo
   B. Omar Bradley
   C. Erwin Rommel
   D. Dwight Eisenhower

35. Produced in 1943, it was the finest German tank of World War II.
   A. *Panzerkampfwagen* VI *Ausf. E*
   B. *Panzerkampfwagen* V *Panther*
   C. *Panzerkampfwagen Tiger Ausf. B*
   D. *Panzerkampfwagen* 17R/18R 730 (f)

36. In any one theater of operations, which US warplane shot down the most enemy aircraft (5,168)?
   A. F6F *Hellcat*
   B. P-51 *Mustang*
   C. SBC *Helldiver*
   D. P-38 *Lightning*

37. Better-known for inventing the RAF's "bouncing bomb," English designer and engineer Sir Barnes Wallis also created "earthquake bombs," such as _____.
   A. "Godzilla" and "Fat Man"
   B. "Cyclops" and "Werewolf"
   C. "Tall Boy" and "Grand Slam"
   D. "Big Bertha" and "Mighty Joe"

38. Approximately how many Japanese aircraft were destroyed during the "Great Marianas Turkey Shoot"?
    A. 120–170
    B. 350–445
    C. 465–580
    D. None of the above

39. Commissioned in 1914, the "Mighty T" saw action in both world wars and was the first US warship to launch aircraft and to mount anti-aircraft guns.
    A. USS *Texas* (BB-35)
    B. USS *Tucson* (BB-22)
    C. USS *Tennessee* (BB-43)
    D. USS *Tuscaloosa* (BB-21)

40. Although *not* a weapon in the traditional sense of the word, it played a key role in the Allies' final victory. Name the British scientist who helped to invent _____.
    A. William Berners-Lee / penicillin
    B. Edgar Douglas Adrian / superglue
    C. Allen Fairchild McPherson / plastic
    D. Robert Alexander Watson-Watt / radar

41. Which technology was introduced on the B-17G in September 1943?
    A. Colmar Auto-Pilot
    B. Bendix Chin Turret
    C. Kodak Data Recorder
    D. Fisher Anti-Lock Brakes

42. "One of the deadliest weapons in the British Army's arsenal," this flame-throwing tank was called the _____. [31]
    A. Cromwell Crisper
    B. Wellington Dragon
    C. King George Oven
    D. Churchill Crocodile

43. A jelly-like substance developed by Harvard scientist Louis Fieser, napalm was first used in _____.
    A. March 1943 when US B-29s incinerated the city of Tokyo
    B. February 1944 when the USAAF bombed the Pacific island of Pohnpei
    C. March 1944 when the RAF attacked German troops in the Falaise Pocket
    D. August 1943 when US soldiers burned a Sicilian wheat field reportedly sheltering German troops

44. How many crew members operated a Japanese Type A-class midget submarine?
    A. One
    B. Two
    C. Four
    D. Seven

45. Built in 1943 at the Philadelphia Navy Yard, the _____ served in three wars and is the most decorated battleship in American history.
    A. USS *Iowa* (BB-61)
    B. USS *Missouri* (BB-63)
    C. USS *Kentucky* (BB-66)
    D. USS *New Jersey* (BB-62)

46. Arguably the world's greatest fighter aircraft, over 35,000 were produced between 1936 and 1945.
    A. Macchi C205
    B. Mitsubishi F6M Troya
    C. Messerschmitt Bf 109E
    D. Mikoyan-Gurevich MiG-1

47. First deployed to the ETO in February 1945, the M26 medium/heavy tank was named in honor of which legendary American general?
    A. Philip Sheridan
    B. John J. Pershing
    C. Stonewall Jackson
    D. George Washington

48. What unusual sobriquet did the Allies give the *Luftwaffe's* Dornier Do 17?
    A. "Flying Cigar"
    B. "Flying Pencil"
    C. "Flying Turnip"
    D. "Flying Sausage"

49. Twenty-three sets of brothers perished aboard this battleship on December 7, 1941.
    A. USS *Nevada* (BB-36)
    B. USS *Arizona* (BB-39)
    C. USS *Maryland* (BB-46)
    D. USS *Oklahoma* (BB-37)

50. Naval historian Mark Peattie described the _____ as "one of the most ingeniously designed fighter planes in aviation history."[32]
    A. A6M *Zero*
    B. F4F *Wildcat*
    C. P51 *Mustang*
    D. Mk. X *Hurricane*

51. Intended as a lightweight alternative to the heavier M1 Garand rifle, it was issued to artillery crews, tankers, and platoon leaders in all theaters of operation.
    A. M1 Carbine
    B. M1917 Colt pistol
    C. M1903 Springfield rifle
    D. M2 Hyde submachine gun

52. Great Britain suffered a devastating blow when these capital ships were sunk by Japanese bombers on December 10, 1941.
    A. HMS *Invincible* and HMS *Nelson*
    B. HMS *Resolution* and HMS *Ark Royal*
    C. HMS *Prince of Wales* and HMS *Repulse*
    D. HMS *King George V* and HMS *Vanguard*

53. The main armament on a US M7 *Priest* was a _____ howitzer.
    A. 75 mm
    B. 88 mm
    C. 90 mm
    D. 105 mm

54. A lightweight and maneuverable Soviet-built fighter, the _____ remained in service until the early 1950s.
    A. Petlyakov Pe-3
    B. Tupolev Tup-6
    C. Yakovlev Yak-3
    D. Lavochkin La-5

55. What was the major drawback to the US M3 *Lee* tank?
    A. Poor acceleration
    B. Lack of firepower
    C. Inadequate side armor
    D. Non-traversing front turret

56. The IJN battleship *Yamato*'s main battery consisted of nine _____ guns.
    A. 12-inch
    B. 15-inch
    C. 18-inch
    D. 19-inch

57. General George Marshall called it "America's greatest contribution to modern warfare."[33]
    A. Plasma
    B. Bazooka
    C. K-ration
    D. Willys jeep

58. What distinguished the German *Mauser* C96 from other military pistols?
    A. Long barrel
    B. Box magazine
    C. Wooden shoulder stock
    D. All of the above

59. Affectionately known as "Big Ben" and the fifth US vessel to bear the name, she was heavily damaged by Japanese bombs during the Philippines campaign.
    A. USS *Intrepid* (CV-11)
    B. USS *Hancock* (CV-19)
    C. USS *Franklin* (CV-13
    D. USS *Oriskany* (CV-34)

60. German Field Marshal Paul von Kleist called the Soviet T-34, "the finest tank in the world."[34] What feature made it such a powerful adversary on the battlefield?
    A. Mobility
    B. Firepower
    C. Sloped armor
    D. All of the above

61. Dubbed _____, this US medium bomber flew the most combat missions (202) during World War II.
    A. "Witchcraft" / B-18 *Bolero*
    B. "Flak-Bait" / B-26 *Marauder*
    C. "Wing Ding" / B-58 *Hustler*
    D. "Ishkabibble" / B-25 *Mitchell*

62. A Soviet attack aircraft, it was considered highly effective against German mechanized forces.
    A. Ilyushin Il-2
    B. Tupolev DB-1
    C. Antonov An-30
    D. Yermolayev Yer-2

63. Name the first US warship sunk by a U-boat on October 31, 1941.
    A. USS *Welles* (DD-257)
    B. USS *Humphreys* (DD-236)
    C. USS *John D. Ford* (DD-228)
    D. USS *Reuben James* (DD-245)

64. Which of the following was the standard infantry rifle of the German Army?
    A. *Gewehr* 41M
    B. *Karabiner* 98K
    C. *Sturmgewehr* 44
    D. *Volkssturmgewehr* 1

65. A light armored vehicle used by American and British forces during the last two years of the war, it replaced the US M6 motor carriage.
    A. M1 *Nomad*
    B. M4 *Retriever*
    C. M6 *Shepherd*
    D. M8 *Greyhound*

66. Germany's first diesel-electric U-boat was the _____.
    A. Type XIII
    B. Type XVI
    C. Type XXI
    D. Type XCI

67. The preferred weapon of US Rangers and British commandos, its rate of fire exceeded 650 rounds-per-minute.
    A. M1 Garand rifle
    B. M3 submachine gun
    C. M1919 Browning machine gun
    D. M1A1 Thompson submachine gun

68. Introduced in March 1945, the Japanese Kawasaki Ki-100 fighter's maximum speed was _____.
    A. 210 mph
    B. 285 mph
    C. 360 mph
    D. 415 mph

69. A USN *Northampton*-class heavy cruiser, she participated in the invasions of North Africa and Normandy but is best remembered as the flagship of FDR and Harry Truman.
    A. USS *Augusta* (CA-31)
    B. USS *Nashville* (CA-29)
    C. USS *Gladwyne* (CA-46)
    D. USS *Philadelphia* (CA-27)

70. Flown by the RAF's 617 Squadron, this heavy bomber could deliver a 14,000 lb. payload.
    A. Avro *Lancaster*
    B. Bristol *Beaufort*
    C. Vickers *Wellesley*
    D. Handley-Page *Halifax*

71. The Browning AN/M2.30.06 caliber machine gun was used in a variety of combat aircraft including all of the following *except* the _____.
    A. TBF *Avenger*
    B. SBD *Dauntless*
    C. TBD *Devastator*
    D. SBF *Rattlesnake*

72. Between 1944 and 1945, only 256 of these Japanese two-seater aircraft were produced by the Aichi Aircraft Company.
    A. E16A floatplane
    B. P1Y two-engine fighter
    C. T6A four-engine bomber
    D. A6M single-engine fighter

73. Created in 1942 and based on the island of Guadalcanal, its official name was Commander, Aircraft, Solomons (AirSols).
    A. Cactus Air Force
    B. Rainbow Air Force
    C. Uncle Sam's Air Force
    D. Star Spangled Air Force

74. Which Allied nation used anti-tank dogs to destroy German armor?
    A. Canada
    B. Australia
    C. Great Britain
    D. Soviet Union

75. The brainchild of a Swiss engineer, the _____ was used by the USAAF to enhance its daylight bombing capabilities.
    A. Sperry Ball Turret
    B. Norden Bombsight
    C. Tyler Radio Compass
    D. Honeywell Auto Pilot

76. How many Japanese ships that participated in the Pearl Harbor operation survived the war?
    A. One
    B. Three
    C. Seven
    D. Twelve

77. Introduced in 1940, it was one in an extensive line of Grumman "felines."
    A. F9F *Panther*
    B. F2D *Tomcat*
    C. F8G *Cougar*
    D. F4F *Wildcat*

78. Which of the following were the sister ships of the German heavy cruiser *Admiral Scheer*?
    A. *Von Schlieffen* and *Munich*
    B. *Germania* and *Hohenzollern*
    C. *Schniewind* and *Von Hindenburg*
    D. *Admiral Graf Spee* and *Deutschland*

79. Attached to the US Twelfth Air Force, the legendary Tuskegee Airmen flew the _____.
    A. P-75 *Eagle* and P-11 *Comanche*
    B. P-39 *Airacobra* and P-40 *Warhawk*
    C. P-51 *Mustang* and P-47 *Thunderbolt*
    D. P-80 *Shooting Star* and P-59 *Airacomet*

80. With no effective weapon to counter German armored vehicles, the British created the Grenade, Hand, Anti-tank device in 1940. What was it more commonly known as?
    A. "Sticky Bomb"
    B. "Mighty Missile"
    C. "London Ticker"
    D. "Grease Grenade"

81. Equipped with a 75 mm main gun and a .50 caliber Browning machine gun, the _____ replaced the less powerful US M3 *Grant*.
    A. M5 *Meade*
    B. M4 *Sherman*
    C. M24 *Chaffee*
    D. M29 *Jackson*

82. The first jet fighter-bomber to engage in air-to-air combat, it was considered a "game changer" by the *Luftwaffe*.
    A. ME 224 *Falke*
    B. ME 231 *Adler*
    C. ME 258 *Kondor*
    D. ME 262 *Schwalbe*

83. In April 1943, the crew of the USN *Casablanca*-class escort carrier _____ became the first US sailors to board and seize an enemy ship since the War of 1812 when they captured the German submarine _____.
    A. USS *Solomons* (CVE-67) / U-271
    B. USS *Corregidor* (CVE-58) / U-388
    C. USS *Manila Bay* (CVE-61) / U-439
    D. USS *Guadalcanal* (CVE-60) / U-505

84. These Italian *Littorio*-class battleships were surrendered to the Allies on September 3, 1943.
    A. *Benedetto Brin* and *Lazio*
    B. *Napoli* and *Regina Elena*
    C. *Italia* and *Vittorio Veneto*
    D. *Roma* and *Antonio Aldini*

85. It was the US fighter aircraft used in the assassination of Admiral Isoroku Yamamoto on April 18, 1943.
    A. P-51 *Mustang*
    B. P-40 *Warhawk*
    C. P-38 *Lightning*
    D. P-66 *Vanguard*

86. Conceived by Ferdinand Porsche, this German tank destroyer first saw action during the Battle of Kursk.
    A. *Panzerjäger Tiger (P)*
    B. *Panzerkampfwagen* I *Ausf. B*
    C. *Panzerkampfwagen* V *Panther*
    D. *Panzerkampfwagen* 38(t) *Ausf.* A

87. Launched in 1944 and named after a US naval aviator killed during the Battle of the Coral Sea, the _____ was the first warship manned by a predominately African American crew.
    A. USS *Mason* (DE-529)
    B. USS *Banfield* (DE-266)
    C. USS *Sylvester* (DE-310)
    D. USS *Finnegan* (DE-307)

88. Named after a nonsensical word coined by an 18th century English actor and playwright, this explosive-laden spinning wheel was designed to breach the German defenses on D-Day.
    A. Panjandrum
    B. Grimgribber
    C. Bletherskate
    D. Twaddledom

89. Which converted steamships served as training aircraft carriers on Lake Michigan?
    A. *Mystic* and *Trojan* / USS *Hawk* (IX-19) and USS *Bigelow* (IX-27)
    B. *Agawam* and *Powhatan* / USS *Norfolk* (IX-37) and USS *Nova* (IX-48)
    C. *Niagara* and *Carrabassett* / USS *Lion* (IX-59) and USS *Bridgewater* (IX-62)
    D. *Seeandbee* and *Greater Buffalo* / USS *Wolverine* (IX-64) and USS *Sable* (IX-81)

THE SECOND WORLD WAR FACT AND QUIZ BOOK

90. Germany's standard issue machine gun, "Hitler's Buzzsaw" fired 1,200 to 1,500 rounds-per-minute.
    A. *Gewehr* 41
    B. *Walther* P39
    C. *Sturmgewehr* 44
    D. *Maschinengerwehr* 42

91. Which US infantry weapon did American artist and illustrator Norman Rockwell immortalize in a 1942 poster for the US War Department?
    A. M1903 Smith & Wesson pistol
    B. M1917 Browning machine gun
    C. M1918 Smith & Wesson revolver
    D. M1941 Johnson light machine gun

92. The Nakajima B5N2 or _____ was considered Japan's most reliable _____ until it was replaced in 1944.
    A. "Oak" / jet fighter
    B. "Jenny" / transport
    C. "Walnut" / pursuit plane
    D. "Kate" / torpedo-bomber

93. What were the painted images located near the nose or cockpit of US military aircraft called?
    A. Kill markings
    B. Victory decals
    C. Mission symbols
    D. All of the above

94. The most widely used troop/cargo glider of the Second World War, the _____, played a crucial role in all major airborne operations in both the ETO and PTO.
    A. CG-15 *Galba*
    B. A-17 *Tiberius*
    C. CG-4 *Hadrian*
    D. XG-1 *Claudius*

95. On which US cruiser were the five Sullivan brothers (Albert, Francis, George, Joseph, and Madison) killed on November 13, 1942?
    A. USS *Juneau* (CL-52)
    B. USS *Atlanta* (CL-51)
    C. USS *Oakland* (CL-95)
    D. USS *San Juan* (CL-54)

96. Inspired by Frenchman Adolphe Kégresse's concept, the _____ was a self-propelled mine developed by Germany as an anti-tank weapon.
    A. Apollo
    B. Goliath
    C. Hercules
    D. Poseidon

97. The most honored US destroyer still in existence, the _____, gained a reputation as "The Ship That Would Not Die."[35]
    A. USS *Laffey* (DD-724)
    B. USS *Barton* (DD-722)
    C. USS *Madison* (DD-425)
    D. USS *Gillespie* (DD-609)

98. Lee Harvey Oswald used this subpar Italian infantry rifle to assassinate President John F. Kennedy on November 22, 1963.
    A. Beretta 38A
    B. Vetterli M1870
    C. Breda Modello 30
    D. Carcano Modello 38

99. What nickname was given to the plutonium device tested at Los Alamos, New Mexico on July 16, 1945?
    A. "Gidget"
    B. "Gopher"
    C. "Gadget"
    D. "Goblin"

100. Approximately how many tanks did the US provide to the Soviet Union under the Lend-Lease Act of 1941?
    A. 10,000
    B. 13,000
    C. 15,000
    D. 18,000

Chapter Four Answers

1. D. Richard L. Williams
2. C. 88 mm
3. C. 385
4. B. Five
5. B. Liberty ships
6. A. Belgian Gates
7. D. "Meat Chopper"
8. A. "Pete"
9. A. Henry Ford
10. C. No. 4 MK I
11. C. USS *Illinois* (BB-65) and USS *Kentucky* (BB-66)
12. C. *Panzerkampfwagen* VIII *Maus*
13. D. "Adams and Eves" and "Panda Bears" and "Hell's Angels"
14. C. Katyusha rocket launcher
15. B. P-38 *Lightning*
16. C. Balloon bombs
17. A. M1 Garand rifle
18. D. A and C
19. C. Hand grenades, flamethrowers, and satchel charges
20. D. USS *Massachusetts* (BB-59)
21. D. "Potato Masher"
22. D. Landing Craft, Vehicle, Personnel (LCVP)
23. C. four x 20 mm Hispano Mk II cannons / 2 x 250lb or 500lb bombs
24. D. Twenty-four
25. B. thirty
26. A. USS *Utah* (BB-31) and USS *Arizona* (BB-39)
27. A. tanks
28. C. A-24 *Banshee*
29. B. "Burp Gun"
30. A. M3 half-track

31. B. Junkers Ju 87
32. D. "Widow Maker"
33. B. Renault FT
34. D. Dwight Eisenhower
35. B. *Panzerkampfwagen* V *Panther*
36. A. F6F *Hellcat*
37. C. "Tall Boy" and "Grand Slam"
38. B. 350–445
39. A. USS *Texas* (BB-35)
40. D. Robert Alexander Watson-Watt / radar
41. B. Bendix Chin Turret
42. D. Churchill Crocodile
43. D. August 1943 when US soldiers burned a wheat field reportedly sheltering German troops in Sicily
44. B. Two
45. D. USS *New Jersey* (BB-62)
46. C. Messerschmitt Bf 109E
47. B. John J. Pershing
48. B. "Flying Pencil"
49. B. USS *Arizona* (BB-39)
50. A. A6M *Zero*
51. A. M1 Carbine
52. C. HMS *Prince of Wales* and HMS *Repulse*
53. D. 105 mm
54. C. Yakovlev Yak-3
55. D. Non-traversing front turret
56. C. 18-inch
57. D. Willys jeep
58. D. All of the above
59. C. USS *Franklin* (CV-13)
60. D. All of the above
61. B. "Flak-Bait" / B-26 *Marauder*
62. A. Ilyushin Il-2

63. D. USS *Reuben James* (DD-245)
64. B. *Karabiner* 98K
65. D. M8 *Greyhound*
66. C. Type XXI
67. D. M1A1 Thompson submachine gun
68. C. 360 mph
69. A. USS *Augusta* (CA-31)
70. A. Avro *Lancaster*
71. D. SBF *Rattlesnake*
72. A. E16A floatplane
73. A. Cactus Air Force
74. D. Soviet Union
75. B. Norden Bombsight
76. A. One
77. D. F4F *Wildcat*
78. D. *Admiral Graf Spee* and *Deutschland*
79. B. P-39 *Airacobra* and P-40 *Warhawk*
80. A. "Sticky Bomb"
81. B. M4 *Sherman*
82. D. ME 262 *Schwalbe*
83. D. USS *Guadalcanal* (CVE-60) / U-505
84. C. *Italia* and *Vittorio Veneto*
85. C. P-38 *Lightning*
86. A. *Panzerjäger Tiger (P)*
87. A. USS *Mason* (DE-529)
88. A. Panjandrum
89. D. *Seeandbee* and *Greater Buffalo* / USS *Wolverine* (IX-64) and USS *Sable* (IX-81)
90. D. *Maschinengewehr* 42
91. B. M1917 Browning machine gun
92. D. "Kate" / torpedo-bomber
93. D. All of the above
94. C. CG-4 *Hadrian*
95. A. USS *Juneau* (CL-52)

96. B. Goliath
97. A. USS *Laffey* (DD-724)
98. D. Carcano Modello 1891
99. C. "Gadget"
100. B. 13,000

CHAPTER FIVE

Conferences And Code Names

1. In the wake of the First World War, the League of Nations was established to _____
   A. "install democratic governments in Germany and Austria-Hungary."
   B. "reestablish the Hapsburgs, Romanovs, and Hohenzollerns dynasties in Europe."
   C. "ensure that Germany would never again make war against its European neighbors."
   D. "promote international cooperation, to ensure the fulfillment of accepted international peace, obligations, and to provide safeguards against war."[36]

2. The Anti-Comintern Pact of 1936 between Germany and Japan was an agreement to _____.
   A. fight communism
   B. combat European Jewry
   C. confront international anarchism
   D. support economic change in Europe

3. Following the Munich Agreement of 1938 between Germany, France, Italy, and Great Britain, which statesman said, "I believe it is peace for our time"?[37]
   A. Benjamin Disraeli
   B. Winston Churchill
   C. David Lloyd George
   D. Neville Chamberlain

4. On September 1, 1939, Germany invaded Poland. When did the plan first come in to being and what was the code name for the operation?
   A. 1926 / Case Blue
   B. 1927 / Case Green
   C. 1928 / Case White
   D. 1929 / Case Yellow

5. "The aim of this operation will be to eliminate the English homeland as a base for the prosecution of the war against Germany and, if necessary, to occupy it completely."[38] What was Hitler's planned invasion of England called?
   A. SEA LION
   B. CROSSFIRE
   C. RED DAWN
   D. GUILLOTINE

6. Who were the signatories of the Tripartite Pact?
   A. Germany, Italy, and Japan
   B. Romania, Yugoslavia, and Italy
   C. China, Great Britain, and France
   D. Soviet Union, Germany, and Finland

7. It was the first large-scale British ground campaign to drive the Italian Army out of Egypt.
   A. Operation COMPASS
   B. Operation CATERHAM
   C. Operation CAMBRIDGE
   D. Operation COMMANDO

8. This New Deal administrator served as FDR's wartime envoy to Great Britain and the Soviet Union.
   A. Cordell Hull
   B. James Byrnes
   C. Harry Hopkins
   D. Wendell Willkie

9. A-GO was the Japanese strategy to _____.
   A. invade the Soviet Union
   B. destroy US naval forces off Saipan
   C. attack the US fleet at Pearl Harbor
   D. block the Chinese invasion of Honshu

10. The Treaty of Moscow ended the Winter War between the Soviet Union and Finland. How long did the conflict last?
    A. 105 days
    B. 126 days
    C. 167 days
    D. 189 days

11. Which member of the Big Three attended the most wartime meetings?
    A. FDR
    B. Joseph Stalin
    C. Harry Truman
    D. Winston Churchill

12. The terms ARGONAUT and CRICKET were associated with which of the following conferences?
    A. Cairo
    B. Malta
    C. First Quebec
    D. Third Moscow

13. Introduced by US Secretary of the Treasury Robert Morgenthau Jr., at the _____, the Morgenthau Plan proposed that Germany be stripped of its heavy industry and become an agrarian state.
    A. First Moscow Conference
    B. Second Quebec Conference
    C. Third Manchester Conference
    D. Fourth Washington Conference

14. What was significant about the Bermuda Conference in April 1943?
    A. It was the first time the plight of Jewish refugees was discussed.
    B. It was the first meeting that involved only US and British military officials.
    C. It was the first time that an action plan had been developed to rescue the Jews in the Warsaw Ghetto.
    D. B and C

15. It was the designation for the first meeting between FDR and Prime Minister Winston Churchill.
    A. OPAL
    B. TOPAZ
    C. GARNET
    D. EMERALD

16. Arrange the following in chronological order.
    1. Yalta Conference
    2. Tehran Conference
    3. Potsdam Conference
    4. Casablanca Conference
    A. 4., 2., 1., 3.
    B. 1., 3., 4., 2.
    C. 2., 3., 1., 4.
    D. 3., 4., 2., 1.

17. Which future US president attended the Potsdam Conference as a foreign correspondent for Hearst Newspapers?
    A. Jimmy Carter
    B. Richard Nixon
    C. John F. Kennedy
    D. George H. W. Bush

18. Name the legendary Glenn Miller song that was also the cryptonym for Allied air operations against German railway targets before D-Day.
    A. "American Patrol"
    B. "Take the A Train"
    C. "Moonlight Serenade"
    D. "Chattanooga Choo Choo"

19. Of the following events, which occurred after the First Moscow Conference?
    A. The US declared war on Japan.
    B. Japanese troops invaded Manchuria.
    C. France sought an armistice with Italy.
    D. British and French troops were evacuated from Dunkirk.

20. It was virtually impossible for FDR and Churchill to insure a free and democratic Poland following the war in Europe. Why?
    A. FDR still sought Stalin's help in fighting the Japanese.
    B. Soviet forces were already well established in the region.
    C. The Poles wanted to become part of the Soviet sphere of influence.
    D. A and B

21. The German plan to invade the Soviet Union was called _____.
    A. TIBERIUS
    B. JUSTINIAN
    C. HERACLIUS
    D. BARBAROSSA

22. A member of the British Conservative Party, who served as Winston Churchill's emissary to France and the Soviet Union during World War II, he succeeded Churchill as prime minister in 1955.
    A. Anthony Eden
    B. Harold Wilson
    C. James Callahan
    D. Harold Macmillan

23. The _____ took place _____.
    A. Tehran Conference / not long after the Cairo Conference
    B. Euro-Power Conference / shortly before the fall of Tobruk
    C. Huntington Conference / during the Allied invasion of Sicily
    D. Second Claridge Conference / right after the Battle of Berlin

24. What was the code name for the Second Quebec Conference?
    A. DECAGON
    B. HEXAGON
    C. OCTAGON
    D. PENTAGON

25. Held in the capitol city of French Equatorial Africa between January 30 and February 8, 1944, its purpose was to determine the future of France's colonial empire.
    A. Kinshasa Conference
    B. Brazzaville Conference
    C. Ouagadougou Conference
    D. Johannesburg Conference

26. FDR's trip to the Casablanca Conference was significant because it was the first time _____.
    A. FDR's dog Fala travelled abroad
    B. a president left the country during wartime
    C. FDR flew in his presidential plane, the "Sacred Cow"
    D. a US president travelled without Secret Service protection

27. All of the following were code words for the Normandy assault beaches except _____.
    A. BLUE
    B. GOLD
    C. OMAHA
    D. SWORD

28. Issued after the First Inter-Allied Conference in 1941, the Declaration of St. James Palace was a policy statement comprised of three resolutions. Which one is false?
    A. The parties supported the creation of a postwar multi-national security force.
    B. The parties pledged that they would enter no separate peace until Germany and Italy had been defeated.
    C. The parties affirmed their alliance and pledged to assist one another in the war against Germany and Italy.
    D. The parties committed to the principle of peace based on the principle of socio- economic freedom for all people.

29. Signed on September 12, 1944, the Allies agreed that Germany would be divided into three zones of occupation.
    A. Geneva Pact
    B. London Protocol
    C. Balfour Declaration
    D. Camp David Accords

30. This was the designation for the Allied invasion of Japan.
    A. SAPPHIRE
    B. DOWNFALL
    C. PROMETHEUS
    D. COMPOSITION

31. Although not considered a binding agreement, the Atlantic Charter did accomplish the following.
    A. It prompted the sale of US war bonds.
    B. It stimulated American interest in foreign affairs.
    C. It solidified the relationship between the US and Great Britain.
    D. It encouraged Americans to support US intervention in Europe.

32. Where did the Potenji River Conference of 1943 take place?
    A. Brazil
    B. Ecuador
    C. Columbia
    D. Argentina

33. The Second Moscow Conference (BRACELET) was held from _____.
    A. May 3 to May 8, 1942
    B. July 25 to July 30, 1942
    C. August 12 to August 17, 1942
    D. September 1 to September 6, 1942

34. Why did the Allies ultimately reject the Morgenthau Plan, a proposal to reorganize postwar Germany?
    A. "It would be viewed as cruel and inhumane by the German people."
    B. "A re-industrialized Germany was vital to the economic recovery of Europe."
    C. "Germany had become a crucially important dike against the westward surge of Soviet communism."[39]
    D. B and C

35. Known as the "Red General," _____ attended only one Allied meeting. Which was it?
    A. Ho Chi Minh / Yalta Conference
    B. Mao Zedong / Peking Conference
    C. Yan Huiqing / Adriatic Conference
    D. Chiang Kai-shek / Cairo Conference

36. According to US historian and author Thomas A. Bailey, "FDR requested that this meeting be called the "Unconditional Surrender Conference."[40]
    A. Cairo
    B. Tehran
    C. Casablanca
    D. Mont Tremblant

37. Operation TOLSTOY was the Allied meeting held in _____ between October 9 and October 18, 1944.
    A. Paris
    B. Rome
    C. Cairo
    D. Moscow

38. Commissioneed in 1931 at the Norfolk Navy Yard, it transported FDR to the Atlantic Conference.
    A. USS *Augusta* (CA-31)
    B. USS *Sacramento* (CA-35)
    C. USS *New Orleans* (CA-32)
    D. USS *Northampton* (CA-26)

39. From July 1 to July 22, 1944, some 700 delegates met at Bretton Woods in the White Mountains of New Hampshire. Its objective was to establish greater economic and political stability in a postwar world. What was/were its major achievement(s)?
    A. International Monetary Fund
    B. Federal Deposit Insurance Corporation
    C. International Bank for Reconstruction and Development
    D. A and C

40. Named after a wild fruit, it was the artificial harbor created for the Normandy invasion.
    A. MULBERRY
    B. CRANBERRY
    C. SALMONBERRY
    D. THIMBLEBERRY

41. As a result of the Bermuda Conference, approximately _____ Jews were rescued from Nazi captivity.
    A. 100,000
    B. 200,000
    C. 800,000
    D. No

42. FDR died thirteen days before hosting the opening session of this summit.
    A. Allied League of States
    B. World Freedom Conference
    C. International Forum on World Peace
    D. United Nations Conference on International Organization

43. Dubbed Operation M, it was the Japanese plan for the invasion of (the) _____.
    A. Hawaii
    B. Borneo
    C. Australia
    D. Philippines

44. Where did Churchill and FDR strategize before attending the Yalta Conference?
    A. Paris
    B. Malta
    C. London
    D. Brussels

45. How did Stalin react when told by President Harry Truman that America had tested the first atomic bomb?
    A. He was unimpressed.
    B. He became visibly upset.
    C. He toasted the US achievement.
    D. He began to sob uncontrollably.

46. This operation called for the mining of the English Channel by the British Royal Navy.
    A. OATMEAL
    B. GERONIMO
    C. SEA BISCUIT
    D. BUTTERMILK

47. All of these were World War II summits *except* the _____.
    A. Dillard Mays Conference
    B. Bretton Woods Conference
    C. Second Claridge Conference
    D. Dumbarton Oaks Conference

48. What territories were ceded to the Soviet Union at the Tehran Conference?
    A. Estonia, Serbia, and Latvia
    B. Latvia, Lithuania, and Estonia
    C. Serbia, Croatia, and Lithuania
    D. Macedonia, Latvia, and Bosnia

49. The cryptonym for German attacks on Allied shipping in the North Atlantic was _____.
    A. *HABICHT*
    B. *BERNHARD*
    C. *NORDMARK*
    D. *TANNENBERG*

50. Identify the major issue that divided the British and Americans at Casablanca.
    A. Where and when should the Western Allies establish a second front?
    B. Should German and Japanese civilians be considered military targets?
    C. How should men and material be allocated across all theaters of operation?
    D. Should biological and chemical weapons be used against Germany and Japan?

51. Which of the following military units came about as a result of the Potenji River Conference?
    A. South American Flotilla
    B. Aracruz Commando Battalion
    C. Brazilian Expeditionary Force
    D. Latin American Defense Brigade

52. It was the German code name for the invasion of Denmark and Norway.
    A. *OST*
    B. *URSULA*
    C. *BODDEN*
    D. *WESERUBUNG*

53. How many nations participated in the Bretton Woods Conference?
    A. Forty-four
    B. Sixty-seven
    C. Eighty-two
    D. Ninety-eight

54. Who was the Canadian prime minister who hosted the First Quebec Conference?
    A. R. B. Bennett
    B. Louis St. Laurent
    C. John Diefenbaker
    D. William Mackenzie

55. Proposed by General Douglas MacArthur, this operation involved the capture of the Japanese base at Rabaul on New Britain Island.
    A. VELVET
    B. ELKTON
    C. FATIGUE
    D. WHIPSAW

56. At Yalta, Stalin agreed to participate in this peacekeeping organization.
    A. NATO
    B. SEATO
    C. Warsaw Pact
    D. United Nations

57. Lasting for a record seventeen days, it was the longest Allied conference of the Second World War.
    A. Adana
    B. Ottawa
    C. Potsdam
    D. Cherchell

58. Which of the following operations called for the invasion of the Italian mainland by the US Fifth Army?
    A. WALLOP
    B. CARPENTER
    C. AVALANCHE
    D. WORKHORSE

59. The _____ took place _____.
    A. Atlantic Conference / before the Pearl Harbor attack
    B. US-British Staff Conference / during the Battle of Britain
    C. Cherchell Conference / before the German invasion of Poland
    D. Second Claridge Conference / right after the Battle of the Ardennes

60. Between August 21 and October 7, 1944, representatives from the US, Great Britain, the Soviet Union, and China met at Dumbarton Oaks to discuss proposals for a postwar peace keeping organization. Where did the meetings take place?
    A. New York
    B. Philadelphia
    C. San Francisco
    D. Washington, DC

61. What was the final conference of World War II?
    A. Leipzig (BRIDGE)
    B. Potsdam (TERMINAL)
    C. Amsterdam (COURIER)
    D. Copenhagen (EXPLORER)

62. This Soviet politician and diplomat took part in all of the major Allied summits *except* _____.
    A. Georgy Malenkov / Yalta
    B. Nikita Khrushchev / Tehran
    C. Vyacheslav Molotov / Venice
    D. Kliment Voroshilov / Casablanca

63. According to US Air Force historian Herman S. Wolk, the decision reached at Casablanca to _____ "marked the beginning of the end of Nazi Germany."[41]
    A. invade Sicily
    B. seek a separate peace agreement with Italy
    C. create an Anglo-American military staff in Washington, DC
    D. conduct a coordinated bombing campaign against Germany

64. The British air and sea operation for the capture of Rangoon during the Burma campaign was named after which movie monster?
    A. DRACULA
    B. GODZILLA
    C. WOLF MAN
    D. FRANKENSTEIN

65. Which of the following events occurred before the Second Quebec Conference?
    A. Bataan Death March
    B. United Nations Declaration
    C. US presidential election of 1940
    D. All of the above

66. The United Nations Monetary and Financial Conference was better known as the _____.
    A. Sagamore Hill Conference
    B. Bletchley Park Conference
    C. Hudson Valley Conference
    D. Bretton Woods Conference

67. Name the plan to defend the Japanese homeland.
    A. HINODE
    B. NIKKOU
    C. SOKONAU
    D. KETSU-GO

68. At the _____, General Dwight Eisenhower was chosen to command the Allied invasion of Europe.
    A. Suez Conference
    B. Tunis Conference
    C. Cairo Conference
    D. Aswan Conference

69. The future president of France, his only wartime meeting with Churchill and FDR occurred at Casablanca.
    A. Rene Coty
    B. Charles de Gaulle
    C. Georges Pompidou
    D. Valery Giscard d'Estaing

70. Initially designated Operation GYMNAST, Operation TORCH was the Allied plan for the _____.
    A. airborne drop on Berlin
    B. invasion of North Africa
    C. blockade of Tokyo Harbor
    D. assassination of Adolf Hitler

71. How many delegates attended the United Nations Conference on International Organization?
    A. 250
    B. 460
    C. 850
    D. 980

72. What did FDR and Churchill promise Stalin if the Soviet Union entered the war against Japan?
    A. The Soviets would be given an occupation zone in Japan.
    B. The Soviets would be permitted to station troops in Italy and Spain.
    C. The Soviets would take possession of Southern Sakhalin and the Kuril Islands.
    D. The Soviets would create a buffer state by annexing a substantial portion of Turkey.

73. Devised by General Omar Bradley, _____ led to the breakout of Allied forces in Normandy.
    A. Operation COBRA
    B. Operation HARPOON
    C. Operation STONEWALL
    D. Operation CORKSCREW

74. TERMINAL was the code name for which Allied conference?
    A. Bernau
    B. Teltow
    C. Potsdam
    D. Stuttgart

75. Known as the Potsdam Declaration, it established the terms of Japan's surrender. The document included all of the following provisions *except* the _____.
    A. occupation by Allied forces
    B. demilitarization of the country
    C. loss of all territorial conquests
    D. imprisonment of Emperor Hirohito

76. J. Robert Oppenheimer called the initial detonation of the atomic bomb TRINITY. The name was inspired by the poetry of the 17th century English writer _____.
    A. Issac Watts
    B. Ben Jonson
    C. John Donne
    D. Aphra Behn

77. Which of these events took place during the Bretton Woods Conference?
    A. The city of Minsk was liberated by Soviet troops.
    B. General Douglas MacArthur "returned" to the Philippines.
    C. An assassination attempt was made on the life of Adolf Hitler.
    D. US B-29s dropped incendiary bombs on Tokyo for the first time.

78. At Dumbarton Oaks, a basic blueprint for the United Nations was introduced. It included all of the following *except* a(n) _____.
    A. Security Council
    B. General Assembly
    C. UN Defense Force
    D. International Court of Justice

79. How many Japanese soldiers were killed during the Battle of Peleliu (Operation STALEMATE II)?
    A. 6,000
    B. 10,000
    C. 11,000
    D. 15,000

80. What was to be Germany's fate at Potsdam?
    A. Its naval fleet would be destroyed.
    B. Its political and military leaders would be tried as war criminals.
    C. Its available resources would be used to rebuild the nations it subjugated.
    D. All of the above

81. At which conference did the Soviet Union demand $20 billion in reparations from Germany?
    A. Yalta
    B. Tehran
    C. London
    D. Casablanca

82. Devised by Field Marshal Bernard Montgomery, _____ was the airborne invasion of the Netherlands.
    A. Operation MACHETE
    B. Operation MATCHBOX
    C. Operation MARKETPLACE
    D. Operation MARKET GARDEN

83. Name the Ivy League institution that owned the estate where the Dumbarton Oaks Conference took place.
    A. Yale University
    B. Brown University
    C. Cornell University
    D. Harvard University

84. Held in Mexico City in early 1945, the Inter-American Conference on Problems of War and Peace (IACPWP) _____.
    A. established guidelines for aiding postwar Germany
    B. signed a treaty of mutual security for the Western Hemisphere
    C. evaluated the buildup of Allied training facilities in Latin America
    D. discussed the role of the United Nations and postwar American economic aid

85. A musical genre, it was also the designation given the Allied buildup in Great Britain for the D-Day invasion.
    A. JAZZ
    B. BOLERO
    C. FLAMENCO
    D. BLUEGRASS

86. Which Latin American country did *not* attend the IACPWP because it failed to declare war on the Axis Powers?
    A. Uruguay
    B. Venezuela
    C. Argentina
    D. Guatemala

87. Conducted in 1941 and attended by officers of the German *Wehrmacht*, the _____ addressed the issue of Jewish resistance in Soviet-occupied territory.
    A. Ozersk Conference
    B. Angren Conference
    C. Mogilev Conference
    D. Smolensk Conference

88. In all, how many Allied divisions participated in the D-Day invasion (Operation OVERLORD)?
    A. Ten
    B. Eleven
    C. Twelve
    D. Fourteen

89. The Declaration of St. James's Palace was also known as _____.
    A. Britannica Accords
    B. Treaty of Amritsar
    C. London Declaration
    D. Commonwealth Pact

90. Which of the following assemblies included at least one member of the Big Three?
    A. US-British Staff Conference
    B. Second Claridge Conference
    C. First Inter-Allied Conference
    D. Greater East Asia Conference

91. In the words of author Joseph N. Mueller, the invasion of _____ "shattered the myth of Japanese invincibility."⁴²
    A. Kiska (Operation COTTAGE)
    B. Tarawa (Operation GALVANIC)
    C. Iwo Jima (Operation DETACHMENT)
    D. Guadalcanal (Operation WATCHTOWER)

92. President Truman's strategy for dealing with the Russians _____.
    A. was similar to that of FDR
    B. damaged his relationship with the US military
    C. led to significant US concessions at Potsdam
    D. caused friction between he and Winston Churchill

93. At the Cairo Conference, Allied leaders determined that after the war, Korea would be _____.
    A. free and independent
    B. stripped of its Pacific colonies
    C. divided into zones of occupation
    D. granted "most favored nation" status

94. What was the code name for a British airborne assault on U-boat pens in France in June 1943?
    A. INDIGO
    B. PLOUGH
    C. LIGHTFOOT
    D. COUGHDROP

95. At the end of the Yalta Conference, basic disagreements remained regarding (the) _____.
    A. German POWs
    B. Czechoslovakian government
    C. war reparations to the Soviet Union
    D. unification of North and South Vietnam

96. Name the only member of the original Big Three to attend the entire Potsdam Conference.
   A. FDR
   B. Joseph Stalin
   C. Charles de Gaulle
   D. Winston Churchill

97. Operation CATECHISM was the RAF mission to destroy the German battleship _____.
   A. *Tirpitz*
   B. *Bismarck*
   C. *Prinz Eugen*
   D. *Scharnhorst*

98. All of the following statements regarding the occupation of Germany are true *except* _____.
   A. there were a total of four zones
   B. all of Berlin would be controlled by the US
   C. at an unspecified date Germany would be reunited
   D. the zones were to be determined by the position of troops at the end of the war

99. This conference is considered the most consequential for shaping the postwar world.
   A. Cairo
   B. Potsdam
   C. Cherchell
   D. Dumbarton Oaks

100. Named after a famous Napoleonic battle, _____ was a joint British and Canadian training exercise in southeastern England in 1941.
   A. Operation TRAFALGAR
   B. Operation WATERLOO
   C. Operation AUSTERLITZ
   D. Operation KAIDANOWO

Chapter Five Answers

1. D. "promote international cooperation, to ensure the fulfillment of accepted international peace, obligations and to provide safeguards against war."
2. A. fight communism
3. D. Neville Chamberlain
4. C. 1928 / Case White
5. A. SEA LION
6. A. Germany, Italy, and Japan
7. A. Operation COMPASS
8. C. Harry Hopkins
9. B. destroy US naval forces off Saipan
10. A. 105 days
11. D. Winston Churchill
12. B. Malta
13. B. Second Quebec Conference
14. A. It was the first time the plight of Jewish refugees was discussed.
15. B. TOPAZ
16. A. 4., 2., 1., 3.
17. C. John F. Kennedy
18. D. "Chattanooga Choo Choo"
19. A. The US declared war on Japan.
20. D. A and B
21. D. BARBAROSSA
22. A. Anthony Eden
23. A. Tehran Conference / not long after the Cairo Conference
24. C. OCTAGON
25. B. Brazzaville Conference
26. B. a president left the country during wartime
27. A. BLUE
28. A. The parties supported the creation of a postwar multi-national security force.

29. B. London Protocol
30. B. DOWNFALL
31. C. It solidified the relationship between the US and Great Britain.
32. A. Brazil
33. C. August 12 to August 17, 1942
34. D. B and C
35. D. Chiang Kai-shek / Cairo Conference
36. C. Casablanca
37. D. Moscow
38. A. USS *Augusta* (CA-31)
39. D. A and C
40. A. MULBERRY
41. D. No
42. D. United Nations Conference on International Organization
43. D. Philippines
44. B. Malta
45. A. He was unimpressed.
46. D. BUTTERMILK
47. A. Dillard Mays Conference
48. B. Latvia, Lithuania, and Estonia
49. C. *NORDMARK*
50. A. Where and when should the Western Allies establish a Second Front?
51. C. Brazilian Expeditionary Force
52. D. *WESERUBUNG*
53. A. Forty-four
54. D. William Mackenzie
55. B. ELKTON
56. D. United Nations
57. C. Potsdam
58. C. AVALANCHE
59. A. Atlantic Conference / before the Pearl Harbor attack
60. D. Washington, DC
61. B. Potsdam (TERMINAL)
62. C. Vyacheslav Molotov / Venice

63. D. conduct a coordinated bombing campaign against Germany
64. A. DRACULA
65. D. All of the above
66. D. Bretton Woods Conference
67. D. KETSU-GO
68. C. Cairo Conference
69. B. Charles de Gaulle
70. B. invasion of North Africa
71. C. 850
72. C. The Soviets would take possession of Southern Sakhalin and the Kuril Islands.
73. A. Operation COBRA
74. C. Potsdam
75. D. imprisonment of Emperor Hirohito
76. C. John Donne
77. A. The city of Minsk was liberated by Soviet troops.
78. C. UN Defense Force
79. B. 10,000
80. D. All of the above
81. A. Yalta
82. D. Operation MARKET GARDEN
83. D. Harvard University
84. D. discussed the role of the United Nations and postwar American economic aid
85. B. BOLERO
86. C. Argentina
87. C. Mogilev Conference
88. A. Ten
89. C. London Declaration
90. B. Second Claridge Conference
91. D. Guadalcanal (Operation WATCHTOWER)
92. C. led to significant US concessions at Potsdam
93. A. free and independent
94. D. COUGHDROP

95. C. war reparations to the Soviet Union
96. B. Joseph Stalin
97. A. *Tirpitz*
98. B. all of Berlin would be controlled by the US
99. B. Potsdam
100. B. Operation WATERLOO

German Chancellor Adolf Hitler meets with eighty-six-year-old President Paul von Hindenburg, March 21, 1933. *Bundesarchiv, Bild 183-S38324*

The *Führer* and Italy's Benito Mussolini in Munich Germany, June 1940. *National Archives*

The Battle of France is over, the Battle of Britain begins. An air observer scans the skies for German aircraft. St. Paul's Cathedral is visible in the background.
National Archives

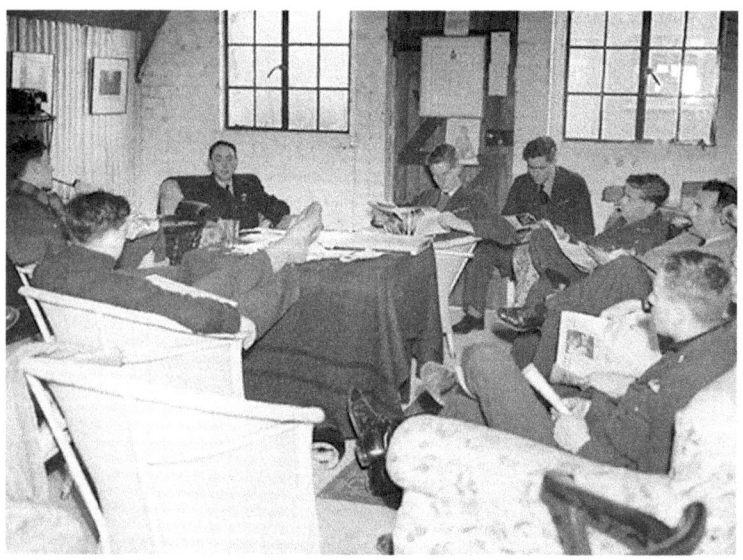

RAF pilots of No. 19 Squadron relax in the crew room during the Battle of Britain, September 1940. *Imperial War Museum*

THE SECOND WORLD WAR FACT AND QUIZ BOOK

President Franklin D. Roosevelt and Prime Minister Winston Churchill seated on the quarterdeck of HMS *Prince of Wales* for a Sunday service during the Atlantic Conference, August 10, 1941. *Imperial War Museum*

Hitler announces Germany's declaration of war against the United States to the *Reichstag*, December 11, 1941. *Bundesarchiv, Bild 183-1987-0703-507*

General Dwight Eisenhower speaks with men of the 101st Airborne Division June 5, 1944. *US Army Signal Corps*

American troops approaching OMAHA Beach, Normandy, France, June 6, 1944. *US Army Signal Corps / National Archives*

THE SECOND WORLD WAR FACT AND QUIZ BOOK

Field Marshal Wilhelm Keitel signing the final surrender terms in Berlin, May 9, 1945. *US Army / National Archives*

Londoners celebrate V-E Day, May 8, 1945. *Imperial War Museum*

WILLIAM E. SCOTT

Air Raid Pearl Harbor! A torpedo hits the USS *West Virginia* (BB-48) on the far side of Ford Island (center). *U.S. Navy NH 50930*

USS *West Virginia* (BB-48) burning in Pearl Harbor. *National Archives*

A USN Douglas SBD-5 *Dauntless* flies over the battleship USS *Washington* (BB-56) en route to the Gilbert Islands, November 12, 1943. *U.S. Navy National Museum of Naval Aviation photo No. 1996.253.680*

Soldiers of the U.S. 7th Infantry Division attack a Japanese blockhouse on Kwajalein (Marshall Islands), February 4, 1944. *National Archives*

U.S. Army soldiers (with the help of an M4 *Sherman* tank) hunt Japanese infiltrators on Bougainville, March 1, 1944. *US Army / National Archives*

Japanese representatives sign the Instrument of Surrender aboard the USS Missouri (BB-63), September 2, 1945. *US Army Signal Corps / Naval Historical Center photo No. SC 213700*

CHAPTER SIX

COMPLETE THE QUOTATION

1. General Omar Bradley: "[General George] Patton was a superb field general and leader—perhaps our best—but a man with _____."⁴³
   A. reckless and dangerous tendencies
   B. many human and professional flaws
   C. a total disregard for his own welfare
   D. no consideration for his fellow officers

2. Field Marshal Erwin Rommel: "The *Führer* must be _____."⁴⁴
   A. a military genius
   B. the devil incarnate
   C. a complete lunatic
   D. the nation's savior

3. Admiral William F. Halsey: "Before we're through with them, the Japanese _____."⁴⁵
   A. language will be spoken only in hell
   B. population will be reduced significantly
   C. military will know the might of American power
   D. emperor will be made to pay for his nation's crimes

4. Captain Yasuji Watanabe: "In all games [Admiral Isoroku] Yamamoto loved to take chances just as he did in naval strategy. He _____."⁴⁶
   A. had a gambler's heart
   B. was gifted but reckless
   C. had a poker player's instincts
   D. was the quintessential risk-taker

5. US Senator Thomas Connally: "How did it happen that our warships were caught like sitting ducks at Pearl Harbor? ... _____?"⁴⁷
   A. Why was this nation blindsided
   B. How could you allow this to happen
   C. Where was the Army, Navy, and Marines
   D. How did they catch us with our pants down

6. Prime Minister Winston Churchill: "I would say to the House, as I said to those who have joined this government: I have nothing to offer but _____."[48]
   A. tears, sweat, and blood
   B. sweat, blood, and tears
   C. blood, toil, tears, and sweat
   D. sweat, tears, toil, and blood

7. General George Patton: "[General Omar] Bradley has many of the attributes which are considered desirable in a general. He wears glasses, has a strong jaw, talks profoundly and _____."[49]
   A. says little
   B. criticizes others
   C. has nothing to say
   D. is an annoying individual

8. Admiral Isoroku Yamamoto: "Should hostilities break out between Japan and the United States, it is not enough that we take Guam and the Philippines, nor even _____…"[50]
   A. Burma and Philadelphia
   B. Australia and New York
   C. Hong Kong and Chicago
   D. Hawaii and San Francisco

9. FDR: "Find out, for God's sake, why _____."[51]
   A. our fleet did not fight back
   B. the ships were tied up in rows
   C. our fleet was vulnerable to attack
   D. the aircraft were lined up like toys

10. Field Marshal Gerd von Rundstedt: "Make peace, _____!"[52]
    A. not war
    B. you idiots
    C. whatever the cost
    D. before it's too late

11. General Dwight Eisenhower: "Sometimes I get so impatient that I want to . . . _____."[53]
    A. take my frustrations out on my staff
    B. resign and let someone else give the orders
    C. climb into a tank and drive directly to Berlin
    D. grab a rifle myself and start fighting Germans

12. Marshal Georgy Zhukov: "If we come to a minefield, our infantry _____."[54]
    A. is not afraid to face death itself
    B. has no regard for its own security
    C. attacks exactly as it were not there
    D. will not stop but keep moving forward

13. General James Doolittle: "There's only one thing that hurts our morale—that's when generals _____."[55]
    A. make decisions above their pay grade
    B. give too much praise for too little effort
    C. are unwilling to admit they made a mistake
    D. come around to see what's the matter with it

14. Adolf Hitler: "Once I really am in power, my first and foremost task will be the _____."[56]
    A. annihilation of the Jews
    B. destruction of the Soviet Union
    C. restructuring of the government
    D. imprisonment of my political rivals

15. Lieutenant Audie L. Murphy: "Let the hill be strewn with corpses so long as I do not have to turn over the bodies and _____."[57]
    A. wonder if he had a family
    B. look at a soldier I just killed
    C. find the familiar face of a friend
    D. become overwhelmed with grief

16. General William Slim: "[Many of] the troops that had been in action for the past few weeks were fought out and could not be relied on to hold anything ...[They] were untrained for the jungle and _____."[58]
    A. feared it more than they did the enemy
    B. loathed it more than they did the Japanese
    C. never should have been there in the first place
    D. should not be blamed for their lack of performance

17. US Secretary of the Navy James Forrestal: "The raising of that flag on Suribachi means _____."[59]
    A. Japan is finished for good
    B. thousands of recruits in the future
    C. a Marine Corps for the next 500 years
    D. our warriors will finally be returning home

18. Field Marshal Bernard Montgomery: "It became obvious to me in the autumn of 1944 ... [that] we were going to 'muck it up.' _____."[60]
    A. I reckon we did
    B. Here are the results
    C. That's exactly what happened
    D. Ike was told this would be the case

19. Admiral William Leahy: "Everybody may have peace if they are willing to pay *any* price for it. Part of this *any* price is slavery, dishonor of your women, _____......"[61]
    A. loss of self-respect
    B. denial of your God
    C. acceptance of defeat
    D. rejection of your values

20. *Reich* Minister of Propaganda Joseph Goebbels: "The best propaganda is that which, as it were, works invisibly, penetrates the whole of life without the public having any knowledge of the _____."⁶²
    A. false rhetoric
    B. misleading tone
    C. propagandistic initiative
    D. implementation of dishonesty

21. General George Marshall: "I don't want you fellows sitting around asking me what to do. _____."⁶³
    A. You know what your duties are
    B. I want you to tell me what to do
    C. That's not what you are paid for
    D. Get off your butts and get to work

22. Admiral Wilhelm Canaris: "I die for my fatherland. I have a clear conscience. I only did my duty to my country when I _____."⁶⁴
    A. fought against the slaughter of the Jews
    B. tried to oppose the criminal folly of Hitler
    C. supported the resistance movement in Berlin
    D. attempted to repudiate the brutal tactics of the Nazis

23. President Harry Truman: "He's [Douglas MacArthur] worse than the Cabots and the Lodges—they at least talked with one another before _____."⁶⁵
    A. they fouled things up
    B. they did as they pleased
    C. they told God what to do
    D. they chose their own path

24. Field Marshal Erich von Manstein: "Even in this hour we think of _____!"[66]
    A. every victorious battle to come
    B. the Fatherland's thirst for victory
    C. our fighting men and of our *Führer*
    D. the German people and their dreams

25. Correspondent Edward R. Murrow: "I don't know whether _____."[67]
    A. Montgomery is fit for command
    B. Eisenhower is a good general or not
    C. Patton should be disciplined or sent home
    D. Marshall is the right man to forge this coalition

26. Admiral Chuichi Nagumo: "The success of our surprise attack on Pearl Harbor will prove to be the _____..."[68]
    A. end of American control
    B. Waterloo of the war to follow
    C. beginning of Japanese domination
    D. undoing of Japan's quest for power

27. General Joseph Stilwell: "I claim we got a hell of a beating. We got run out of Burma, and it is humiliating as hell. _____."[69]
    A. It isn't fair to the men who died there
    B. I alone take full responsibility for what happened
    C. It isn't the fault of one soldier or even one field commander
    D. I think we ought to find out what caused it, go back, and retake it

28. Adolf Hitler: "Stalingrad is to be held _____."[70]
    A. at any cost
    B. with all means
    C. to the last man
    D. with our blood

29. Commander Logan Ramsay: "Air raid Pearl Harbor! _____!"[71]
    A. This is no drill
    B. This is only a test
    C. This is the real thing
    D. This is a war warning

30. General Harold Alexander: "Sir, it is my duty to report that the Tunisian campaign is over… _____."[72]
    A. Now on to our next adventure
    B. Herr Rommel has been defeated
    C. The bloody Hun has been vanquished
    D. We are masters of the North African shores

31. FDR: "Almighty God: Our sons, pride of our Nation, this day have set upon a mighty endeavor, a struggle to preserve our Republic, our religion, and our civilization, and to set free a suffering humanity. Lead them straight and true; give strength to their arms, stoutness to their hearts, _____…"[73]
    A. concern for their task
    B. patience in their mission
    C. dedication to their cause
    D. steadfastness in their faith

32. General Hermann Hoth: "The Russians have learnt a lot since 1941. They have learnt the _____."[74]
    A. keys to victory
    B. art of war from us
    C. technique of urban fighting
    D. meaning of sacrifice and discipline

33. US Senator Arthur H. Vandenberg: "The commander-in-chief should have instant power to act, and _____."[75]
    A. act he should
    B. he should act
    C. needs to insist upon it
    D. can't bother with Congress

34. Admiral Isoroku Yamamoto: "In the first six to twelve months of a war with the United States and Great Britain, I will run wild and win victory after victory, But then, if war continues after that, _____."[76]
    A. we will be in a fight for survival
    B. I have no expectation of success
    C. there may be difficult times ahead
    D. a Japanese victory will become elusive

35. General Lucius Clay: "We did all right because we made so many of them ... But we never had a _____."[77]
    A. tank that equaled the German tank
    B. rifle that equaled the Japanese rifle
    C. mine that equaled the British mine
    D. pistol that equaled the Italian pistol

36. *Reich* Minister of Armaments Albert Speer: "In the burning and devastated cities, we daily experienced the direct impact of war. It spurred us to do our utmost ...the bombing and the hardships that resulted from them did not _____."[78]
    A. sap the will of our glorious leader
    B. weaken the morale of the populace
    C. destroy the enthusiasm of our troops
    D. extinguish the spirit of the German people

37. Colonel Paul W. Tibbets: "If I ever have any grandchildren, I doubt if I'll get a chance to tell them about the [atomic] bomb. By that time I'll be a pretty old-fashioned fellow and _____."[79]
    A. they'll be telling me
    B. they won't be interested
    C. this will be ancient history
    D. they will teach this in school

38. General Tomoyuki Yamashita: "We have just received your reply. The Japanese Army will _____."[80]
    A. accept only total victory
    B. will attack in fifteen minutes
    C. receive your general's sword
    D. consider nothing but surrender

39. Admiral Chester Nimitz: "Among the Americans who served on Iwo Island, uncommon valor was _____."[81]
    A. a common virtue
    B. present in each man
    C. an ordinary occurrence
    D. the normal state of affairs

40. Prime Minister Clement Atlee: "The British people now realize the danger with which they are faced and know that in the event of a German victory everything they have built up will be destroyed. The Germans kill _____."[82]
    A. not only men, but ideas
    B. not only soldiers, but dreams
    C. not only people, but innocence
    D. not only their enemies, but hope

41. General Douglas MacArthur: "It was close; but that's the way it is in war. You win or lose, live or die—and _____."[83]
    A. therefore you must win
    B. the latter is unthinkable
    C. that is what war is all about
    D. the difference is just an eyelash

42. Minister of Foreign Affairs Vyacheslav Molotov: "Only a fool _____."[84]
    A. would attack us
    B. launches a winter offensive
    C. would stage an assault on Moscow
    D. chooses to go war with the Soviet Union

43. Admiral Samuel Eliot Morison: "No military event in our or any other country's history has been the subject of such exhaustive research as the _____."[85]
    A. invasion of Normandy
    B. air assault on Pearl Harbor
    C. stunning victory at Midway
    D. development of the atomic bomb

44. Prime Minister Fumimaro Konoye: "The thing that brought about the determination to make peace was the _____."[86]
    A. incessant raids by your aircraft
    B. prolonged bombing by the B-29s
    C. devastating effects of the atomic bomb
    D. futility of continuing a war we could not win

45. General Mark Clark: "...Here was our only conquest; all we asked of Italy was enough of her soil in which to _____."[87]
    A. defeat Mussolini
    B. establish a beachhead
    C. bury our gallant dead
    D. defeat the Nazi invaders

46. Field Marshal Wilhelm Keitel: "...The truth was that nobody would have been able to replace me, because each one knew that he would end up _____."88
    A. facing a firing squad
    B. just as much a wreck as I
    C. doing the *Führer's* bidding
    D. hanging from the end of a rope

47. Admiral Ernest King: "I didn't like the atom bomb or _____."89
    A. any part of it
    B. understand our motivation
    C. its use against the Japanese
    D. using it against our enemies

48. Prime Minister Winston Churchill: "Hitler knows that he will have to break us in this Island or lose the war...Let us therefore brace ourselves to our duties, and so bear ourselves that, if the British Empire and its Commonwealth last for a thousand years, men will still say, _____."90
    A. *This* was their finest hour
    B. *They* did what had to de done
    C. *Their* sacrifices were not in vain
    D. *They* answered the call when needed

49. General Dwight Eisenhower: "Soldiers, Sailors, and Airmen of the Allied Expeditionary Force: You are about to embark on the Great Crusade, toward with we have striven these many months...Your task will not be an easy one. Your enemy is well-trained, well equipped and battle-hardened. He _____..."91
    A. will fight savagely
    B. will give no quarter
    C. will never surrender
    D. will test your training

50. Field Marshal Erwin Rommel: "May Almighty God help me in the coming year, as in the past, to justify the faith in me of the *Führer* and the _____."[92]
   A. Nazi Party
   B. German people
   C. men of the *Afrika Korps*
   D. troops defending the fatherland

51. Admiral William F. Halsey: "Hit hard, hit fast, _____!"[93]
   A. hit often
   B. hit courageously
   C. hit without mercy
   D. hit with determination

52. General Percy Hobart: "Why piddle about making porridge with artillery, and then send men to drown themselves in it for a hundred yards of No Man's Land? _____!"[94]
   A. An Airborne assault is the way to go
   B. Tanks mean advances of miles at a time not yards
   C. Armor can help troops reach their objectives much faster
   D. We should depend on the battleship boys with their big guns

53. US Senator Robert Taft: "An invasion of the United States by the German Army is as fantastic as would be _____."[95]
   A. Christmas in August
   B. a snowstorm in the Mojave Desert
   C. the New York Yankees losing the World Series
   D. an invasion of Germany by the American Army

54. General Adolf Galland: "From the very first moment of the [Normandy] invasion, the Allies had absolute air supremacy. Therefore, the enemy, our own troops, and the population asked the obvious question, '_____?'"[96]
   A. When will this end
   B. Where is the *Luftwaffe*
   C. Why won't this war end
   D. Will we see German planes

55. President Ronald Reagan: "These are the boys of Pointe du Hoc. These are the men who took the cliffs. These are the champions who helped free a continent. These are the _____."⁹⁷
    A. men who epitomize bravery
    B. heroes who helped end a war
    C. survivors of the Great Crusade
    D. victorious defenders of freedom

56. Admiral Sir Andrew Cunningham: "PM [Prime Minister Winston Churchill] now most optimistic and placing great faith in the new bomb. He now thinks it is a good thing that the Russians should know about it, and it may make _____."⁹⁸
    A. it easier to deal with them
    B. them a little more humble
    C. Stalin think twice about Berlin
    D. them less demanding in the long-run

57. General Leslie Groves: "He's a genius. A real genius…Why, [J. Robert] Oppenheimer knows about everything. He can talk to you about anything you bring up. Well, not exactly He doesn't know anything about _____."⁹⁹
    A. art
    B. music
    C. sports
    D. fishing

58. *Reich* Minister of Foreign Affairs Joachim von Ribbentrop: "I know for a fact that this idea of the Jews causing the war and the Jews being so all-important is nonsense. _____."¹⁰⁰
    A. Of this I am certain
    B. But that was Hitler's idea
    C. It is Pure and utter nonsense
    D. This is the crux of the matter

59. Colonel George Taylor: "On a landing operation, there are two classes of men that may be found on the beach, those who are already dead and _____."¹⁰¹
   A. those who need a push
   B. those who are about to die
   C. those who are afraid to move
   D. those who need to forge ahead

60. General Brian Horrocks: "…It is only now that I realize fully just how great he [Field Marshal Alan Brooke] was. We regarded him as a _____…"¹⁰²
   A. capable leader of men
   B. powerful force of nature
   C. skilled tactician and strategist
   D. highly efficient military machine

61. FDR: "We should come as close to unconditional surrender as we can, followed by _____."¹⁰³
   A. a fair deal for the Japanese people
   B. good treatment of the Italian populace
   C. severe punishment of the Nazi leadership
   D. the trial and execution of Italian war criminals

62. Prime Minister Winston Churchill: "No American will think it wrong of me if I proclaim—that to have the United States at our side was to me the greatest joy…Hitler's fate was sealed, Mussolini's fate was sealed, as for the Japanese, _____."¹⁰⁴
   A. they were finished
   B. they ceased to exist
   C. they were unable to continue
   D. they would be ground to powder

63. Vice President Richard Nixon: "[General Douglas] MacArthur spoke to me eloquently about it …MacArthur you see was a soldier. He believed in using force _____…"[105]
    A. if diplomacy failed
    B. when absolutely necessary
    C. only against military targets
    D. if the odds were in his favor

64. Admiral Mitsumasa Yonai: "It seems that the army is losing confidence in the war situation. The army is very afraid of how the Soviets will move. Therefore, they want to prolong the Neutrality Pact; ask the Soviets to be an intermediary; and _____."[106]
    A. end the Great Asian War
    B. preserve Japan's monarchy
    C. negotiate a surrender agreement
    D. have the bombing of Japanese cities stopped

65. General George Patton: "Ike is more British than the British and is putty in their hands. _____."[107]
    A. Oh, God, for John J. Pershing
    B. Cripes, Ike needs to listen to reason
    C. Geez, I wish Stonewall Jackson were here
    D. Damn him, we need a George Washington

66. *Reich* Marshal Hermann Göring: "No enemy bomber can reach the Ruhr. If one reaches the Ruhr, my name is _____."[108]
    A. Meyer
    B. Becker
    C. Wagner
    D. Schmidt

67. Correspondent Ernie Pyle: "…You feel small in the presence of dead men, and ashamed at being alive, and _____."[109]
    A. you are speechless
    B. you feel insignificant
    C. you want to be invisible
    D. you don't ask silly questions

68. Premier Joseph Stalin: "God is on your side? Is He a conservative? The Devil's on my side, _____."[110]
    A. he's a loyal Bolshevik
    B. he's a trusted Marxist
    C. he's a patriot of Russian
    D. he's a good Communist

69. General Omar Bradley: "Six hours after the [D-Day] landings, we held _____."[111]
    A. one yard of sand
    B. five yards of hell
    C. ten yards of beach
    D. eleven yards of chaos

70. Minister of Foreign Affairs Shigenori Togo: "His Majesty the Emperor, mindful of the fact that the present war daily brings greater evil and sacrifice upon the peoples of all belligerent powers, _____…"[112]
    A. wants peace at any cost
    B. hopes for a speedy end to hostilities
    C. craves the benefits of a tranquil world
    D. desires from his heart that it may be quickly terminated

71. President George W. Bush: "That road to V-E Day was hard and long and traveled by weary and valiant men. And history will always record where that road began. It began here, _____."113
    A. on the sands of North Africa
    B. in the hallowed halls of the US Capitol
    C. on the narrow streets and wide boulevards of Paris
    D. with the first footprints on the beaches of Normandy

72. Air Marshal Arthur Harris: "I do not personally regard the whole of the remaining cities of Germany worth the bones of one _____."114
    A. Royal Fusilier
    B. Dragoon Guard
    C. British Grenadier
    D. English Carabineer

73. General Leonard T. Gerow: "In my opinion, the War Department had sent ample warnings to the overseas commanders…to _____."115
    A. notify their naval and military assets
    B. alert their respective commands for war
    C. inform their units of pending belligerent action
    D. warn their subordinates regarding possible hostilities

74. Prime Minister Neville Chamberlain: "I don't agree…that we should make peace with Germany in order to resist Russia. I still regard Germany as _____…"116
    A. our arch enemy
    B. Public Enemy No. 1
    C. our primary nemesis
    D. the stone in our shoe

75. US Secretary of State Joseph C. Grew: "If some indication can now be given the Japanese that they themselves, when once thoroughly defeated and rendered impotent to wage war in the future, will be permitted to determine _____..."[117]
   A. their own future political structure
   B. which form of government they wish to have
   C. how former government officials should be punished
   D. in conjunction with the Allies, their own economic structure

76. General Yoshijiro Umezu: "It is all very well to be cautious, but if we are too cautious _____."[118]
   A. the Americans will pounce
   B. we will miss our opportunity
   C. our hard work will be for naught
   D. may the gods of war have mercy on us

77. US Senator Daniel K. Inouye: "I gave this arm to fight fascists. If my country wants the other one to fight communists, it can have it. What _____?"[119]
   A. is the cost of freedom
   B. are you prepared to give
   C. price are you willing to pay
   D. does your conscience tell you

78. *Reich* Protector of Bohemia and Moravia Reinhard Heydrich: "It is natural that people do not want to be involved with us too much. There is no problem down to the smallest egotistical longing which the _____..."[120]
   A. *SS* cannot manage
   B. *Führer* cannot solve
   C. *Wehrmacht* cannot fix
   D. *Gestapo* cannot handle

79. General Henry Arnold: "We are getting a rash of aces elsewhere and losing them in many cases because the individual score _____."[121]
    A. blinds them to their true mission
    B. cannot defeat a determined enemy
    C. means more than the squadron score
    D. is more significant than unit cohesion

80. Colonel Claus von Stauffenberg: "We took this challenge before our Lord and our conscience, and it must be done, because this man, Hitler, _____."[122]
    A. he is Satan himself
    B. he is the ultimate evil
    C. he is the destroyer of worlds
    D. he is the incarnation of the devil

81. Admiral Harold Stark: "This dispatch is to be considered a war warning. Negotiations with Japan looking toward stabilization of conditions in the Pacific have ceased. An aggressive move by Japan is expected _____..."[123]
    A. at any moment
    B. possibly this weekend
    C. by the end of the month
    D. within the next few days

82. Prime Minister Édouard Daladier: "If the blood of France and Germany flows again, as it did twenty-five years ago, in a longer and even more murderous war, each of the two peoples will fight with confidence in its own victory, but the most certain victors will be the..."[124]
    A. rich and the powerful
    B. warmongers and industrialists
    C. forces of destruction and barbarism
    D. generations that emerge from the rubble

83. General Curtis LeMay: "The atomic bomb had nothing to do with _____."[125]
   A. defeating the Japanese
   B. securing a lasting peace
   C. the end of the war at all
   D. Russia's entry into the war

84. Admiral Isoroku Yamamoto: "The Army talks big, but if war came and there were large-scale air raids, _____."[126]
   A. the living would envy the dead
   B. I cannot imagine what would occur
   C. there's no telling what would happen
   D. life as we know it would cease to exist

85. US Secretary of State James F. Byrnes: "The ultimate form of government of Japan shall be established by the _____."[127]
   A. international community
   B. government of the United States
   C. military commission of Allied nations
   D. freely expressed will of the Japanese people

86. General Hideki Tojo: "It is natural that I should bear entire responsibility for the war in general, and, needless to say, _____..."[128]
   A. I can not do otherwise
   B. I am prepared to do so
   C. I will accept the blame
   D. I admit my involvement

87. Captain Henry P. Crowe: "Goddamn it, you'll never get the Purple Heart hiding in a foxhole! _____!"[129]
   A. Follow me
   B. Get your asses in gear
   C. Let's make a fight of it
   D. You can't win down there

88. Adolf Hitler: "The soldiers on the Eastern Front fight far better. The reason they give in so easily in the West is simply the fault of _____..."[130]
    A. our incompetent generals
    B. that stupid Geneva Convention
    C. your inability to lead men in battle
    D. the despicable cowards in our ranks

89. US Assistant Secretary of War John J. McCloy: "…We ought to have our heads examined if we don't explore some other method by which we can terminate this war than just by _____…"[131]
    A. a massive air assault on Berlin
    B. another conventional attack and landing
    C. using a weapon such as the atomic bomb
    D. a coordinated invasion of the home islands

90. General Tomoyuki Yamashita: "How could we win _____?"[132]
    A. when you had all that
    B. when the odds were against us
    C. when we lacked the means to continue
    D. when your air force was leveling our cities

91. President Barack Obama: "We tell this story for the old soldiers who pull themselves a little straighter today to salute _____."[133]
    A. comrades who freed a continent
    B. brothers who never made it home
    C. heroes who missed the final victory
    D. friends who will never see tomorrow

92. Field Marshal Erwin Rommel: "Believe me, Lang, the first twenty-four hours of the invasion will be decisive…the fate of Germany depends on the outcome…for the Allies, as well as Germany, _____."[134]
    A. it will be the longest day
    B. time will be a major factor
    C. it will be the ultimate battle
    D. this day will decide the future

93. US Secretary of the Navy Frank Knox: "If war eventuates with Japan, it is believed easily possible that hostilities would be initiated by a surprise attack upon the fleet or the _____."¹³⁵
    A. West Coast of the US
    B. naval base at Pearl Harbor
    C. US military garrison on Corregidor
    D. aircraft at Hickam and Wheeler Fields

94. Prime Minister Winston Churchill: "I told you hard things at the beginning of these last five years; you did not shrink, and I should be unworthy of your confidence and generosity if I did not still cry: Forward, unflinching, unswerving, indomitable, till the whole task is done and _____."¹³⁶
    A. we can return to our loved ones
    B. the whole world is safe and clean
    C. we are rid of the Nazis and Fascists
    D. the planet has been purged of hatred

95. J. Robert Oppenheimer: "We didn't know beans about the military situation in Japan. We didn't know whether they could be caused to surrender by other means or whether the _____…"¹³⁷
    A. war would go on and on
    B. invasion was really inevitable
    C. atomic bomb would have to be used
    D. Soviet Union needed to get involved

96. *Reichsführer-SS* Heinrich Himmler: "I hope to see the very concept of Jewry _____."¹³⁸
    A. totally destroyed
    B. expunged forever
    C. universally eradicated
    D. completely obliterated

97. General James Gavin: "Soldiers of the 505th Combat Team: Tonight you embark upon a combat mission for which our people and the free people of the world have been waiting for two years... You will spearhead the landing of an American Force _____..."[139]
   A. on the shores of Japan
   B. upon the island of Sicily
   C. on the beaches of Normandy
   D. near the capital of the Philippines

98. Field Marshal Sir Alan Brooke: "He [General Dwight Eisenhower] literally knows nothing of the _____."[140]
   A. art of warfare
   B. men he is sending into battle
   C. requirements of a commander in action
   D. effort needed to hold a coalition together

99. Admiral Ernest King: "Well, it's all over. _____."[141]
   A. I need to find a new hobby
   B. I think I will go fishing today
   C. I expect the future will be uneventful
   D. I wonder what I'm going to do tomorrow

100. General Franz Halder: "Bad weather has grounded the *Luftwaffe* and now we must stand by and watch countless thousands of the enemy _____."[142]
   A. slip through the jaws of our trap
   B. getting away to England under our noses
   C. skipping merrily across the English Channel
   D. escaping to safety in order to fight another day

Chapter Six Answers

1. B. many human and professional flaws
2. C. a complete lunatic
3. A. language will be spoken only in hell
4. A. had a gambler's heart
5. D. How did they catch us with our pants down
6. D. sweat, tears, toil, and blood
7. A. says little
8. D. Hawaii and San Francisco
9. B. the ships were tied up in rows
10. B. you idiots
11. D. grab a rifle myself and start fighting Germans
12. C. attacks exactly as it were not there
13. D. come around to see what's the matter with it
14. A. annihilation of the Jews
15. C. find the familiar face of a friend
16. A. feared it more than they did the enemy
17. C. a Marine Corps for the next 500 years
18. A. I reckon we did
19. B. denial of your God
20. C. propagandistic initiative
21. B. I want you to tell me what to do
22. B. tried to oppose the criminal folly of Hitler
23. C. they told God what to do
24. C. our fighting men and of our *Führer*
25. B. Eisenhower is a good general or not
26. C. Waterloo of the war to follow
27. D. I think we ought to find out what caused it, go back and retake it
28. B. with all means
29. A. This is no drill
30. D. We are masters of the North African shores

31. D. steadfastness in their faith
32. B. art of war from us
33. B. he should act
34. B. I have no expectation of success
35. A. tank that equaled the German tank
36. B. weaken the morale of the populace
37. A. they'll be telling me
38. D. consider nothing but surrender
39. A. a common virtue
40. A. not only men but ideas
41. D. the difference is just an eyelash
42. A. would attack us
43. B. air assault on Pearl Harbor
44. B. prolonged bombing by the B-29s
45. C. bury our gallant dead
46. B. just as much a wreck as I
47. A. any part of it
48. A. *This* was their finest hour
49. A. will fight savagely
50. B. German people
51. A. hit often
52. B. Tanks mean advances of miles at a time not yards
53. D. an invasion of Germany by the American Army
54. B. Where is the *Luftwaffe*
55. B. heroes who helped end a war
56. B. them a little more humble
57. C. sports
58. B. But that was Hitler's idea
59. B. those who are about to die
60. D. highly efficient military machine
61. B. good treatment of the Italian populace
62. D. they would be ground to powder
63. C. only against military targets

THE SECOND WORLD WAR FACT AND QUIZ BOOK

64. A. end the Great Asian War
65. A. Oh, God, for John J. Pershing
66. A. Meyer
67. D. you don't ask silly questions
68. D. he's a good Communist
69. C. ten yards of beach
70. D. desires from his heart that it may be quickly terminated
71. D. with the first footprints on the beaches of Normandy
72. C. British Grenadier
73. B. alert their respective commands for war
74. B. Public Enemy No. 1
75. A. their own future political structure
76. B. we will miss our opportunity
77. B. are you prepared to give
78. D. *Gestapo* cannot handle
79. C. means more than the squadron score
80. B. he is the ultimate evil
81. D. within the next few days
82. C. forces of destruction and barbarism
83. C. the end of the war at all
84. C. there's no telling what would happen
85. D. freely expressed will of the Japanese people
86. B. I am prepared to do so
87. A. Follow me
88. B. that stupid Geneva Convention
89. B. another conventional attack and landing
90. A. when you had all that
91. B. brothers who never made it home
92. A. it will be the longest day
93. B. naval base at Pearl Harbor
94. B. the whole world is safe and clean
95. B. invasion was really inevitable
96. D. completely obliterated

97. B. upon the island of Sicily
98. C. requirements of a commander in action
99. D. I wonder what I'm going to do tomorrow
100. B. getting away to England under our noses

CHAPTER SEVEN

G.I. JARGON

1. ACK-ACK:
   A. Pimples
   B. Baked beans
   C. Machine gun
   D. Truck backfire

2. ALBATROS:
   A. Fish
   B. Loser
   C. Snitch
   D. Chicken

3. ARMOURED COW:
   A. Skim milk
   B. Breast milk
   C. Whole milk
   D. Canned milk

4. ARMY BANJO:
   A. Shovel
   B. Bayonet
   C. Hammer
   D. Screwdriver

5. ARMY STRAWBERRIES:
   A. Prunes
   B. Strawberries
   C. New recruits
   D. Hemorrhoids

6. ASPARAGUS STICK:
   A. Trench knife
   B. Hand grenade
   C. Bangalore torpedo
   D. Submarine periscope

7. AXLE GREASE:
    A. Butter
    B. Hair tonic
    C. Mayonnaise
    D. Cooking oil

8. BABY:
    A. Relish
    B. Ketchup
    C. Onions
    D. Mustard

9. BAGS OF MYSTERY:
    A. Sausages
    B. K-rations
    C. Prostitutes
    D. Walkie-talkie

10. BAIL OUT:
    A. Excuse
    B. Retreat
    C. Court martial
    D. Parachute jump

11. BARKER:
    A. Bazooka
    B. Artillery
    C. Staff sergeant
    D. Air raid siren

12. BARRACKS 13:
    A. Foxhole
    B. Hospital
    C. Guardhouse
    D. Medic station

13. BATH TUB:
    A. Submarine
    B. Bomb crater
    C. Helmet liner
    D. Motorcycle sidecar

14. BATTERY ACID:
    A. Coffee
    B. Quicksand
    C. Orange juice
    D. Pepto-Bismol

15. BEAST:
    A. Tough guy
    B. Ugly woman
    C. German tank
    D. West Point cadet

16. BEHAVIOR REPORT:
    A. Court-martial
    B. Letter to a girl
    C. Fitness evaluation
    D. Psychiatric report

17. BELLY ROBBER:
    A. Ulcer
    B. Diarrhea
    C. Mess sergeant
    D. Army surgeon

18. BEND THE THROTTLE:
    A. Urinate
    B. Talk too much
    C. Someone who lies
    D. To fly or drive fast

19. BIBLE:
    A. Magazine
    B. Newspaper
    C. Weapons manual
    D. Army regulations

20. BIG JOHN:
    A. Recruit
    B. Chaplain
    C. Platoon sergeant
    D. Commanding general

21. BLACK STRAP:
    A. Tea
    B. Coffee
    C. Scotch
    D. Whiskey

22. BLISTERFOOT:
    A. Sinner
    B. Defector
    C. Fighter pilot
    D. Infantryman

23. BLITZES:
    A. Air patrols
    B. Tank assault
    C. Depth charges
    D. Bayonet attack

24. BLOW YOUR TOP:
    A. Desert your post
    B. Lose your temper
    C. Divulge information
    D. Strike a superior officer

25. BOB-TAIL:
    A. Flying ace
    B. Enemy agent
    C. Dishonorable discharge
    D. Someone who takes chances

26. BOG-POCKET:
    A. Tightwad
    B. Spendthrift
    C. German prisoner
    D. Demolitions expert

27. BOODLE:
    A. Candy
    B. Liquor
    C. Ammunition
    D. Stolen money

28. BOUDOIR:
    A. Latrine
    B. Bunker
    C. Mess hall
    D. Squad tent

29. BOWLEGS:
    A. Civilians
    B. Cavalrymen
    C. Collaborators
    D. Correspondents

30. BRASS HATS:
    A. Senators
    B. Navy fliers
    C. Staff officers
    D. Congressmen

THE SECOND WORLD WAR FACT AND QUIZ BOOK

31. BUGGY:
    A. Staff Car
    B. Destroyer
    C. Half-track
    D. Battleship

32. BULLY BEEF:
    A. Spam
    B. Pastrami
    C. Liverwurst
    D. Corned beef

33. BURN AND TURN:
    A. Poker
    B. Solitaire
    C. Pinochle
    D. Blackjack

34. BUTCH:
    A. Medical officer
    B. Latrine orderly
    C. Gas station attendant
    D. Motor pool mechanic

35. BUTTON CHOPPER:
    A. Salute
    B. Laundry
    C. Pen knife
    D. Doorbell

36. CANS:
    A. Gloves
    B. Breasts
    C. Destroyers
    D. Headphones

37. CARE BOY:
    A. Co-pilot
    B. Mailman
    C. Tank driver
    D. Paratrooper

38. CAT'S BEER:
    A. Milk
    B. Urine
    C. Water
    D. Coffee

39. CHINA CLIPPER:
    A. Repairman
    B. Dishwasher
    C. Civilian pilot
    D. Loose woman

40. COCK PIT FOG:
    A. Vertigo
    B. Dyslexia
    C. Unconscious
    D. Mentally lost

41. COFFEE COOLER:
    A. Liar
    B. Misfit
    C. Loafer
    D. Cream

42. COPENHAGEN:
    A. Sneezing
    B. Chewing snuff
    C. Smoking a pipe
    D. Blowing bubbles

THE SECOND WORLD WAR FACT AND QUIZ BOOK

43. COSMOLINES:
    A. Spies
    B. Artillery
    C. Veterans
    D. Imposters

44. COUSIN:
    A. Sister
    B. Brother
    C. Farm boy
    D. Close friend

45. CROSS BAR HOTEL:
    A. Pillbox
    B. Brothel
    C. Ambulance
    D. Guardhouse

46. CRUMB HUNT:
    A. Rifle inspection
    B. Kitchen inspection
    C. Uniform inspection
    D. Barracks inspection

47. DAY ROOM:
    A. Bedroom
    B. Pool room
    C. Waiting room
    D. Recreation room

48. DECODE:
    A. To confess
    B. To explain
    C. To criticize
    D. To apologize

49. DEVIL'S PIANO:
    A. Barbed wire
    B. Machine gun
    C. Air raid siren
    D. Contact mine

50. DIT DA ARTIST:
    A. Singer
    B. Magician
    C. Photographer
    D. Radio Operator

51. DOGFACE:
    A. Ugly man
    B. Corpsman
    C. Enlisted man
    D. Canine handler

52. DOG ROBBER:
    A. Orderly
    B. Scavenger
    C. Male nurse
    D. General's aide

53. DOG SHOW:
    A. Target practice
    B. Military parade
    C. Beauty pageant
    D. Foot inspection

54. DOODLE BUG:
    A. Pistol
    B. Battleship
    C. Aircraft carrier
    D. Reconnaissance car

55. DOPES OFF:
    A. Acts stupid
    B. Falls asleep
    C. Takes drugs
    D. Falls in love

56. DOUGHBOY:
    A. Cook
    B. Waiter
    C. Bank clerk
    D. Infantryman

57. DOUGH PUNCHER:
    A. Girlfriend
    B. Army baker
    C. Grave digger
    D. Troublemaker

58. DRY RUN:
    A. Surgery
    B. Aborted flight
    C. Desert warfare
    D. Dress rehearsal

59. DUD:
    A. Prude
    B. Movie
    C. Womanizer
    D. Unexploded shell

60. FAT FRIENDS:
    A. Balloons
    B. Depth charges
    C. Atomic bombs
    D. Wealthy buddy

61. FATIGUES:
    A. Boots
    B. Underwear
    C. Work clothes
    D. Dress uniform

62. FILE:
    A. Typewriter
    B. Jackhammer
    C. Waste basket
    D. Loose woman

63. FIRST GRADER:
    A. Seabee
    B. Truck driver
    C. Master Sergeant
    D. Annapolis graduate

64. FIRST MAN:
    A. Private
    B. Captain
    C. Lieutenant
    D. First Sergeant

65. FLYING BOXCAR:
    A. Fighter
    B. Bomber
    C. Hand grenade
    D. Reconnaissance plane

66. GENERAL'S CAR:
    A. Tricycle
    B. Roller skates
    C. Wheel barrel
    D. Horse and wagon

67. GINK:
    A. Glue
    B. Mustard
    C. Lamb stew
    D. Stupid person

68. GLAMOUR BOY:
    A. Draftee
    B. War hero
    C. Movie star
    D. College graduate

69. GOLD-FISH:
    A. Trout
    B. Salmon
    C. Sea Bass
    D. Flounder

70. GRANDMA GEAR:
    A. Galoshes
    B. Low gear
    C. Bloomers
    D. Pocketbook

71. HANGER WARRIOR:
    A. Hotshot pilot
    B. Chief Signalman
    C. Machinist's mate
    D. Aircraft mechanic

72. HASH BURNER:
    A. Cook
    B. Stove
    C. Hamburger
    D. Flamethrower

73. JAWBREAKER:
    A. Ice
    B. Candy
    C. Biscuit
    D. Diamond

74. JESUS:
    A. Rifle
    B. Helmet
    C. Major
    D. Chaplain

75. JOE:
    A. Buddy
    B. Soldier
    C. Dentist
    D. Boy friend

76. JUICE JERKER:
    A. Bartender
    B. Electrician
    C. Petty officer
    D. Radio operator

77. KITE:
    A. Airplane
    B. Dirigible
    C. Troop glider
    D. Barrage balloon

78. LANDING GEAR:
    A. Legs
    B. Wheels
    C. Prophylactic
    D. Combat boots

79. LEAD POISONING:
    A. Bullet
    B. Napalm
    C. Infection
    D. Tin plate

80. LOOSENERS:
    A. Prunes
    B. Scissors
    C. Tweezers
    D. Suppositories

81. MAE WEST:
    A. Brassiere
    B. Pontoons
    C. Flotation vest
    D. Inflatable raft

82. MARFAK:
    A. Butter
    B. Onions
    C. Turnips
    D. Spaghetti

83. MEAT WAGON:
    A. Bus
    B. Fire truck
    C. Trolley car
    D. Ambulance

84. MISERY PIPE:
    A. Bugle
    B. Cigar
    C. Bazooka
    D. Trumpet

85. MITT-FLOPPER:
    A. Glove
    B. Skillet
    C. Traitor
    D. Yes-man

86. MOTORIZED FRECKLES:
    A. Insects
    B. Pimples
    C. Search light
    D. Chicken pox

87. MOUSETRAP:
    A. Cheese
    B. Tunnel
    C. Submarine
    D. Teller mine

88. NORTH DAKOTA RICE:
    A. Lice
    B. Snow
    C. Wheat
    D. Hot cereal

89. PEP TIRE:
    A. Pizza
    B. Cookie
    C. Pancake
    D. Doughnut

90. PIG SNOUT:
    A. Ham
    B. Gas mask
    C. Ugly nurse
    D. Oxygen mask

91. POCKET LETTUCE:
    A. Lint
    B. Money
    C. Sandwich
    D. Playing cards

92. SUPERMAN SUIT:
    A. Naked
    B. Overalls
    C. Underwear
    D. Swim trunks

93. SWACKED:
    A. Confused
    B. Wounded
    C. Intoxicated
    D. Shell shocked

94. SWOOP:
    A. Napalm
    B. Dynamite
    C. Roast beef
    D. Quick sand

95. TABLE MUSCLE:
    A. Fat
    B. Tough guy
    C. Arm wrestler
    D. Company boxer

96. TIGER MEAT:
    A. Veal
    B. Beef
    C. Pork
    D. Chicken

97. TIN PICKLE:
    A. Cigar
    B. Rocket
    C. Bazooka
    D. Torpedo

98. TUB:
    A. Ship
    B. Major
    C. Admiral
    D. Scout car

99. WARD MAN:
    A. Lawyer
    B. Doctor
    C. Brother
    D. Hospital attendant

100. YARD BIRD:
    A. Drunk
    B. Convict
    C. Raw recruit
    D. Carrier pigeon

Chapter Seven Answers

1. C. Machine gun
2. D. Chicken
3. D. Canned milk
4. A. Shovel
5. A. Prunes
6. D. Submarine periscope
7. A. Butter
8. D. Mustard
9. A. Sausages
10. D. Parachute jump
11. B. Artillery
12. C. Guardhouse
13. D. Motorcycle sidecar
14. A. Coffee
15. D. West Point cadet
16. B. Letter to a girl
17. C. Mess sergeant
18. D. To fly or drive fast
19. D. Army regulations
20. A. Recruit
21. B. Coffee
22. D. Infantryman
23. A. Air patrols
24. B. Lose your temper
25. C. Dishonorable discharge
26. A. Tightwad
27. A. Candy
28. D. Squad tent
29. B. Cavalrymen
30. C. Staff officers
31. A. Staff car
32. D. Corned beef

33. D. Blackjack
34. A. Medical officer
35. B. Laundry
36. D. Headphones
37. C. Tank driver
38. A. Milk
39. B. Dishwasher
40. D. Mentally lost
41. C. Loafer
42. B. Chewing snuff
43. B. Artillery
44. D. Close friend
45. D. Guardhouse
46. B. Kitchen inspection
47. D. Recreation room
48. B. To explain
49. B. Machine gun
50. D. Radio operator
51. C. Enlisted man
52. A. Orderly
53. D. Foot inspection
54. D. Reconnaissance car
55. A. Acts stupid
56. D. Infantryman
57. B. Army baker
58. D. Dress rehearsal
59. D. Unexploded shell
60. A. Balloons
61. C. Work cloths
62. C. Waste basket
63. C. Master Sergeant
64. D. First Sergeant
65. B. Bomber
66. C. Wheel barrel

67. D. Stupid person
68. A. Draftee
69. B. Slamon
70. B. Low gear
71. D. Aircraft mechanic
72. A. Cook
73. C. Biscuit
74. D. Chaplain
75. B. Soldier
76. B. Electrician
77. A. Airplane
78. A. Legs
79. A. Bullet
80. A. Prunes
81. C. Flotation vest
82. A. Butter
83. D. Ambulance
84. A. Bugle
85. D. Yes-man
86. A. Insects
87. C. Submarine
88. D. Hot cereal
89. D. Doughnut
90. B. Gas mask
91. B. Money
92. C. Underwear
93. C. Intoxicated
94. B. Dynamite
95. A. Fat
96. B. Beef
97. D. Torpedo
98. D. Scout car
99. D. Hospital attendant
100. C. Raw recruit

CHAPTER EIGHT
HOLLYWOOD GOES TO WAR

1. Henry Fonda starred as Lieutenant Douglas Roberts in the 1955 motion picture *Mr. Roberts*. Who starred in the original 1948 Broadway production?
   A. Dan Dailey
   B. Henry Fonda
   C. Jack Lemmon
   D. Robert Walker

2. Adapted from a novel by William Wharton, it marked the acting debut of Gary Sinise and featured a young Ethan Hawke as Sergeant Will Knott.
   A. *Winter Soldiers*
   B. *The Forest Green*
   C. *A Midnight Clear*
   D. *Peace on the Earth*

3. Released one month after the start of World War II, it was the first American film to depict a simulated concentration camp in Nazi Germany.
   A. *Blood and Iron*
   B. *Sentinels of Evil*
   C. *Bonfires of Death*
   D. *Hitler: Beast of Berlin*

4. The most highly decorated soldier in American history, _____ portrayed himself in *To Hell and Back*.
   A. Ralph Meeker
   B. James Stewart
   C. Audie Murphy
   D. Jason Robards

5. Can you name the real-life general who was the inspiration for Gregory Peck's character in *Twelve O'Clock High*?
   A. Ira Eaker
   B. Lauris Norstad
   C. George Kenney
   D. Frank Armstrong

6. In the opening scene of the anti-war epic *The Victors*, two US soldiers are standing guard outside of a supply depot. Who are they?
   A. Eli Wallach and Peter Fonda
   B. Jim Hutton and Michael Callan
   C. Vince Edwards and Jim Mitchum
   D. George Hamilton and George Peppard

7. The companion piece to Clint Eastwood's Oscar-nominated *Flags of Our Fathers* was _____.
   A. *Island in the Sky*
   B. *None but the Brave*
   C. *Letters from Iwo Jima*
   D. *To the Shores of Tripoli*

8. Which Hollywood icons allegedly turned down the role of General Joseph "Vinegar Joe" Stilwell in *1941*?
   A. Burt Reynolds and Al Pacino
   B. Roy Scheider and Gene Hackman
   C. Charlton Heston and John Wayne
   D. John Travolta and Dustin Hoffman

9. On September 2, 1945, these future actors watched the Japanese surrender ceremony from the deck of the submarine tender USS *Proteus* (AS-19) in Tokyo Bay.
   A. Tony Curtis and Larry Storch
   B. Rock Hudson and Lee Van Cleef
   C. Andy Griffith and Jack Nicholson
   D. Charles Durning and Dick van Dyke

10. Although the setting for the cinematic classic *Casablanca* was set in Morrocco, it was actually filmed in _____.
    A. Reno, Nevada
    B. Tucson, Arizona
    C. Burbank, California
    D. Santa Fe, New Mexico

11. Loosely based on actual events, it chronicled the twenty-fifth and final mission of a B-17 crew.
    A. *Memphis Belle*
    B. *Unsung Heroes*
    C. *The War Lovers*
    D. *Ships With Wings*

12. A 1940 masterpiece, *The Great Dictator* parodied which 20th Century tyrant?
    A. Adolf Hitler
    B. Joseph Stalin
    C. Francisco Franco
    D. Benito Mussolini

13. "When the order came to retreat, one man stayed" was the tagline for _____.[143]
    A. *Hacksaw Ridge*
    B. *Suicide Battalion*
    C. *Uncommon Glory*
    D. *Along Came a Hero*

14. This future US senator from California appeared as Private "Pop" Stazak in the 1949 war drama *Battleground*.
    A. John Hodiak
    B. Ronald Reagan
    C. Wendell Corey
    D. George Murphy

15. A US destroyer and a German U-boat engage in a deadly game of cat and mouse in the South Atlantic.
    A. *Gray Lady Down*
    B. *Submarine Attack*
    C. *The Enemy Below*
    D. *We Dive At Dawn*

16. What was the name of G Company's commanding officer in *From Here to Eternity*?
    A. Rolland "Rocky" Garnett
    B. Byron "Bull Dog" Erskine
    C. Dana "Dynamite" Holmes
    D. Harold "Hurricane" Flagg

17. Co-founded in 1942 by _____, the Hollywood Canteen provided food and entertainment to servicemen and women free of charge.
    A. Bette Davis and John Garfield
    B. Marlene Dietrich and Bob Hope
    C. Carole Lombard and Clark Gable
    D. Rita Hayworth and Humphrey Bogart

18. President John F. Kennedy selected him to play the skipper in *PT-109*.
    A. Edd Byrnes
    B. Troy Donahue
    C. Grant Williams
    D. Cliff Robertson

19. Tom Sizemore gave a convincing performance as the tough-talking and edgy Sergeant Mike Horvath in *Saving Private Ryan*. Who did Steven Spielberg initially consider for the role?
    A. Eric Roberts
    B. Kevin Dillon
    C. Harvey Keitel
    D. Michael Madsen

20. John Wayne's character in *Flying Leathernecks* was based on USMC Medal of Honor recipient _____.
    A. Major Joseph Foss
    B. Captain John Smith
    C. Major George Axtell
    D. Captain Loren Everton

21. A B-29 tail-gunner during World War II, his tough guy persona made him a screen legend for nearly five decades.
    A. Rod Steiger
    B. John Garfield
    C. Anthony Quinn
    D. Charles Bronson

22. Three of the following actors from *Bad Day at Black Rock* also appeared in *The Dirty Dozen*. Who were they?
    A. Robert Ryan, Spencer Tracy, and Dean Jagger
    B. Lee Marvin, Robert Ryan, and Ernest Borgnine
    C. Walter Brennan, Robert Webber, and Clint Walker
    D. Ernest Borgnine, John Ericson, and Robert Ryan

23. Funnyman Don Rickles made his screen debut in the tense 1958 naval drama _____.
    A. *Crimson Tide*
    B. *Torpedo Alley*
    C. *Operation Pacific*
    D. *Run Silent Run Deep*

24. This Italian crooner from Steubenville, Ohio, shared top billing with Marlon Brando and Montgomery Clift in *The Young Lions*.
    A. Vic Damone
    B. Dean Martin
    C. Frankie Laine
    D. Tony Bennett

25. Directed by Melvin Frank, _____ profiled the career of Colonel Paul W. Tibbetts, the pilot of the "Enola Gay."
    A. *Wild Blue Yonder*
    B. *Decision at Dawn*
    C. *Above and Beyond*
    D. *The Wings of Eagles*

26. Who was known as "Old Yellow Stain" in Edward Dmytryk's *The Caine Mutiny*?
    A. José Ferrer
    B. Van Johnson
    C. Fred McMurray
    D. Humphrey Bogart

27. Name the choral conductor who wrote the music and the cast member who wrote the lyrics to "Away He Went," the haunting sea shanty from *The Gallant Hours*, the 1960 biopic about the wartime experiences of Admiral William F. Halsey.
    A. Robert Shaw / Dennis Weaver
    B. Kenneth Fulton / James Cagney
    C. Roger Wagner / Ward Costello
    D. Jerry Blackstone / Richard Jaeckel

28. In *The Guns of Navarone*, this Allied commando was injected with the "truth serum" scopolamine.
    A. Major Roy Franklin
    B. Corporal John Miller
    C. Petty Officer Casey Brown
    D. Lieutenant Andrew Stevens

29. Released by Metro-Goldwyn-Mayer (MGM) in 1978, _____ hypothesized that General George S. Patton died as a result of a murder conspiracy.
    A. *Brass Target*
    B. *Executive Action*
    C. *Death in Heidelberg*
    D. *The Algonquin Project*

30. A British colonel matches wits with his Japanese counterpart in *The Bridge on the River Kwai*. Who was the motion picture's esteemed director?
    A. David Lean
    B. Peter Brook
    C. Guy Hamilton
    D. Anthony Asquith

31. Which future US president signed Major Clark Gable's discharge papers on June 12, 1944?
    A. Harry Truman
    B. Ronald Reagan
    C. Lyndon Johnson
    D. Dwight Eisenhower

32. One of the last films produced at RKO Pictures, it was based on the novel by Pulitzer Prize-winning author Norman Mailer.
    A. *The Siege of Moscow*
    B. *The Armies of the Night*
    C. *The Naked and the Dead*
    D. *The Solitude Before Dawn*

33. Her performance as Mrs. Kay Miniver, the matriarch of a middle-class English family during World War II, earned her an Academy Award for Best Actress.
    A. Greer Garson
    B. Loretta Young
    C. Joan Crawford
    D. Barbara Stanwyck

34. What do the letters A-V-G stand for in the 1942 movie *Flying Tigers?*
    A. All Volunteers Group
    B. Allied Voluntary Group
    C. Ancillary Veterans Group
    D. American Volunteer Group

35. An aggressive and determined Colonel Robert T. Frederick whips a ragtag group of American and Canadian soldiers into an elite fighting force.
    A. *Operation Misfits*
    B. *Satan's Juggernaut*
    C. *Hell or High Water*
    D. *The Devil's Brigade*

36. Born Ralph Nathaniel Twisleton-Wykeham-Fiennes, he portrayed the sadistic SS commandant _____ in *Schindler's List*.
    A. Amon Göth
    B. Josef Kramer
    C. Christian Wirth
    D. Heinrich Schwarz

37. "When 400,000 men couldn't go home, home came for them" was the tagline for which motion picture?[144]
    A. *Anzio*
    B. *Inchon*
    C. *Dunkirk*
    D. *Stalingrad*

38. James Garner is offered the opportunity to be the first fatality on OMAHA Beach in Arthur Hiller's _____.
    A. *Imitation Hero*
    B. *Darby's Rangers*
    C. *What a Way to Go!*
    D. *The Americanization of Emily*

39. Which wartime comedy included the characters "Big Joe" and "Crapgame" and "Oddball"?
    A. *Go For Broke*
    B. *Kelly's Heroes*
    C. *Pork Chop Hill*
    D. *Operation Bikini*

40. In *The Great Escape,* Richard Attenborough was "Big X" and Donald Pleasance was "The Forger." Who was "The Mole"?
    A. Nigel Stock
    B. Angus Lennie
    C. James Coburn
    D. David McCallum

41. An Irish nun and a US Marine must learn to coexist on a Japanese-held island in the South Pacific.
    A. *Say One For Me*
    B. *God Is My Co-Pilot*
    C. *Between Heaven and Hell*
    D. *Heaven Knows, Mr. Allison*

42. *Lawrence of Arabia's* Peter O'Toole gave a chilling performance as a German officer suspected of murdering a prostitute in _____.
    A. *Cross of Iron*
    B. *In the Shadows*
    C. *Murder in Warsaw*
    D. *The Night of the Generals*

43. Museum curators, art dealers, and an architect are tasked with finding paintings, sculptures, and other priceless artifacts stolen by the Nazis.
    A. *National Treasure*
    B. *In Which We Serve*
    C. *Operation Van Gogh*
    D. *The Monuments Men*

44. Which film does *not* depict the 1942 assassination of *SS Obergruppenführer* Reinhard Heydrich, "The Butcher of Prague"?
    A. *Anthropoid*
    B. *Demon of Death*
    C. *The Assassination*
    D. *Hangmen Also Die!*

45. Based on a Harry Brown novel, *A Walk in the Sun* introduced American audiences to Canadian-born character actor _____.
    A. Glenn Ford
    B. John Ireland
    C. Hume Cronyn
    D. Raymond Burr

46. In the final scene of Darryl F. Zanuck's *The Longest Day*, who said "He's dead. I'm crippled. You're lost. Do you suppose it's always like that? I mean war."[145]
    A. Henry Fonda
    B. Richard Burton
    C. Stuart Whitman
    D. Edmund O'Brien

47. Directed by the legendary Raoul Walsh and starring Errol Flynn, it is considered one of the finest World War II movies of the 1940s.
    A. *Northern Pursuit*
    B. *The Dawn Patrol*
    C. *Objective, Burma!*
    D. *Desperate Journey*

48. Who was the first convict to die in *The Dirty Dozen*?
    A. Trini Lopez
    B. Clint Walker
    C. John Cassavetes
    D. Donald Sutherland

49. A Grammy-winning vocalist, _____ played con artist Private Corby in *Hell Is for Heroes*.
    A. Gene Pitney
    B. Bobby Darin
    C. Del Shannon
    D. James Darren

50. This British rocker portrayed Major Jack "Strafer" Cellier in the POW drama *Merry Christmas, Mr. Lawrence*.
    A. Ringo Starr
    B. Mick Jagger
    C. David Bowie
    D. Eric Clapton

51. For his rendition of defense attorney Hans Rolfe in *Judgment at Nuremberg*, _____ received the Oscar for Best Actor at the 34th Academy Awards.
    A. Omar Sharif
    B. Curt Jurgens
    C. Horst Buchholz
    D. Maximilian Schell

52. Which real-life member of the 101st Airborne Division was the inspiration for *Saving Private Ryan*?
    A. James "Irish" Ryan
    B. Henry "Moose" Moore
    C. Edward "Tank" Sullivan
    D. Frederick "Fritz" Niland

53. Author and critic Chris Fujiwara lauded this 1957 Soviet war romance "as one of the most brilliant works from a brief and still-challenging period of cinematic experimentation and discovery—a period it inaugurated."[146]
    A. *The Cranes Are Flying*
    B. *The Alive and the Dead*
    C. *The Children Must Fight*
    D. *The Dawns Here Are Quiet*

54. *The Shamrock Spitfire* tells the true-life story of _____, the Irish fighter ace who became the youngest _____ in RAF history.
    A. Ian Dobie / flying officer
    B. Cyril Babbage / squadron leader
    C. John Hemingway / group captain
    D. Brendan Finucane / wing commander

55. What is the English translation of *Tora! Tora! Tora!*?
    A. Fire! Fire! Fire!
    B. Tiger! Tiger! Tiger!
    C. Attack! Attack! Attack!
    D. Surprise! Surprise! Surprise!

56. Disillusioned by the war, a USAAF bombardier feigns illness to avoid flying combat missions.
    A. *Catch-22*
    B. *Bombardier*
    C. *Tail-Gunner Joe*
    D. *Command Decision*

57. The *Halls of Montezuma* marked the acting debut of these future TV stars.
    A. Jack Webb and Neville Brand
    B. Forrest Tucker and Jack Palance
    C. Skip Homeier and Martin Milner
    D. Richard Boone and Robert Wagner

58. Which 2004 foreign film chronicled the final days of Adolf Hitler?
    A. *Downfall*
    B. *The Corporal*
    C. *Hitler's Bunker*
    D. *The Evil Below*

59. German sniper Erwin König and Soviet sniper Vasily Zaitsev duel for supremacy during the Battle of Stalingrad.
    A. *Sworn to Kill*
    B. *The Lion in Winter*
    C. *Enemy at the Gates*
    D. *Catch Me If You Can*

60. In the movie version of Charles Fuller's Pulitzer Prize-winning play, Captain Richard Davenport is given seventy-two hours to investigate the murder of an African American drill sergeant in wartime Louisiana.
    A. *Flashpoint*
    B. *Dark Passage*
    C. *A Soldier's Story*
    D. *The Cost of Victory*

61. What was the nickname of Sergeant Joe Gunn's M3 *Lee* tank in *Sahara*?
    A. "Rosie"
    B. "Daisy"
    C. "Lulubelle"
    D. "Josephine"

62. Adolf Hitler offered a $5,000 bounty to anyone who could capture this Hollywood idol.
    A. Clark Gable
    B. Bing Crosby
    C. John Wayne
    D. Gary Cooper

63. "Captain, you're about to be caught in a vacuum between a peacetime Navy and a wartime Navy. Six months from now, they'll be making admirals out of captains who exhibit some guts. But right now, they're only reacting to the Pearl Harbor disaster, and punishment is the order-of-the-day…" The above dialogue is from which motion picture?[147]
    A. *Day of Infamy*
    B. *In Harm's Way*
    C. *Across the Pacific*
    D. *The Final Countdown*

64. A decorated World War II veteran, he played the cowardly Captain Erskine Cooney in the 1956 drama *Attack!*.
    A. Lee Marvin
    B. Jack Palance
    C. Eddie Albert
    D. Buddy Ebsen

65. Colonel Franz von Waldheim's efforts to smuggle priceless works of art out of France are thwarted by Resistance leader Paul Labiche in John Frankenheimer's _____.
    A. *48 Hours*
    B. *The Train*
    C. *Showdown*
    D. *5:15 to Nice*

66. In this adaptation of Jack Higgins's best-selling novel, a group of German paratroopers led by Colonel Kurt Steiner attempt to kidnap Winston Churchill from a small English village.
    A. *Dangerous Liaison*
    B. *Race Against Time*
    C. *Operation Crosshairs*
    D. *The Eagle Has Landed*

67. Which slapstick duo starred in Universal Picture's *Buck Privates*?
    A. Burns and Allen
    B. Laurel and Hardy
    C. Martin and Lewis
    D. Abbott and Costello

68. Although it featured a star-studded cast that included Henry Fonda, Robert Ryan, and Telly Savalas, _____ was filled with historical inaccuracies and publicly denounced by former President Dwight Eisenhower.
    A. *A Bridge Too Far*
    B. *Battle of the Bulge*
    C. *The Bridge at Remagen*
    D. *D-Day the Sixth of June*

69. This Canadian-American teen idol wrote the theme song for and made a cameo appearance in *The Longest Day*.
    A. Paul Anka
    B. Sal Mineo
    C. Tommy Sands
    D. Robert Wagner

70. A Rodgers and Hammerstein musical, it featured actual World War II battle footage.
    A. *Morituri*
    B. *South Pacific*
    C. *Flower Drum Song*
    D. *The Teahouse of the August Moon*

71. Which alumnus of the Ringling Bros. and Barnum & Bailey Clown College impersonated the voice of FDR in *Darkest Hour*?
    A. Barry Bostwick
    B. David Strathairn
    C. Kenneth Branagh
    D. Edward Hermann

72. On the set of _____, twenty-year-old actress Mia Farrow meets her soon-to-be husband, fifty-year-old Frank Sinatra.
    A. *Kings Go Forth*
    B. *Von Ryan's Express*
    C. *Cast a Giant Shadow*
    D. *Hiding in Plain Sight*

73. A sex symbol of the 1960s, she was a German spy in *Armored Command*.
    A. Tina Louise
    B. Julie Newmar
    C. Raquel Welch
    D. Ursula Andress

74. The celebrated American broadcaster Edward R. Murrow played himself in which 1960 British film?
    A. *Night of the Fox*
    B. *Above the Waves*
    C. *Sink the Bismarck!*
    D. *Damn the Defiant!*

75. Featuring Richard Todd and Michael Redgrave, _____ depicted the exploits of the RAF's 617 Squadron.
    A. *Angels in the Air*
    B. *The Dam Busters*
    C. *We Dive at Dawn*
    D. *Theirs Is the Glory*

76. Which prayer did Major Julian Cook repeat over and over in *A Bridge Too Far*?
    A. "Lord, give me grace…"
    B. "Glory be to the Father…"
    C. "Hail Mary, full of grace…"
    D. "God grant me the serenity…"[148]

77. Name the Ukrainian-born filmmaker who appeared as Oberst von Scherbach in Billy Wilder's *Stalag 17*.
    A. Fritz Lang
    B. Anatole Litvak
    C. Otto Preminger
    D. Sergei Bondarchuk

78. What Japanese-occupied island was the backdrop for *The Thin Red Line*?
    A. Peleliu
    B. Tarawa
    C. Okinawa
    D. Guadalcanal

79. A versatile and debonair leading man, _____ graduated from the Royal Military College at Sandhurst and served with a British reconnaissance detachment during World War II.
    A. Ray Milland
    B. David Niven
    C. George Sanders
    D. Stewart Granger

80. *No Man Is an Island* was a 1962 movie about George Tweed, a USN radioman marooned on enemy-held Guam. Who portrayed Tweed?
    A. Nick Adams
    B. David Janssen
    C. Jeffrey Hunter
    D. Anthony Perkins

81. In the psychological thriller _____, Nazis drug and kidnap Major Jefferson Pike to learn the details of the Normandy invasion.
    A. *36 Hours*
    B. *Midnight Passage*
    C. *Strangers When We Meet*
    D. *The Quiller Memorandum*

82. Based on the book *The Death of a City*, _____ chronicles Polish musician Wladyslaw Szpilman's life in the Warsaw Ghetto.
    A. *Intermezzo*
    B. *The Pianist*
    C. *Angela's Ashes*
    D. *La Vie En Rose*

83. What did Liam Neeson place on Oskar Schindler's grave in the final scene of *Schindler's List*?
    A. Ashes
    B. Roses
    C. Twigs
    D. Stones

84. The title of this motion picture is from a quote by US naval hero John Paul Jones.
    A. *In Harm's Way*
    B. *Fire When Ready*
    C. *Damn the Torpedoes*
    D. *The Sea Shall Have Them*

85. His performance in *The Best Years of Our Lives* earned him two Academy Awards for the same role.
    A. Dana Andrews
    B. Harold Russell
    C. Frederick March
    D. Hoagy Carmichael

86. An ill-mannered and slovenly coast watcher battles the Japanese Navy, a French school teacher, and her seven pupils on a tiny Pacific island.
    A. *Father Goose*
    B. *Teacher's Pet*
    C. *Yours, Mine and Ours*
    D. *Please Don't Eat the Daisies*

87. Nicknamed the "King of Cool," _____ replaced this future member of the "Rat Pack" in *Never So Few*.
    A. Paul Newman / Joey Bishop
    B. Robert Vaughn / Dean Martin
    C. James Coburn / Peter Lawford
    D. Steve McQueen / Sammy Davis Jr.

88. What was the first Hollywood production filmed in postwar Germany?
    A. *Fall of Berlin*
    B. *Berlin Express*
    C. *Escape to Berlin*
    D. *A Berlin Romance*

89. In the third installment of the Indiana Jones series, who did Indy meet?
    A. *Indiana Jones and the Last Crusade* / Adolf Hitler
    B. *Indiana Jones and the Dial of Destiny* / Hideki Tojo
    C. *Indiana Jones and the Crown of Thorns* / Charles De Gaulle
    D. *Indiana Jones and the Raiders of the Lost Ark* / Winston Churchill

90. Which Australian-born actor took the role of Winston Churchill in Quentin Tarantino's *Inglorious Basterds*?
    A. Rod Taylor
    B. Guy Pearce
    C. Jeffrey Rush
    D. Simon Baker

Match the film character with the actor.

91. _____ Max Rothman (*Max*)	A.	Brad Pitt
92. _____ Gus Smith (*Lifeboat*)	B.	Daniel Craig
93. _____ Tuvia Bielski (*Defiance*)	C.	John Cusack
94. _____ Kay Walsh (*Swing Shift*)	D.	Goldie Hawn
95. _____ Linda Voss (*Shining Through*)	E.	Terence Stamp

96.	_____ John Lawrence (*The Frogmen*)	F.	William Bendix
97.	_____ Buzz Rickson (*The War Lovers*)	G.	Melanie Griffith
98.	_____ Henry Faber (*Eye of the Needle*)	H.	Steve McQueen
99.	_____ General Ludwig Beck (*Valkyrie*)	I.	Richard Widmark
100.	_____ Sergeant "Wardaddy" Collier (*Fury*)	J.	Donald Sutherland

Chapter Eight Answers

1. B. Henry Fonda
2. C. *A Midnight Clear*
3. D. *Hitler: Beast of Berlin*
4. C. Audie Murphy
5. D. Frank Armstrong
6. D. George Hamilton and George Peppard
7. C. *Letters From Iwo Jima*
8. C. Charlton Heston and John Wayne
9. A. Tony Curtis and Larry Storch
10. C. Burbank, California
11. A. *Memphis Belle*
12. A. Adolf Hitler
13. A. *Hacksaw Ridge*
14. D. George Murphy
15. C. *The Enemy Below*
16. C. Dana "Dynamite" Holmes
17. A. Bette Davis and John Garfield
18. D. Cliff Robertson
19. D. Michael Madsen
20. B. Captain John Smith
21. D. Charles Bronson
22. B. Lee Marvin, Robert Ryan, and Ernest Borgnine
23. D. *Run Silent Run Deep*
24. B. Dean Martin
25. C. *Above and Beyond*
26. D. Humphrey Bogart
27. C. Roger Wagner / Ward Costello
28. A. Major Roy Franklin
29. A. *Brass Target*
30. A. David Lean
31. B. Ronald Reagan
32. C. *The Naked and the Dead*

33. A. Greer Garson
34. D. American Volunteer Group
35. D. *The Devil's Brigade*
36. A. Amon Göth
37. C. *Dunkirk*
38. D. *The Americanization of Emily*
39. B. *Kelly's Heroes*
40. B. Angus Lennie
41. D. *Heaven Knows, Mr. Allison*
42. D. *The Night of the Generals*
43. D. *The Monuments Men*
44. B. *Demon of Death*
45. B. John Ireland
46. B. Richard Burton
47. C. *Objective, Burma!*
48. A. Trini Lopez
49. B. Bobby Darin
50. C. David Bowie
51. D. Maximilian Schell
52. D. Frederick "Fritz" Niland
53. A. *The Cranes Are Flying*
54. D. Brendan Finucane / wing commander
55. B. Tiger! Tiger! Tiger!
56. A. *Catch-22*
57. D. Richard Boone and Robert Wagner
58. A. *Downfall*
59. C. *Enemy at the Gates*
60. C. *A Soldier's Story*
61. C. "Lulubelle"
62. A. Clark Gable
63. B. *In Harm's Way*
64. C. Eddie Albert
65. B. *The Train*
66. D. *The Eagle Has Landed*
67. D. Abbott and Costello

68. B. *Battle of the Bulge*
69. A. Paul Anka
70. B. *South Pacific*
71. B. David Strathairn
72. B. *Von Ryan's Express*
73. A. Tina Louise
74. C. *Sink the Bismarck!*
75. B. *The Dam Busters*
76. C. "Hail Mary, full of grace…"
77. C. Otto Preminger
78. D. Guadalcanal
79. B. David Niven
80. C. Jeffrey Hunter
81. A. *36 Hours*
82. B. *The Pianist*
83. B. Roses
84. A. *In Harm's Way*
85. B. Harold Russell
86. A. *Father Goose*
87. D. Steve McQueen / Sammy Davis Jr.
88. B. *Berlin Express*
89. A. *Indiana Jones and the Last Crusade* / Adolf Hitler
90. A. Rod Taylor
91. C. John Cusack
92. F. William Bendix
93. B. Daniel Craig
94. D. Goldie Hawn
95. G. Melanie Griffith
96. I. Richard Widmark
97. H. Steve McQueen
98. J. Donald Sutherland
99. E. Terence Stamp
100. A. Brad Pitt

Chapter Nine
The Living Room War

1. An Academy Award-winning actor of stage and screen, _____ narrated the British-produced series *The World at War*.
   A. Sir John Gielgud
   B. Sir Laurence Olivier
   C. Sir Ralph Richardson
   D. Sir Cedric Hardwicke

2. You won't become a castaway if you answer this question correctly: Which episode of *Gilligan's Island* had a World War II theme?
   A. "Mine Hero"
   B. "Forward March"
   C. "So Sorry, My Island Now"
   D. All of the above

3. In 1966, CBS canceled the espionage series *Jericho* after sixteen weeks. Why?
   A. TV and film writers were on strike.
   B. Cast members demanded more money.
   C. A devastating fire shutdown production.
   D. The show could not compete with ABC's *Batman*.

4. Who were the actors who portrayed Captain Philip Queeg in the 1988 and 2023 TV versions of the 1954 Broadway play *The Caine Mutiny Court-Martial*?
   A. Larry Hagman and Ted Danson
   B. Brad Davis and Keifer Sutherland
   C. John Schneider and David Duchovny
   D. Wayne Rogers and Andrew McCarthy

5. "Seven Against the Sea" was the pilot for which long-running comedy?
   A. *Island Rescue*
   B. *Ensign Pulver*
   C. *McHale's Navy*
   D. *Operation Snafu*

6. A short-lived 1950s war drama, it explored US submarine operations in the South Pacific.
   A. *Dive!*
   B. *Sea Hunt*
   C. *Down Periscope*
   D. *The Silent Service*

7. Do you remember the word that appeared in the title of every episode of *The Rat Patrol*?
   A. "Raid"
   B. "Assault"
   C. "Mission"
   D. "Operation"

8. Seriously wounded during the Allied invasion of Anzio, he later became a famous TV lawman.
   A. James Arness
   B. Andy Griffith
   C. Hugh O'Brian
   D. Stuart Whitman

9. Real-life fighter ace Gregory "Pappy" Boyington made a cameo appearance as _____ in season one of *Baa Baa Black Sheep*.
   A. Colonel Jonathan Buell
   B. General Charles Mathis
   C. Colonel Robert Gibbons
   D. General Harrison Kenlay

10. The last surviving cast member of *Hogan's Heroes*, he replaced Sergeant James Kinchloe in the show's final season.
    A. Sergeant Richard Baker
    B. Sergeant Alvin Jefferson
    C. Sergeant Emmett Brewer
    D. Sergeant Bruce Pettigrew

11. Prior to the theatrical release of *Redtails* in 2012, the story of African American pilots in the ETO was explored in HBO's _____.
    A. *The Tuskegee Heroes*
    B. *The Tuskegee Legacy*
    C. *The Tuskegee Airmen*
    D. *The Tuskegee Experiment*

12. Which ABC series was inspired by the motion picture *The Dirty Dozen*?
    A. *Eight Iron Men*
    B. *Operation Bravo*
    C. *The Glory Brigade*
    D. *Garrison's Gorillas*

13. Can you name the decorated Vietnam veteran who played legendary Colonel Robert F. Sink in *Band of Brothers*?
    A. Dale Dye
    B. Chuck Norris
    C. R. Lee Ermey
    D. William Sadler

14. Name *The Godfather* consigliere who guest starred in three episodes of *Combat!*.
    A. Al Pacino
    B. James Caan
    C. Robert Duvall
    D. Marlon Brando

15. It was the long-awaited sequel to the extraordinarily successful miniseries *The Winds of War*.
    A. *Tide of Battle*
    B. *War and Peace*
    C. *A Time to Recall*
    D. *War and Remembrance*

16. A 2001 made-for-TV drama, _____ featured Kenneth Branagh and Stanley Tucci as the architects of the "Final Solution."
    A. *Pogrom*
    B. *Holocaust*
    C. *Conspiracy*
    D. *Annihilation*

17. In *Casablanca*, Humphrey Bogart portrayed the same character as the star of the TV reboot.
    A. David Soul
    B. Lee Majors
    C. James Brolin
    D. Peter Strauss

18. This *McHale's Navy* cast member died of an apparent heart attack while swimming in his Beverly Hills pool.
    A. Joe Flynn
    B. Ken Ritter
    C. Billy Sands
    D. Gary Vinson

19. What was the name of Colonel Joe Gallagher's B-17 on *Twelve O'Clock High*?
    A. "Shady Lady"
    B. "Piccadilly Lily"
    C. "Swamp Ghost"
    D. "Blonde Bomber"

20. Before playing an undercover agent on *Blue Light*, _____ co-starred opposite Julie Andrews and Richard Burton in the Broadway production of *Camelot*.
    A. Hal Linden
    B. Dean Jones
    C. Robert Goulet
    D. Theodore Bikel

21. Produced by Garry Marshall, it was the 1940s version of *Laverne and Shirley*.
    A. *Sassy Lassies*
    B. *Goodtime Girls*
    C. *Devilish Dames*
    D. *Naughty Nymphs*

22. Best remembered as the patriarch of *The Addams Family*, _____ commanded a submarine on *Operation Petticoat*.
    A. Al Lewis
    B. John Astin
    C. Fred Gwynne
    D. Jackie Coogan

23. *McHale's Navy* spawned two motion pictures. Name them.
    A. *McHale's Navy* and *McHale's Navy Wins the War*
    B. *McHale's Navy* and *McHale's Navy Joins the Army*
    C. *McHale's Navy* and *McHale's Navy Joins the Air Force*
    D. *McHale's Navy* and *McHale's Navy Goes to Hollywood*

24. Which POW on *Hogan's Heroes* survived the Holocaust?
    A. Leon Askin
    B. John Banner
    C. Robert Clary
    D. Cynthia Lynn

25. The HBO miniseries *The Pacific* starred Rami Malek as Corporal Merriell Shelton. What was Shelton's nickname?
    A. "Snafu"
    B. "Gunny"
    C. "Manny"
    D. "Hillbilly"

26. How many episodes of *Combat!* aired between 1962 and 1967?
    A. 111
    B. 133
    C. 152
    D. 167

27. Before playing Private Bernie Lucavich on *The Gallant Men*, Roland La Starza was a(n) _____.
    A. carpenter
    B. prizefighter
    C. truck driver
    D. house painter

28. Narrated by Meryl Streep, the 2017 Netflix TV series _____ chronicled the wartime contributions of acclaimed filmmakers Frank Capra, John Ford, John Huston, George Stevens, and William Wyler.
    A. *Five Came Back*
    B. *The Fearless Five*
    C. *Five the Hard Way*
    D. *Then There Were Five*

29. A stand-up comedian turned late night talk show host, Jimmy Fallon made a blink-and-you'll-miss-him appearance in _____.
    A. *The Pacific*
    B. *Island at War*
    C. *Band of Brothers*
    D. *In Pursuit of Peace*

30. Who reprised his film role in the TV version of *The Wackiest Ship in the Army*?
    A. Mike Kellin
    B. Gary Collins
    C. Jack Warden
    D. Robert Morse

31. All of the following science fiction programs aired episodes with a World War II theme *except* _____.
    A. *Star Trek*
    B. *Galactica*
    C. *The Invaders*
    D. *Voyage to the Bottom of the Sea*

32. Tom Selleck delivered a surprisingly strong performance as General Dwight Eisenhower in the 2004 historical drama _____.
    A. *Ike: The War Years*
    B. *Ike: Man of Destiny*
    C. *Ike: Hour of Decision*
    D. *Ike: Countdown to D-Day*

33. With a musical score by renowned composer Richard Rodgers, the groundbreaking NBC series _____, set the standard for all future World War II documentaries.
    A. *Call to Duty*
    B. *Victory at Sea*
    C. *Why We Fight*
    D. *Legion of Honor*

34. An accomplished comedy magician, _____ was Torpedoman Lester Gruber on *McHale's Navy*.
    A. Billy Sands
    B. Edson Stroll
    C. Tim Conway
    D. Carl Ballantine

35. In this ABC made-for-TV movie, Ben Gazzara commanded a hard-luck US division following the D-Day invasion.
    A. *Fast Forward*
    B. *Lucky Forward*
    C. *Fireball Forward*
    D. *Diamond Forward*

36. The flirtatious host of *Family Feud*, he was Corporal Peter Newkirk on *Hogan's Heroes*.
    A. Ray Combs
    B. Bob Eubanks
    C. John O'Hurley
    D. Richard Dawson

37. A BBC production, it focused on female POWs in a Japanese internment camp.
    A. *Tenko*
    B. *Nancy Wake*
    C. *Wish Me Luck*
    D. *The Last Bastion*

38. Who took the Deborah Kerr role in the TV version of *From Here to Eternity*?
    A. Jill St. John
    B. Natalie Wood
    C. Barbara Hershey
    D. Stephanie Powers

39. Captain Wallace Binghamton's favorite expression on *McHale's Navy* was _____.[150]
    A. "McHale, you idiot!"
    B. "I could just scream!"
    C. "Great jumping Jehoshaphat!"
    D. "This can't be happening again!"

40. In which episode of *Band of Brothers* does the audience learn who was the first commanding officer of "Easy" Company?
    A. "Points"
    B. "Currahee"
    C. "Day of Days"
    D. "Why We Fight"

41. Long before joining the crew of *Star Trek*, _____ served with the Canadian Army on D-Day.
    A. James Doohan
    B. Leonard Nimoy
    C. DeForest Kelley
    D. William Shatner

42. Where did the British drama *A Family at War* take place?
    A. Cardiff, Wales
    B. Killarney, Ireland
    C. Liverpool, England
    D. Melbourne, Australia

43. The leather aviator's jacket worn by Bob Crane on *Hogan's Heroes* was previously worn by Frank Sinatra in _____.
    A. *Von Ryan's Express*
    B. *Cast A Giant Shadow*
    C. *From Here to Eternity*
    D. *The Manchurian Candidate*

44. An award-winning documentarian, he produced the PBS series' *The War* and *The U.S. and the Holocaust*.
    A. Ken Burns
    B. Paul Devlin
    C. Ross McElwee
    D. Michael Gibson

45. Which of the following was Commander Victor "Pug" Henry's favorite naval vessel in *The Winds of War*?
    A. Cruiser
    B. Battleship
    C. Destroyer
    D. Submarine

46. Arguably the most popular character in soap opera history, he played Captain Hans Dietrich on *The Rat Patrol*.
    A. Eric Braeden
    B. Peter Bergman
    C. Gary Raymond
    D. Doug Davidson

47. He was Captain Jim Benedict on *The Gallant Men* and later Special Agent Tom Colby on *The FBI*.
    A. Bruce Simon
    B. Philip Abbott
    C. Stephen Brook
    D. William Reynolds

48. These South Philly heartthrobs made guest appearances on *Combat!*.
    A. Fabian Forte and Ricky Nelson
    B. James Darren and Paul Petersen
    C. Chubby Checker and Al Martino
    D. Bobby Rydell and Frankie Avalon

49. Based on the exploits of the famed "Red Ball Express," this ABC series included the talented trio of Hilly Hicks, Ed Begley Jr., and Stu Gilliam as Corporal Carter "Sweet" Williams.
    A. *Drive*
    B. *Roll Out*
    C. *Fast Forward*
    D. *Thunder Alley*

50. She portrayed Kay Summersby, General Dwight Eisenhower's driver and personal secretary in the miniseries *Ike: The War Years*.
    A. Lee Remick
    B. Tippi Hedren
    C. Elizabeth Ashley
    D. Suzanne Pleshette

51. What was Lieutenant Brian Ash's occupation on *Danger UXB*?
    A. Combat engineer
    B. Tank commander
    C. Infantry instructor
    D. Bomb disposal officer

52. The son of a famous composer and conductor, _____ won two Emmy Awards for his work on *Hogan's Heroes*.
    A. Larry Hovis
    B. John Banner
    C. Howard Caine
    D. Werner Klemperer

53. "In the heat of battle not all soldiers can be heroes" was the tagline for the HBO film _____.[149]
    A. *Path to War*
    B. *Into the Storm*
    C. *Gardens of Stone*
    D. *When Trumpets Fade*

54. All of the following comedic actors guest starred on *Combat!* except _____.
    A. Ted Knight
    B. Jack Carter
    C. Frank Gorshin
    D. Buddy Hackett

55. On *Foyle's War*, what did Christopher Foyle do for a living?
    A. Novelist
    B. Fighter pilot
    C. Music teacher
    D. Police detective

56. Featuring Stacey Keach and Richard Thomas, _____ examined the tragic circumstances surrounding the sinking of the USS *Indianapolis* (CA-35) in July 1945.
   A. *Survival: The Men of the USS Indianapolis*
   B. *Dangerous Waters: The USS Indianapolis Tragedy*
   C. *Mission of the Shark: The Saga of the USS Indianapolis*
   D. *Deadly Encounter: Surviving the USS Indianapolis Disaster*

57. Who was the *Saturday Night Live* cast member, who played Wheels Dawson on the '60s sitcom *Roll Out?*
   A. Flip Wilson
   B. Cleavon Little
   C. Eddie Murphy
   D. Garrett Morris

58. The third and final installment of Steven Spielberg's World War II trilogy was _____.
   A. *Lions in the Sky*
   B. *Masters of the Air*
   C. *The Mighty Eighth*
   D. *With Wings of Eagles*

59. John Ratzenberger of *Cheers*-fame made his TV debut on this BBC produced program.
   A. *Secret War*
   B. *Pathfinders*
   C. *Jenny's War*
   D. *Piece of Cake*

60. What was the name of the PT base on *McHale's Navy?*
   A. Taratupa
   B. Shangri-La
   C. Buna Road
   D. Mystic Cove

61. All of these books were the basis for *The Pacific* except _____.
    A. *Pacific Crucible*
    B. *With the Old Breed*
    C. *Helmet for My Pillow*
    D. *Red Blood, Black Sand*

62. Starring William Devane as Sergeant Milt Warden and Kim Basinger as Lorene Rogers, it was an NBC weekly series in 1980.
    A. *The Undefeated*
    B. *From Here to Eternity*
    C. *War and Remembrance*
    D. *Hitler: Reign of Terror*

63. This quiz book will self-destruct in ten seconds if you fail to answer the following question: Which member of the *Mission: Impossible* team starred as Major Frank Whittaker on ABC's *Court Martial*?
    A. Steven Hill
    B. Greg Morris
    C. Peter Graves
    D. Martin Landau

64. In the 1974 TV movie *The Execution of Private Slovik*, why was Slovik put to death?
    A. He deserted his post.
    B. He committed treason.
    C. He struck a superior officer.
    D. He murdered a fellow soldier.

65. On the February 4, 1965 episode of this animated series, prehistoric cavemen were trained as slave laborers by a Nazi war criminal.
    A. *Astro Boy*
    B. *Underdog*
    C. *Jonny Quest*
    D. *Mighty Mouse*

66. Best-known for his role as Leland McKenzie on *L.A. Law*, he portrayed General Dwight Eisenhower in *The Last Days of Patton*.
    A. Alan Rachins
    B. Harry Hamlin
    C. Richard Dysart
    D. Michael Tucker

67. Ecuadorian-born Albert Paulsen made guest appearances on all of the following series *except* _____.
    A. *Combat!*
    B. *The Rat Patrol*
    C. *Hogan's Heroes*
    D. *Twelve O'Clock High*

68. What color was the submarine USS *Sea Tiger* on *Operation Petticoat*?
    A. Pink
    B. Green
    C. Lavender
    D. Turquoise

69. Blacklisted in the 1950s by the House Un-American Activities Committee, _____ later went on to write music for films and TV programs including *Hogan's Heroes*.
    A. Jack Eliot
    B. Ray Evans
    C. Jerry Fielding
    D. Randy Newman

70. Ron Harper, the star of *Garrison's Gorillas*, attended which Ivy League university?
    A. Brown
    B. Cornell
    C. Harvard
    D. Princeton

71. Who was Seaman Happy Haines on *McHale's Navy* and Captain Merrill Stubing on *Love Boat?*
    A. Tim Conway
    B. Bernie Kopell
    C. Gavin MacLeod
    D. Harvey Korman

72. This acclaimed ABC anchorman narrated the CBS made-for-TV movie *Escape from Sobibor.*
    A. Ted Koppel
    B. Peter Jennings
    C. Frank Reynolds
    D. Howard K. Smith

73. Containing lost archival footage from Hollywood director William Wyler, the 2018 HBO documentary _____ focused on the heroic exploits of the US Eighth Air Force.
    A. *Sky Gods*
    B. *Air Warriors*
    C. *Into the Fight*
    D. *The Cold Blue*

74. Name the wartime drama that featured the characters "Casino" and "Chief."
    A. *Satan's Soldiers*
    B. *The Gallant Men*
    C. *Garrison's Gorillas*
    D. *Baa Baa Black Sheep*

75. In the 1983 production *The Scarlet and the Black,* Academy Award-winning actor _____ played Father Hugh O'Flaherty, a Vatican priest who rescued countless numbers of Jews and POWs from the clutches of the Nazis.
    A. John Voight
    B. Gregory Peck
    C. Richard Dreyfuss
    D. Christopher Plummer

76. Which of the following US senators hosted an episode of the 1956 anthology series *Navy Log*?
    A. Thomas C. Hart
    B. John F. Kennedy
    C. Howard H. Baker
    D. Lyndon B. Johnson

77. On *Hogan's Heroes*, what codename did the POWs use when communicating with Allied headquarters?
    A. "Papa Bear"
    B. "Goldilocks"
    C. "Donald Duck"
    D. "Mickey Mouse"

78. Two of the original cast members from *The Dirty Dozen* were also in the 1987 TV movie *The Dirty Dozen: The Deadly Mission*. Who were they?
    A. Jim Brown and Robert Ryan
    B. Ernest Borgnine and Telly Savalas
    C. George Kennedy and Clint Walker
    D. Robert Webber and Charles Bronson

79. It was Sergeant Troy's favorite expression on *The Rat Patrol*.
    A. "Head out!"
    B. "Let's roll!"
    C. "Hit the road!"
    D. "Let's shake it!"[151]

80. You'll travel through another dimension if you can answer this question: Which episode of Rod Serling's *The Twilight Zone* told the story of a US infantry officer who possessed the uncanny ability to predict which of his men would be killed in action?
    A. "Harbinger of Death"
    B. "Judgement in Battle"
    C. "Valley of the Shadow"
    D. "The Purple Testament"

81. American composer and arranger Dominic Frontiere's theme credits included _____.
    A. *Foyle's War* and *Danger UXB*
    B. *Band of Brothers* and *The Pacific*
    C. *The Rat Patrol* and *Twelve O'Clock High*
    D. *Baa Baa Black Sheep* and *Garrison's Gorillas*

82. Who said "I see nothing!" on *Hogan's Heroes*?[152]
    A. Sergeant Hans Schultz
    B. Colonel Wilhelm Klink
    C. General Albert Burkhalter
    D. Major Wolfgang Hochstetter

83. A 2022 BBC offering, _____ depicted a real-life British commando unit that operated behind enemy lines.
    A. *SAS: Rogue Heroes*
    B. *Eastern Approaches*
    C. *SIS: Code of Secrecy*
    D. *The Wellington Boys*

84. Which *Combat!* stars made guest appearances on Dick Clark's *American Bandstand* in 1965?
    A. Rick Jason and Vic Morrow
    B. Jack Hogan and Tom Lowell
    C. Pierre Jalbert and Dick Peabody
    D. Conlan Carter and Steven Rogers

85. The skipper of a USN destroyer escort on *Convoy*, he served as US ambassador to Mexico in the Reagan administration.
    A. Mel Ferrer
    B. John Gavin
    C. Mike Connors
    D. Cesar Romero

86. "Brothers in war…rivals in love" was the tagline for _____.[153]
    A. *Colditz*
    B. *Swing Shift*
    C. *Piece of Cake*
    D. *Fall From Grace*

87. Can you name the four-part drama that featured a Catholic priest who joined the French Resistance following the fall of France?
    A. *State of Grace*
    B. *The Watchman*
    C. *Sins of the Father*
    D. *Monsignor Renard*

88. Where was the 918th Bomb Group stationed on *Twelve O'Clock High*?
    A. Archbury, England
    B. Briton Ferry, Wales
    C. Cherrywood, Ireland
    D. East Kilbride, Scotland

89. A member of New Kids on the Block, _____ portrayed Second Lieutenant Carwood Lipton on *Band of Brothers*.
    A. Jordan Miller
    B. Danny Wood
    C. Joey McIntyre
    D. Donnie Wahlberg

90. Which Emmy-winning actor narrated the History Channel documentary series *The Color of War*?
    A. Brian Cox
    B. Keith David
    C. Peter Coyote
    D. Liev Schreiber

Match the TV character with the actor.

91. _____ Midge Forrest (*Pearl*)   A. Jack Hogan
92. _____ Rudi Weiss (*Holocaust*)   B. Roger Davis
93. _____ Dora Basilone (*The Pacific*)   C. Polly Bergen
94. _____ Rhoda Henry (*The Winds of War*)   D. Austin Butler
95. _____ Captain Felix Sparks (*The Liberator*)   E. Leila Goldini
96. _____ Private William G. Kirby (*Combat!*)   F. Tim Conway
97. _____ Lieutenant Anne Morgan (*Broadside*)   G. Bradley James
98. _____ Major Gale Cleven (*Masters of the Air*)   H. Kathleen Nolan
99. _____ Ensign Charles Parker (*McHale's Navy*)   I. Joseph Bottoms
100. _____ Private Roger Gibson (*The Gallant Men*)   J. Angie Dickinson

CHAPTER NINE ANSWERS

1. B. Sir Laurence Olivier
2. D. All of the above
3. D. The show could not compete with ABC's *Batman*.
4. B. Brad Davis and Keifer Sutherland
5. C. *McHale's Navy*
6. D. *The Silent Service*
7. A. "Raid"
8. A. James Arness
9. D. General Harrison Kenlay
10. A. Sergeant Richard Baker
11. C. *The Tuskegee Airmen*
12. D. *Garrison's Gorillas*
13. A. Dale Dye
14. C. Robert Duvall
15. D. *War and Remembrance*
16. C. *Conspiracy*
17. A. David Soul
18. A. Joe Flynn
19. B. "Piccadilly Lily"
20. C. Robert Goulet
21. B. *Goodtime Girls*
22. B. John Astin
23. C. *McHale's Navy* and *McHale's Navy Joins the Air Force*
24. C. Robert Clary
25. A. "Snafu"
26. C. 152
27. B. prizefighter
28. A. *Five Came Back*
29. C. *Band of Brothers*
30. A. Mike Kellin
31. C. *The Invaders*
32. D. *Ike: Countdown to D-Day*

33. B. *Victory at Sea*
34. D. Carl Ballantine
35. C. *Fireball Forward*
36. D. Richard Dawson
37. A. *Tenko*
38. B. Natalie Wood
39. B. "I could just scream!"
40. B. "Currahee"
41. A. James Doohan
42. C. Liverpool, England
43. A. *Von Ryan's Express*
44. A. Ken Burns
45. B. Battleship
46. A. Eric Braeden
47. D. William Reynolds
48. D. Bobby Rydell and Frankie Avalon
49. B. *Roll Out*
50. A. Lee Remick
51. D. Bomb disposal officer
52. D. Werner Klemperer
53. D. *When Trumpets Fade*
54. D. Buddy Hackett
55. D. Police detective
56. C. *Mission of the Shark: The Saga of the USS Indianapolis*
57. D. Garrett Morris
58. B. *Masters of the Air*
59. A. *Secret War*
60. A. Taratupa
61. A. *Pacific Crucible*
62. B. *From Here to Eternity*
63. C. Peter Graves
64. A. He deserted his post.
65. C. *Jonny Quest*
66. C. Richard Dysart

67. C. *Hogan's Heroes*
68. A. Pink
69. C. Jerry Fielding
70. D. Princeton
71. C. Gavin MacLeod
72. D. Howard K. Smith
73. D. *The Cold Blue*
74. C. *Garrison's Gorillas*
75. B. Gregory Peck
76. B. John F. Kennedy
77. B. "Goldilocks"
78. B. Ernest Borgnine and Telly Savalas
79. D. "Let's shake it!"
80. D. "The Purple Testament"
81. C. *The Rat Patrol* and *Twelve O'Clock High*
82. A. Sergeant Hans Schultz
83. A. *SAS: Rogue Heroes*
84. C. Pierre Jalbert and Dick Peabody
85. B. John Gavin
86. A. *Colditz*
87. D. *Monsignor Renard*
88. A. Archbury, England
89. D. Donnie Wahlberg
90. C. Peter Coyote
91. J. Angie Dickinson
92. I. Joseph Bottoms
93. E. Leila Goldini
94. C. Polly Bergen
95. G. Bradley James
96. A. Jack Hogan
97. H. Kathleen Nolan
98. D. Austin Butler
99. F. Tim Conway
100. B. Roger Davis

CHAPTER TEN

THE WAY WE WERE: 1939–1945

1939

1. The average price of a new house was _____.
   A. $1,900
   B. $2,450
   C. $3,800
   D. $4,150

2. Belgian Sylvère Maes won this cycling classic for the second time.
   A. Giro d'Italia
   B. Paris-Roubaix
   C. Tour de France
   D. Milan-San Remo

3. General Francisco Franco's troops conquered the Spanish city of _____.
   A. Seville
   B. Madrid
   C. Granada
   D. Barcelona

4. What well-known technology company was founded?
   A. Microsoft
   B. LG Electronics
   C. Hewlett-Packard
   D. Texas Instruments

5. The following celebrities were born *except* _____.
   A. Jon Voight
   B. Marvin Gaye
   C. George Hamilton
   D. Francis Ford Coppola

6. In which South American country did a devastating earthquake kill 30,000 people?
   A. Peru
   B. Chile
   C. Brazil
   D. Ecuador

7. Cardinal Eugenio Pacelli (Pius XII) became the 260th pope of the Roman Catholic Church. Who was his predecessor?
   A. Pius XI
   B. John XXIII
   C. Benedict XIV
   D. Clement XXII

8. The University of Tennessee defeated the University of Oklahoma 17-0 in the _____.
   A. Cotton Bowl
   B. Orange Bowl
   C. Liberty Bowl
   D. Holiday Bowl

9. All of these films premiered *except* _____.
   A. *King Kong*
   B. *Stagecoach*
   C. *The Wizard of Oz*
   D. *Gone With the Wind*

10. Prior to the outbreak of World War II, the Women's Auxiliary Air Force was created in _____.
    A. France
    B. Denmark
    C. Soviet Union
    D. Great Britain

11. Boxer Joe Louis defended his heavyweight title by knocking out _____ in the first round.
    A. Arturo Godoy
    B. Clarence Burman
    C. John Henry Lewis
    D. Bill Patrick Donovan

12. African American contralto Marian Anderson was denied the right to sing in Washington, DC, by which organization?
    A. Sons of Liberty
    B. Alliance for Women's Rights
    C. Patriotic Order of the United States
    D. Daughters of the American Revolution

13. The following celebrities died *except* _____.
    A. Will Rogers
    B. Amelia Earhart
    C. Sigmund Freud
    D. Douglas Fairbanks

14. Nicknamed the "Iron Horse," this New York Yankee retired after being diagnosed with ALS or amyotrophic lateral sclerosis.
    A. Babe Ruth
    B. Lou Gehrig
    C. Jimmy Reese
    D. Ben Chapman

1940

15. A leading Marxist and a dominant force behind the Russian Revolution of 1917, he was assassinated in Mexico City.
    A. Leon Trotsky
    B. Mikhail Frunze
    C. Nikolai Zinoviev
    D. Georgy Chicherin

16. Elected to an unprecedented third term, FDR defeated _____.
    A. Alf Landon
    B. Herbert Hoover
    C. Wendell Willkie
    D. Thomas E. Dewey

17. Which superhero comic book was published for the first time?
    A. Batman
    B. Superman
    C. Captain America
    D. Wonder Woman

18. A new automobile sold for _____.
    A. $700
    B. $850
    C. $900
    D. $1,050

19. The following celebrities were born *except* _____.
    A. Al Pacino
    B. Ringo Starr
    C. Mick Jagger
    D. Nancy Sinatra

20. She became the first African American to win an Academy Award.
    A. Daisy Buford
    B. Ethel Waters
    C. Josephine Baker
    D. Hattie McDaniel

21. The world's population reached _____.
    A. 2.569 billion
    B. 3.963 billion
    C. 4.387 billion
    D. 5.217 billion

22. At your local movie house, a ticket cost _____.
    A. five cents
    B. twelve cents
    C. fifteen cents
    D. twenty-five cents

23. Created by Dupont researcher Wallace Carothers, this material was used in the production of women's stockings.
    A. Latex
    B. Nylon
    C. Rayon
    D. Cotton

24. A future World Golf Hall-of-Famer, he won the PGA Championship for the first time.
    A. Sam Snead
    B. Byron Nelson
    C. Gene Sarazen
    D. Johnny Revolta

25. The following celebrities died *except* _____.
    A. Tom Mix
    B. Virginia Woolf
    C. F. Scott Fitzgerald
    D. Neville Chamberlain

26. Recorded by Tommy Dorsey and his orchestra with vocals by Frank Sinatra and the Pied Pipers, it remained at No. 1 on *Billboard* for twelve weeks.
    A. "Moonlight Serenade"
    B. "Dancing in the Dark"
    C. "Sentimental Journey"
    D. "I'll Never Smile Again"

27. Which city was the first to televise the Republican National Convention?
    A. Boston, Massachusetts
    B. Los Angeles, California
    C. Chattanooga, Tennessee
    D. Philadelphia, Pennsylvania

1941

28. A gallon of vitamin D milk sold for _____.
    A. fifteen cents
    B. nineteen cents
    C. fifty-four cents
    D. sixty-two cents

29. "Yes, It's the Most Famous Understatement in America" was the advertising slogan for which brand of whiskey?[154]
    A. Jack Daniels
    B. Yellowstone
    C. Old Forester
    D. Wild Turkey

30. The following celebrities were born *except* _____.
    A. Bob Dylan
    B. Ann-Margret
    C. Neil Diamond
    D. Paul McCartney

31. Roy J. Plunkett received U.S. patent No. 2,230,654 for his invention. What was it?
    A. Teflon
    B. Penicillin
    C. Hula Hoop
    D. Ball-point pen

32. Designed by John Russell Pope, the_____ officially opened in Washington, DC.
    A. National Archives
    B. Library of Congress
    C. National Gallery of Art
    D. Civil War Memorial Museum

33. Written by composer Irving Berlin, it became a Christmas standard.
    A. "White Christmas"
    B. "Frosty the Snowman"
    C. "Rudolph the Red-Nosed Reindeer"
    D. "Have Yourself a Merry Little Christmas"

34. Name the organization created to entertain US troops.
    A. AFS
    B. USO
    C. ASC
    D. GTS

35. Arguably America's favorite candy, it was introduced by the Mars Company. Since 2003, it has been sold in over one hundred countries.
    A. Kit Kat
    B. M&M's
    C. Almond Joy
    D. Peanut Chews

36. Known as "The Yankee Clipper," Joe DiMaggio began his fifty-six-game hitting streak against the _____.
    A. Detroit Tigers
    B. St. Louis Browns
    C. Chicago White Sox
    D. Washington Senators

37. It cost _____ per academic year at Harvard University.
    A. $270
    B. $395
    C. $420
    D. $615

38. Which brand of coffee was advertised as the "Most Popular Cup in My Trophy Room!"?[155]
    A. A&P
    B. Folgers
    C. Nescafe
    D. Maxwell House

39. The following celebrities died *except* _____.
    A. Lou Gehrig
    B. James Joyce
    C. Marcus Garvey
    D. John Barrymore

40. Initially penned by Hollywood columnist Hedda Hopper, it became an American cinematic classic.
    A. *Citizen Kane*
    B. *Sergeant York*
    C. *The Grapes of Wrath*
    D. *It's a Wonderful Life*

41. Gradually declining since the implementation of the New Deal, the average unemployment rate for the year was _____.
    A. 7.1%
    B. 9.9%
    C. 10.3%
    D. 12.5%

1942

42. At the 14th Academy Awards, _____ won the Oscar for Best Picture.
    A. *One Foot in Heaven*
    B. *Hold Back the Dawn*
    C. *All That Money Can Buy*
    D. *How Green Was My Valley*

43. Which city cancelled night-time baseball games for the duration of World War II?
    A. Chicago, Illinois
    B. New York, New York
    C. Los Angeles, California
    D. Pittsburgh, Pennsylvania

44. The following celebrities were born *except* _____.
    A. Bill Murray
    B. Jimi Hendrix
    C. Harrison Ford
    D. Muhammad Ali

45. At your local Walgreens, a bottle of Coca-Cola sold for _____.
    A. one cent
    B. five cents
    C. seven cents
    D. eleven cents

46. In Boston, Massachusetts, a fast-moving fire at this popular nightspot killed 492 patrons.
    A. Latin Quarter
    B. Coconut Grove
    C. Stardust Lounge
    D. Rendezvous Club

47. The minimum draft age was lowered from twenty-one to _____.
    A. fifteen
    B. sixteen
    C. eighteen
    D. nineteen

48. RCA Victor awarded its first "gold record" for Glenn Miller's _____.
    A. "In the Mood"
    B. "String of Pearls"
    C. "Pennsylvania 6-5000"
    D. "Chattanooga Choo Choo"

49. Nominated for three Oscars, it was Walt Disney's fifth animated film.
    A. *Bambi*
    B. *Dumbo*
    C. *Fantasia*
    D. *Pinocchio*

50. A nine-time All-Star and a five-time World Series champion, he won the American League MVP Award with eighteen home runs, 103 RBIs, and a batting average of .322.
    A. Hank Bauer
    B. Joe Gordon
    C. Ted Williams
    D. Joe DiMaggio

51. Kellogg's introduced this brand of cereal.
    A. Corn Pops
    B. Raisin Bran
    C. Fruit Loops
    D. Apple Jacks

52. "Speed the Materials of War in Victory Bound Convoys" was the slogan of which company?[156]
    A. Acme Truck Carrier
    B. Federal Motor Truck
    C. Prime Transportation
    D. Old Dominion Freight Line

53. The sale of US war bonds raised an estimated _____.
    A. $10 billion
    B. $11 billion
    C. $12 billion
    D. $13 billion

54. A jelly-like substance, it was developed by Harvard University chemist Louis F. Fieser.
    A. Latex
    B. Phosilin
    C. Napalm
    D. Giudice

55. The following celebrities died *except* _____.
    A. W. C. Fields
    B. Carole Lombard
    C. George M. Cohan
    D. Roland "Bunny" Berigan

56. Under the direction of _____, work began on developing the world's first atomic bomb (Manhattan Project).
    A. Richard I. Jones
    B. Leslie R. Groves
    C. William A. Ryder
    D. George K. Douglas

57. The future star of such films as *Showboat*, *The Barefoot Contessa*, and *On the Beach*, she wed actor Mickey Rooney in a private California ceremony. Their marriage ended in divorce in 1943. Who was she?
    A. Lana Turner
    B. Ava Gardner
    C. Veronica Lake
    D. Rita Hayworth

1943

58. Mandatory gasoline rationing began in which city?
    A. Ottawa, Canada
    B. London, England
    C. Phoenix, Arizona
    D. Detroit, Michigan

59. The following celebrities were born *except* _____.
    A. John Denver
    B. Newt Gingrich
    C. Peter O'Toole
    D. Robert De Niro

60. At the 15th Academy Awards, _____ won the Oscar for Best Actor.
    A. Bing Crosby
    B. James Cagney
    C. Walter Pigeon
    D. Ronald Colman

61. Completed in less than two years at a cost of $83 billion, it is America's largest office building.
    A. Aon Center
    B. The Pentagon
    C. US Steel Tower
    D. Empire State Building

62. The undefeated University of Tulsa Golden Hurricanes were upset by (the) _____ 14-7.
    A. University of Tennessee
    B. Michigan State University
    C. University of Texas at El Paso
    D. West Virginia State University

63. Mayor Edward Kelly opened this city's new subway system.
    A. Chicago, Illinois
    B. Portland, Oregon
    C. Seattle, Washington
    D. Baltimore, Maryland

64. Average yearly wages reached _____.
    A. $1,800
    B. $2,000
    C. $2,500
    D. $3,000

65. Can you name the English actor who was killed when his civilian aircraft was shot down by German fighters over the Atlantic Ocean?
    A. John Laurie
    B. Nigel Bruce
    C. Leslie Howard
    D. Cedric Hardwicke

66. In Montana, _____ people perished following a coal mine explosion.
    A. thirty-one
    B. fifty-eight
    C. seventy-four
    D. ninety-seven

67. A Rodgers and Hammerstein musical, it opened on Broadway at the St. James Theatre.
    A. *Carousel*
    B. *Showboat*
    C. *Oklahoma!*
    D. *Kiss Me, Kate*

68. Due to a copper shortage, the US Mint began producing pennies made of _____.
    A. iron
    B. steel
    C. nickel
    D. titanium

69. Built by Philadelphia contractor John McShain, this historic landmark was completed at a cost of $3 million.
    A. Mount Rushmore
    B. Lincoln Memorial
    C. Washington Monument
    D. Thomas Jefferson Memorial

70. Founded by Chicago Cubs owner P. K. Wrigley, they were the inspiration for the film *A League of Their Own*.
    A. The Southern Female Slow-Pitch Union
    B. The Girls Amateur Baseball Consortium
    C. The Ladies Major League Softball Federation
    D. The All-American Girls Professional Baseball League

71. The following celebrities died *except* _____.
    A. Frank Nitti
    B. H. G. Wells
    C. Nikola Tesla
    D. Beatrix Potter

72. Still sold today, it was invented by Richard James and inducted into the National Toy Hall of Fame in 2000.
    A. Slinky
    B. Frisbee
    C. Lincoln Logs
    D. Etch A Sketch

1944

73. In the 30th edition of the Rose Bowl, the University of Southern California defeated the previously unbeaten _____ by a score of 29-0.
    A. University of Alabama
    B. University of Wisconsin
    C. University of Washington
    D. University of Notre Dame

74. The following celebrities were born *except* _____.
    A. Diana Ross
    B. Rudy Giuliani
    C. Michael Douglas
    D. Arnold Schwarzenegger

75. At the 16th Academy Awards, Paul Lukas took home the Oscar for Best Actor in _____.
    A. *Uncertain Glory*
    B. *Address Unknown*
    C. *Watch on the Rhine*
    D. *Experiment Perilous*

76. Born in Somerset, Kentucky, and representing the District of Columbia, she was the first redhead to be crowned Miss America.
    A. Venus Ramey
    B. Shirley Ballard
    C. Betty Jane Rase
    D. Paulina McKevitt

77. A future Nobel laureate, he became the first African American appointed to the US State Department.
    A. W. W. Law
    B. Ralph Bunche
    C. Clarence Bacote
    D. John Wesley Dobbs

78. *Time*'s "Man of the Year" was _____.
    A. Harry Truman
    B. George Marshall
    C. Winston Churchill
    D. Dwight Eisenhower

79. Life expectancy in America reached _____ for men and _____ for women.
    A. 60.8 / 61.9
    B. 61.5 / 62.6
    C. 62.7 / 64.9
    D. 63.6 / 66.8

80. Bing Crosby played a singing priest in the heartwarming motion picture _____.
    A. *Going My Way*
    B. *The Bells of St. Mary*
    C. *Angels in the Outfield*
    D. *The Right Hand of God*

81. The Games of the XIII Olympiad were cancelled because of the Second World War. Which city was scheduled to host the event?
    A. Tokyo, Japan
    B. Madrid, Spain
    C. Dublin, Ireland
    D. London, England

82. All of these were popular baby names *except* _____.
    A. Patricia
    B. William
    C. Barbara
    D. Kenneth

83. The C-64 *Norseman* flying big band leader _____ to a performance in Paris went missing somewhere over the English Channel. His remains were never found.
    A. Artie Shaw
    B. Glenn Miller
    C. Harry James
    D. Woody Herman

84. Written by Nat King Cole and performed by the King Cole Trio, it was a popular tune on the Harlem Hit Parade.
    A. "It Had to Be You"
    B. "Straighten Up and Fly Right"
    C. "You Always Hurt the One You Love"
    D. "Would You Like to Swing On A Star"

85. The following celebrities died *except* _____.
    A. Henry Ford
    B. Edwin Stanley
    C. Manuel Quezon
    D. Wendell Willkie
    1945

86. Which Warner Brothers character made his debut in the cartoon *Odor-able Kitty*?
    A. Daffy Duck
    B. Bugs Bunny
    C. Pepé Le Pew
    D. Foghorn Leghorn

87. An ounce of gold was valued at _____.
    A. $18.65
    B. $29.40
    C. $37.25
    D. $42.50

88. While flying in inclement weather, a military aircraft crashed into this New York City skyscraper.
    A. Flatiron Building
    B. Chrysler Building
    C. Woolworth Building
    D. Empire State Building

89. The following celebrities were born *except* _____.
    A. Tom Petty
    B. Steve Martin
    C. Eric Clapton
    D. Goldie Hawn

90. A future actress and politician, she was crowned the 19th Miss America.
    A. Anita Bryant
    B. Bess Myerson
    C. Dorothy Johnson
    D. Virginia Freeland

91. Movies at your local theater included all of the following *except* _____.
    A. *State Fair*
    B. *Anchors Away*
    C. *The Lost Weekend*
    D. *Beauty and the Beast*

92. A devastating hurricane and subsequent fire destroyed 366 aircraft at the _____ in Florida.
    A. Miami Naval Air Station
    B. Pensacola Naval Air Station
    C. Richmond Naval Air Station
    D. Tallahassee Naval Air Station

93. Which US secretary of state received the Noble Peace Prize?
    A. Cordell Hull
    B. Frank Kellogg
    C. Dean Acheson
    D. Henry Stimson

94. An American gymnast and inventor, George Nissen received a patent for this high-flying device.
    A. Trapeze
    B. Pogo stick
    C. Trampoline
    D. Vaulting box

95. Future rock 'n' roll legend _____ made his first public appearance at the Mississippi-Alabama Fair and Dairy Show.
    A. Elvis Presley
    B. Chuck Berry
    C. Gene Vincent
    D. Jerry Lee Lewis

96. One pound of _____ cost twenty-one cents.
    A. Goldfish
    B. Cheese Nips
    C. Wheat Thins
    D. Ritz Crackers

97. The longest-running news information program in TV history made its radio debut on the Mutual Broadcasting System.
    A. *Meet the Press*
    B. *You Are There*
    C. *Face the Nation*
    D. *Person to Person*

98. Which company was *not* founded in 1945?
    A. Mattel
    B. U-Haul
    C. Minute Maid
    D. Pottery Barn

99. A juicy porterhouse steak at your local butcher shop sold for _____ a pound.
    A. ten cents
    B. forty cents
    C. sixty cents
    D. eighty cents

100. The following celebrities died *except* _____.
    A. Anne Frank
    B. Jerome Kern
    C. David Lloyd George
    D. George Bernard Shaw

Chapter Ten Answers

1. C. $3,800
2. C. Tour de France
3. D. Barcelona
4. C. Hewlett-Packard
5. A. Jon Voight
6. B. Chile
7. A. Pius XI
8. B. Orange Bowl
9. A. *King Kong*
10. D. Great Britain
11. C. John Henry Lewis
12. D. Daughters of the American Revolution
13. A. Will Rogers
14. B. Lou Gehrig
15. A. Leon Trotsky
16. C. Wendell Willkie
17. C. Captain America
18. B. $850
19. C. Mick Jagger
20. D. Hattie McDaniel
21. C. 4.387 billion
22. D. twenty-five cents
23. B. Nylon
24. B. Byron Nelson
25. B. Virginia Woolf
26. D. "I'll Never Smile Again"
27. D. Philadelphia, Pennsylvania
28. C. fifty-four cents
29. C. Old Forester
30. D. Paul McCartney
31. A. Teflon
32. C. National Gallery of Art

33. A. "White Christmas"
34. B. USO
35. B. M&M's
36. C. Chicago White Sox
37. C. $420
38. A. A&P
39. D. John Barrymore
40. A. *Citizen Kane*
41. B. 9.9%
42. D. *How Green Was My Valley*
43. B. New York, New York
44. A. Bill Murray
45. B. five cents
46. B. Coconut Grove
47. C. eighteen
48. D. "Chattanooga Choo Choo"
49. A. *Bambi*
50. B. Joe Gordon
51. B. Raisin Bran
52. B. Federal Motor Truck
53. D. $13 billion
54. C. Napalm
55. A. W. C. Fields
56. B. Leslie R. Groves
57. B. Ava Gardner
58. A. Ottawa, Canada
59. C. Peter O'Toole
60. B. James Cagney
61. B. The Pentagon
62. A. University of Tennessee
63. A. Chicago, Illinois
64. B. $2,000
65. C. Leslie Howard
66. C. seventy-four

67. C. *Oklahoma!*
68. B. steel
69. D. Thomas Jefferson Memorial
70. D. The All-American Girls Professional Baseball League
71. B. H. G. Wells
72. A. Slinky
73. C. University of Washington
74. D. Arnold Schwarzenegger
75. C. *Watch on the Rhine*
76. A. Venus Ramey
77. B. Ralph Bunche
78. D. Dwight Eisenhower
79. D. 63.6 / 66.8
80. A. *Going My Way*
81. D. London, England
82. D. Kenneth
83. B. Glenn Miller
84. B. "Straighten Up and Fly Right"
85. A. Henry Ford
86. C. Pepé Le Pew
87. C. $37.25
88. D. Empire State Building
89. A. Tom Petty
90. B. Bess Myerson
91. D. *Beauty and the Beast*
92. C. Richmond Naval Air Station
93. A. Cordell Hull
94. C. Trampoline
95. A. Elvis Presley
96. D. Ritz Crackers
97. A. *Meet the Press*
98. D. Pottery Barn
99. B. forty cents
100. D. George Bernard Shaw

Appendix

Did You Know?

1. In 1938, *Time* named Adolf Hitler its "Man of the Year."

2. With the coming of war in 1939 and the inevitable food shortages that would follow, Londoners euthanized an estimated 750,000 of their cats, dogs, and other household pets.

3. During the Battle of Britain, the German *Luftwaffe* bombed the city of London for fifty-seven consecutive nights.

4. Introduced by Germany in 1940, *Rettungsbojen* or "rescue buoys" were dropped in the English Channel to be used by downed *Luftwaffe* airmen as safe havens while awaiting recovery. Anchored to the sea floor, the structures were large enough to hold up to four people, as well as food, water, blankets, and dry clothing.

5. Between April and May 1940, the Soviet Secret Police murdered 22,000 Polish military officers and intellectuals in what became known as the Katyn Massacre.

6. In August 1941, a nineteen-year-old *Spitfire* pilot with the Royal Canadian Air Force named John Gillespie Magee Jr. authored a poem entitled "High Flight." Several months after composing the sonnet, Magee was killed on a training mission over Roxholm, England. In tribute to Magee, "High Flight" has been quoted by presidents, inscribed on the headstones of astronauts and aviators, and was recited by Sir Laurence Olivier at the funeral of fellow actor Tyrone Power.

7. The war in the Pacific began a full seventy minutes before the first Japanese aircraft appeared over Pearl Harbor when the USS *Ward* (DD-139) dropped depth charges on what it believed was an enemy submarine operating outside of the harbor entrance.

8. According to presidential lore, FDR rode to the US Capitol on December 8, 1941, in Al Capone's bulletproof limousine to deliver his "Day of Infamy" speech and to ask Congress for a declaration of war.

9. Following FDR's Pearl Harbor address, the Senate and House of Representatives voted 470-1 to declare war on Japan. The only dissenting vote was cast by Representative Jeanette Rankin from Montana.

10. Japan did not achieve all of its objectives at Pearl Harbor because it failed to destroy any aircraft carriers, submarines, or oil facilities.

11. Sergeant Wilson R. DeAngelo was the first and only serviceman to receive both the Army and Navy Medals of Honor for a single act of valor during the Battle of Guadalcanal.

12. FDR established the Volunteer Port Security Force (VPSF) in February 1942 to assist in the protection of the US mainland. Along with the USCG, the VPSF helped to secure piers, warehouses and other waterfront facilities from sabotage. Among the notable volunteers were Hollywood actor Humphrey Bogart and Boston Pops Orchestra conductor Arthur Fiedler.

13. Two months after America entered World War II, the US Congress created a law establishing national daylight savings time to conserve on fuel and promote national security and defense. Known as "war time," the law was repealed in 1945.

14. On August 15, 1942, twelve-year-old Calvin Graham walked into his local recruiting office and joined the USN. He later received the Bronze Star and the Purple Heart for injuries sustained during the Naval Battle of Guadalcanal.

15. While escorting a flight of B-17s on a bombing mission over Oschersleben, Germany, a P-51 pilot named Major James H. Howard, single-handedly and without regard for his own welfare, engaged a formation of thirty *Luftwaffe* fighters. For his bravery against overwhelming odds, Howard was awarded the Medal of Honor.

16. In order to confuse the Germans as to the actual location of the

cross-channel invasion, the Allies used fake radio transmissions, double agents, and even concocted a bogus army under the command of General George Patton.

17. On D-Day, the town of Bedford, Virginia, population 3,000, made the ultimate sacrifice when twenty of its young men were killed on OMAHA Beach.

18. Captain Leonard "Max" Schroeder Jr. of Company C, 2nd Battalion, 4th Regiment, 4th Infantry Division was the first Allied soldier to step foot on Normandy's UTAH Beach.

19. In September 1944, Second Lieutenant Reba Z. Whittle became the first and only female POW in the ETO.

20. Second Lieutenant Martin James Monti became the first known American to defect to the Nazis in October 1944.

21. On April 14, 1945, the German submarine U-1206 sank in the North Atlantic when its toilet malfunctioned.

22. During the campaign to retake the Philippines, Sergeant John R. McKinney single handedly repelled some one hundred Japanese soldiers who were attempting to overrun his position. For his heroic efforts, he was presented the Medal of Honor by President Harry Truman.

23. Stanislawa Leszczynska, a Polish midwife, delivered more than 3,000 babies while imprisoned at Auschwitz.

24. Jakob Nacken, the German Army's tallest soldier, stood seven feet three inches tall.

25. US tankers tied logs to the front and sides of their M4 *Shermans* to create the illusion of added protection from the superior firepower of German armor.

26. Adolf Hitler's half-nephew, William Patrick Hitler, immigrated to America eight months before the start of World War II and served as a pharmacist's mate in the USN until 1947.

27. Max Heiliger was the fictious name used by the *Nazis* to establish bank accounts for the purpose of laundering the confiscated bank notes, gold, and jewelry of concentration camp victims.

28. Considered one of Great Britain's greatest double agents, Spanish-born Juan Pujol Garcia supplied the Germans with false information from 1942 to 1944. His duplicity was so convincing that he was awarded the Iron Cross (Second Class) by Adolf Hitler.

29. At age eighty-eight, Nikolai Morozov served briefly as a sniper in the Soviet Red Army. He is believed to be the oldest person to fight in World War II.

30. Margot Wolk was among fifteen young German women to be recruited by the *SS*, to taste-test Adolf Hitler's food. The last surviving food tester, she died in 2014 at the age of 97.

31. On average, British soldiers were rationed three sheets of toilet paper a day, while their American counterparts received twenty-two sheets.

32. The *Sonderkommando Elbe* was a special unit of the *Luftwaffe* tasked with ramming US bombers with their *Messerschmitt* Bf 109Gs.

33. M&M's were sold exclusively to the US military during World War II. They were not made available to the general public until after the war.

34. Private Wojtek was your typical army recruit. He enjoyed guzzling beer, smoking cigarettes, and never failed to salute a superior officer. He served with the Polish 22nd Artillery Supply Company and participated in the Battle of Monte Cassino. In 1963, he died at the Edinburgh Zoo in

Scotland. Oh, did I forget to mention Wotjek was a 500 lb. Syrian brown bear?

35. Best remembered as the granite-faced coach who led the Dallas Cowboys to two Super Bowl titles, Second Lieutenant Tom Landry flew thirty combat missions with the US Eighth Air Force.

36. Some homesick GIs replaced the wooden handles or grips on their Colt M1911A1 pistols with pieces of clear acrylic (Plexiglass or Lucite) to insert a photo of their girlfriend, wife, children, or dog. Hence the name "sweetheart grips."

37. Virginia Patton, who portrayed Jimmy Stewart's sister-in-law in *It's a Wonderful Life*, was the real-life niece of General George Patton.

38. In 1924, the Oklahoma-based 45th Infantry Division began wearing a red diamond-shaped shoulder patch with a yellow swastika (a Native American symbol) in the center. With the rise of *Nazi* Germany in the 1930s, the swastika was replaced with a yellow Thunderbird.

39. Several of today's well-known European-based companies including Audi, Bayer, BMW, Daimler-Benz/Mercedes-Benz, Porsche, and Volkswagen utilized forced labour from Nazi concentration camps.

40. The "V" in Germany's V-1 rocket stood for "Vendetta."

41. Between 13,000 and 15,000 US airmen died in training accidents during the war.

42. The US government used thirty-four-year-old Colorado native Mary Babnik Brown's "blonde locks" to create the crosshairs for aircraft bombsights.

43. First Sergeant Anton Hilberath is the only German POW buried in Arlington National Cemetery, Section 15, Lot 347.

44. According to estimates from the US National Park Service, one gallon of oil leaks from the USS *Arizona* (BB-39) every day.

45. Veterans who served on the USS *Arizona* (BB-39) during the Pearl Harbor attack, and who wish to spend eternity with their shipmates, are permitted to have their ashes deposited by divers beneath one of her sunken gun turrets.

46. Private Charley Havlat was the last American soldier killed in the ETO.

47. The last American soldier killed in the PTO was Sergeant Anthony J. Marchione.

48. For exhibiting bravery above and beyond the call of duty, 473 members of the US armed forces were awarded Medals of Honor during World War II. Of those recipients, only seven were African American.

49. The Nazis boasted that the Third Reich would last for 1,000 years. In reality, it lasted only 4,156 days.

50. Private Teruo Nakamura became the last known Japanese soldier to officially surrender on December 18, 1974.

Abbreviations and Acronyms

ABC	American Broadcasting Company
AEF	American Expeditionary Force
ANC	Army Nurse Corps
AS	Auxiliary Submarine Tender
BB	Battleship
BBC	British Broadcasting Corporation
CA	Heavy Cruiser
CBS	Columbia Broadcasting System
CL	Light Cruiser
CV	Aircraft Carrier
CVE	Escort Aircraft Carrier
CVL	Light Aircraft Carrier
DAP	German Worker's Party
DD	Destroyer
DE	Destroyer Escort
ETO	European Theater of Operations
FDR	Franklin D. Roosevelt
HBO	Home Box Office
HMS	His/Her Majesty's Ship
IACPWP	Inter-American Conference on Problems of War and Peace
IJA	Imperial Japanese Army
IJN	Imperial Japanese Navy
LCA	Landing Craft, Assault
LCVP	Landing Craft, Vehicle, Personnel
LSFF	Landing Ship, Flotilla Flagship
LST	Landing Ship, Tank

LVT	Landing Vehicle, Tracked
NATO	North Atlantic Treaty Organization
MGM	Metro-Goldwyn-Mayer
MPH	Miles Per Hour
NBC	National Broadcasting Company
POTUS	President of the United States
POW	Prisoner of War
PTO	Pacific Theater of Operations
RAF	Royal Air Force
SS	*Schutzstaffel*
SEATO	Southeast Asia Treaty Organization
SA	*Sturmabteilung*
UN	United Nations
US	United States
USA	United States Army
USAAF	United States Army Air Forces
USASC	United States Army Signal Corps
USCG	United States Coast Guard
USMA	United States Military Academy
USMC	United States Marine Corps
USMM	United States Merchant Marine
USN	United States Navy
USNA	United States Naval Academy
USNR	United States Naval Reserve
USO	United Service Organizations
USS	United States Ship
WAC	Women's Army Corps
WASP	Women Airforce Service Pilots
WAVES	Women Accepted for Volunteer Emergency Service

Acknowledgements

During a teaching career that began with Ronald Reagan in the White House and ended with President Barack Obama, I was both fortunate and blessed to have taught many gifted students including Chris Allen, Bill Avington, Stewart Barbera, Tony Braithwaite, Steve Calabro, David Chermol, John Connors, Craig Dimitri, Jake Ennis, Dave Falcone, Jenna Ficchi, Sean Gabaree, Nick Groch, Joseph Ingemi, Joe Kain, Katie Karsh, Lan Le, Mike Liberati, Diana Lim, Jenny Ly, Brian Mann, George Marsden, John Martino, Jackie McBride, Dave Mingey, Phil Press, John Regan, Katie Schlegel, Marc Schuster, Jason Schwartz, Jeremy Simon, Robert Sola, Lyndsay Taylor, Matt Thomas, Cherie Walters, Greg Wheelan, Donald Woods, Tim Wright, Patrick Zaleski, and Eric Zalewski.

For their support and friendship through the years, I would also like to acknowledge George Bell, MD, Sue Belding, Tom Belzer, Jerry Bennett, Reverend Barry Boyle, SJ, Bill Brennan, Joseph "Brownie" Brown, H. James Burgwyn, PhD, Betty Carboy, Louis Casciato, MS, Jeffrey Celebre, PhD, Charlotte Clarkson, Earl Davenport, Sister Immaculata DiBlasi, SHCJ, William Dienna, John Fawcett, MD, Tom Fitzpatrick, Eileen Frampton, Jane Frampton, Charles Ghapthion, Steve Ghicondes, Chris Glielmi, Robert Gorski, John Groch, John Gruber, Beverly Hadwal, Thomas Heston, PhD, Victor Jouet, Karen Katrinak, Dennis Kent, Kevin Kitchenman, Cheryl Thomas Leinheiser Chuck Longo, Paul Lynch, Kendall Mattern, Noah May, MD, Levi McCall, Dolores McPoyle, Albert Melfi Sr., Joseph Micucci, PhD, Reverend Joseph Michini, SJ, John Milewski, John and Catherine Moore, William D. and Ella Moore, Nancy Moule, Rick Orme, George and Doris Parsons, Andrew Pauls, Ben Peters, PhD, Herb Popp, Mari Preis, Patti Proud, Daniel Patrick Scott, Pa-C, Edward and Ruth Scott, William and Helen Scott, Reverend Frank Skechus, SJ, Maryanne Sola, Carl Staub, MD, Reverend Vince Taggart, SJ, Jerry Taylor, Andrew Tyler, Richard

Webster, PhD, Alice Welsh, Kerry Wetzel, Curt Wrzeszczynski, Carmella Young, and Al Zimmerman.

A very special thank you to Nell Chennault Calloway, granddaughter of General Claire Chennault and Director of the Chennault Aviation and Military Museum in Monroe, Louisiana for her kind words of advice and encouragement and for diligently reviewing my manuscript.

To my wife Diane, for allowing me to pursue my passion and for tolerating my eccentricities, thank you.

Finally, I was inspired to write this book by the courageous and self-effacing young men and women who left their farms, small towns, and big cities across America to face a world at war. For those who served, it would be the greatest and most frightening experience of their lives. Among those answering the call to arms were the residents of Delaware County, PA, where I was raised: **George Abramides, United States Marine Corps (USMC)** ☆ William H. Ackerman, United States Army (USA) ☆ Alfred J. Adams Jr., USA ☆ John Joseph Adams Jr., USA ☆ Joseph H. Adams III, USMC ☆ Joseph E. Adamski, USN ☆ Thomas Newkirk Aiken, USMC ☆ Walter Edward Albright, USA ☆ Alex E. Alexander, United States Navy (USN) ☆ Webster S. Allyn, United States Army Air Forces (USAAF) ☆ Andrew Joseph Ammazzaorsi, USN ☆ Robert H. Ammon, USAAF ☆ George A. Anastasio, USN ☆ Matthew M. Anderson, USA ☆ Victor J. Anderson, USAAF ☆ William J. Anderson, USA ☆ Pasquale J. Angelina Jr., USA ☆ Edmund Francis Anzalone, USAAF ☆ Joseph S. Archacki, USMC ☆ John Paul Archdeacon, USN ☆ Jack F. Ardery, USA ☆ John C. Ardes, USA ☆ Dillwyn Ashenfelder, USA ☆ Philip H. Atwood Jr., USN ☆ Robert Barclay Averell, USA ☆ **Kenneth S. Babe, USA** ☆ Kenneth Babkirk, USN ☆ Ignatius Joseph Bail, USA ☆ William Struthers Bailey, USN ☆ Ernest C. Baker, USAAF ☆ George M. Baker, USA ☆ John Baker, USMC ☆ George Baksi, USA ☆ Raymond J. Ballone, USA ☆ Michael Balock, USA ☆ Richard P. Bannerman, USAAF ☆ Thomas Raymond Baraldi, USN ☆ Joseph James Barnes, USN ☆ George R. Barone Sr., USN ☆ Charlotte Barr, USA ☆ Joseph Barr, USA ☆ John F. Barrett, USAAF ☆ Lewin Bennett Barringer, USAAF ☆ Edward Joseph Barry, USMC ☆ Eugene F. Barry, USN ☆ Arthur F. D. Bartholomew, USMC ☆ Frank J. Basara, USA ☆ Paul G. Basehore Jr., USA ☆ Robert Bassett, USN ☆ James Arthur Bateman Jr., USN ☆ Olive C. Bateman, USA ☆ Donald A. Bath, USAAF

☆ William H. Bathgate, USAAF ☆ Hiram E. Battersby, USAAF ☆ Charles H. Bauer, USA ☆ Harry O. Baxter, USA ☆ Charles Becht, USA ☆ Charles A. Beck, USMC ☆ Charles W. Beck, USAAF ☆ Paul Becker, USAAF ☆ Edward W. Beebe, USMC ☆ John W. Beiswanger Jr., USA ☆ Joseph F. Bell, USA ☆ John B. Bellace, USA ☆ Julian Benson Jr., USAAF ☆ Woodie Benson, USN ☆ David Lionel Berman, USA ☆ William A. Bernero, USA ☆ Richard F. Betzler, USA ☆ Delmont R. Beuttel, USN ☆ Carl D. Bevis, USN ☆ Anthony J. Bianelli, USA ☆ Charles Bieri, USA ☆ Stanley Bilker, USMC ☆ John A. Bissinger, USN ☆ Joseph Bissinger, USA ☆ Martin G. Bissinger, USA ☆ Robert D. Bitler, USMC ☆ Joseph E. Bizyozez, USMC ☆ Peter Black, USAAF ☆ Frederick J. Blackburn, USA ☆ Elwin M. Blackstone, USA ☆ James Douglas Blackwood Jr., USN ☆ John Vincent Blake, USA ☆ Mark Charles Bluebello, USA ☆ Miles J. Blunt Jr., USA ☆ Kenneth Paul Bluzard, USN ☆ Stephen R. Bluzard, USMC ☆ Daniel T. Bonaventure, USA ☆ Vincent J. Bonina, USAAF ☆ Joseph W. Bonkowski, USA ☆ Paul W. Bonsall, USN ☆ Anthony Bonshock, USN ☆ David A. Boone Jr., USN ☆ Donald F. Boorse Sr., USN ☆ William N. "Bokey" Borak Sr., USN ☆ James Andrew Borderieux, USN ☆ Albert F. Borth Jr., USA ☆ Howell Bosbyshell Jr., USA ☆ Harold J. Boston, USA ☆ Albert R. Bothner, USN ☆ Joseph C. Boughner Jr., USN ☆ Al Bowe, USA ☆ Donald W. Bowley, USAAF ☆ James Bowman, USA ☆ Robert Hathaway Boyer Jr., USA ☆ Frank Boyko, USA ☆ Francis R. Boyle, USA ☆ John J. Boyle, USN ☆ Bill Bradfield, USN ☆ Brian Bradfield, USMC ☆ Jack Bradfield, USA ☆ Thomas A. Bradford, USAAF ☆ John J. Bradley Sr., USAAF ☆ William Bradley, USA ☆ Leonard J. Bramble, USAAF ☆ George F. Branson, USA ☆ Frank "Duke" Braun, USA ☆ William O. "Bill" Braxton, USN ☆ Robert L. Breswick, USA ☆ Roland S. Briean Jr., USA ☆ Natale Joseph Brisgone, USN ☆ Manuel P. Britto, USN ☆ Sidney F.T. Brock, USA ☆ Francis D. Broderick, USAAF ☆ George Brodeur Sr., USN ☆ James J. Brogan, USN ☆ Daniel Bronson, USMC ☆ Harry J. "Isaac" Broomall, USA ☆ Blaine D. Brown, USA ☆ Dale William Brown, USA ☆ George Brown, USA ☆ Harold W. Brown, USA ☆ Harry Randolph Brown, USA ☆ James P. Brown, USMC ☆ John J. Brown, USA ☆ Malvin L. Brown, USA ☆ Norman Edward Brown, USAAF ☆ Philip B. Brown, USMC ☆ Thomas J. "T-Bird" Brown, USA ☆ James Brunone, USA ☆ A.J. Bruton, USA ☆ James Clement Bruton, USN ☆ Sophie Brzozowski, USMC ☆ Stanley A. Brzozowski, USN ☆ Richard R. Bucher,

USMC ☆ Albert A. Buckoski, USA ☆ Edward Buffman, USN ☆ Matthew Jacob Buraczynski, USN ☆ Gerald P. Burdette, USMC ☆ Elmer J. Burke Jr., USAAF ☆ Francis P. Burke, USMC ☆ Roy O. Burlew Jr., USA ☆ Albert Burnett, USA ☆ Clarence Burns Jr., USMC ☆ Mason Kirby Burr, USN ☆ Joseph P. Butler Sr., USA ☆ Lewis Benner Butt, USAAF ☆ Ray R. Butts, USA ☆ **Francis "Smitty" Caldwell, USN** ☆ Paul D. Caldwell, USA ☆ William Morris Calhoun, USN ☆ Henry A. Callahan, USA ☆ Louis N. Camilli, USMC ☆ Joseph Campagna, USA ☆ Earl C. Campbell, USMC ☆ James J. Campbell, USA ☆ Zachariah T. Campbell, USA ☆ Arlington W. Canizares, USAAF ☆ Giles J. Cannon, USA ☆ Vincent N. Capelli, United States Coast Guard (USCG) ☆ Joseph Patrick Caponi, USA ☆ Mario F. Cappelli, USN ☆ Albert J. Caracchi, USA ☆ Nicholas Joseph Caramanico, USA ☆ Joseph J. Carbine, USAAF ☆ Pat Cardelli, USA ☆ Alfred C. Cardoza, USA ☆ Hugh J. Carducci, USA ☆ John G. "Johnnie" Carducci, USN ☆ Robert E. Carney, USA ☆ Thomas J. Carr Jr., USA ☆ William B. Carr, USMC ☆ Arthur William Carson, USMC ☆ Harold E. Carter Jr., USMC ☆ John Casertano, USAAF ☆ Charles H. Cassidy Jr., USA ☆ Frederick E. Cassidy, USA ☆ Francis J. Catania, USAAF ☆ Nicholas F. Catania, USA ☆ Barron Chandler, USN ☆ Raymond W. Chandler, USA ☆ Harry Chaykun, USN ☆ Abraham Chazin, USMC ☆ John J. Chester, USA ☆ James S. Cheyney Jr., USA ☆ Pasquale D. Chiacchiere, USA ☆ John J. Chiarolanza, USA ☆ Nicholas Chiavari, USAAF ☆ William Edward Chipman, USN ☆ Paul Chorney, USA ☆ Vernon N. Churchman, USA ☆ James Stanley J. Ciesielka, USA ☆ Clement Francis Cioeta, USA ☆ John D. Cipollone, USA ☆ Philip A. Citerone, USAAF ☆ Carrington Clark, USN ☆ George W. Clark, USA ☆ Lehman A. Clark, USAAF ☆ Walter F. Clifford, USAAF ☆ Reece Thomas Cobourn, USA ☆ Anthony Coccia, USA ☆ Ernest Harold Cocking Jr., USAAF ☆ Arthur Edward Colby Jr., USN ☆ Ralph M. Colflesh, USAAF ☆ Joseph J. Coll, USA ☆ John J. Collins, USA ☆ Domenic L. Colodonato, USN, ☆ Walter J. Coney, USA ☆ Walt Conley, USMC ☆ Charles A. Connell, USA ☆ Harold Connett Jr., USN ☆ Bernard Leo Connor Jr., USMC ☆ John J. Connors, USA ☆ Sebastian Conte, USA ☆ Robert J. Conway, USAAF ☆ James A. Conwell, USMC ☆ Bruce Cook, USAAF ☆ Louis J. Cooke, USA ☆ Anthony J. Coppa Jr., USA ☆ Walter Harry Copple, USN ☆ Robert Bell Coppock, USA ☆ Phillip J. Corbett, USN ☆ Vincent J. Cornacchio, USA ☆ Charles Franklin Cornog, USMC ☆ Anthony A.

THE SECOND WORLD WAR FACT AND QUIZ BOOK

Corradetti, USAAF ✯ William T. Costello, USA ✯ Robert A. Coughenour Jr., USAAF ✯ Anthony Leslie Cowan, USA ✯ Edward Cowan, USN ✯ Harry Cowan, USA ✯ Howard Cowan, USA ✯ John A. Cowan, USA ✯ Joseph T. Cowan, USA ✯ Lawrence P. Cowan, USA ✯ Lewis W. Cowan, USA ✯ Sargent X. Cox, USAAF ✯ Vernon R. Coxen, USAAF ✯ Charles J. Craig, USAAF ✯ Herbert E. Cressman, USN ✯ Frank "Jake" Cresta, USN ✯ Gus Joseph Cristofaro, USAAF ✯ Nick J. Crocetto, USA ✯ Vincent A. Cropper, USN ✯ John J. Crowley, USA ✯ Maurice Fulmer Crowley, USAAF ✯ John J. "Jack" Cruice, USA ✯ Thomas Stanley Cunerd, USN ✯ William H. Cunningham, USN ✯ Emanuel A. Curcio Sr., USN ✯ Bernard Charles Custer, USN ✯ John E. Czukiewski, USA ✯ **Edward C. Dale Jr., USN** ✯ Alvin Daley, USA ✯ Joseph B. Daliessio Jr., USMC ✯ George "Chief" Dalton, USN ✯ Carl Daly, USA ✯ John Filomeno "Phil" D'Amicantonio, USA ✯ George Edward Danenhauer, USN ✯ Joseph J. Davies, USMC ✯ Bob Davis, USN ✯ Wilbert "Bip" Davis, USMC ✯ Wilfred Austin "Utt" Davis, USAAF ✯ George E. Davisson, USA ✯ John J. Deasey Jr., USA ✯ Clarence DeBold, USN ✯ George T. Delgott, USA ✯ Daniel T. Delgrippo, USA ✯ James Thomas DeLizzio, USA ✯ Joseph A. Delloso, USA ✯ Earl R. DeLong, USMC ✯ Edward Joseph Delviscio, USMC ✯ John T. DeMarco, USA ✯ John D. DeMartini, USN ✯ Peter "Pat" Demski, USA ✯ John E. Dennin, USN ✯ Joseph F. DePaul, USA ✯ John David Depew Sr., USMC ✯ Louis V. DeRico, USA ✯ Leonard F. DeStefano Sr., ✯ William E. Detwiler, USMC ✯ James A. Devine, USA ✯ Albert J. "Bertie" De Virgilio, USMC ✯ Joseph DeVito, USMC ✯ Joseph Francis Devlin, USN ✯ Leslie Clarke Dew, USMC ✯ John A. Diamond, USMC ✯ Anthony DiBenedetto, USA ✯ Joseph V. Dicampli, USN ✯ Armando E. DiCarlo, USCG ✯ George J. Dick, USA ✯ John M. Dickinson Jr., USN ✯ Francis DiDonato, USN ✯ Dewitt L. Dietrich, USMC ✯ Bernard P. DiFrancesco Jr., USA ✯ Joseph DiFranks, USAAF ✯ Michael C. Di Furio, USA ✯ Joseph A. Diggins, USA ✯ Anthony G. DiIorio Sr., USA ✯ Nicholas A. DiMarcello, USA ✯ Phillip DiNenno, USA ✯ George A. Dinkelacker, USAAF ✯ Herman P. DiNocola, USA ✯ Gulio F. Di Pangrazio, USA ✯ Lawrence DiSipio, USA ✯ Donald M. Dix, USN ✯ Joseph L. Doak, USAAF ✯ John T. "Pepper" Dodds, USA ✯ Steve J. Domenick, USA ✯ Ed Donnelly, USAAF ✯ Fred Donnelly, United States Merchant Marine (USMM) ✯ Charles B. Donohue, USMC ✯ Robert W. Donovan, USA ✯ Nicholas Doperak, USA ✯ Theodore

Joseph Dorosh, USA ☆ Walter Edward Dorricott Jr., USN ☆ Carl R. Dougherty, USN ☆ Joseph J. Dougherty, USA ☆ David Douglas Sr., USAAF ☆ Norm Douglas, USN ☆ Eugene Downey, USAAF ☆ Edward "Ducky" Doyle, USN ☆ John J. Doyle, USN ☆ William J. Draper, USMC ☆ Stanley Driadon, USN ☆ Robert C. Driscoll, USA ☆ Elton Lee Dryden Sr., USN ☆ Jack Duke, USAAF ☆ Howard B. Duff Jr., USN ☆ Charles H. Duffield Jr., USAAF ☆ James T. Duffy Jr., USMC ☆ Robert J. Duffy, USAAF ☆ Theodore "Ted" Dugan, USA ☆ James B. Dunn, USMC ☆ Wesley E. Dunning, USAAF ☆ Carl E. Dunphy, USA ☆ Charles T. Durkin, USA ☆ **Frederick B. Eager, USN** ☆ Edward J. Early, USMC ☆ William Earnest, USN ☆ Richard A. Ebersole, USMC ☆ Charles W. Eckels Jr., USA ☆ Robert Stedman Eddy, USA ☆ Gilbert Gregory Edgar Jr., USN ☆ Clifford D. Edgcumbe, USN ☆ Charles V. Ednie, USMC ☆ James G. Eisenberger, USA ☆ Patrick Elia, USA ☆ William P. Ellington, USMC ☆ Clyde C. Elmes Jr., USN ☆ William P. Elzey, USMC ☆ Lawrence C. Emmertz, USN ☆ Frank J. Ennis Jr., USMC ☆ Arthur A. Erickson Jr., USAAF ☆ Arvid Ericson, USMC ☆ John Philip Eubank Jr., USAAF ☆ William Charles Evan, USAAF ☆ Angelo Evangelista, USA ☆ Albert A. Ewald, USAAF ☆ Charles E. Ewart, USA ☆ **Florindo A. Fabiani, USA** ☆ William Fabris, USCG ☆ James J. Facciolo, USA ☆ Ralph J. Falcone, USA ☆ Albert Fallon, USMC ☆ James F. Fallon, USAAF ☆ Michael Fatzinick, USA ☆ Furry P. Fecondo, USA ☆ Kenneth I. Feeck, USA ☆ Hugh Paul Feeley, USMC ☆ Rhollo Rodney Fees, USN ☆ Willis Fehr Jr., USN ☆ Charles Thomas Fellona, USA ☆ Raymond P. Feltey, USMC ☆ Willard W. Felton, USA ☆ Horace Goff Ferguson Jr., USN ☆ John A. Ferrante, USA ☆ Edward Morris Fiander, USA ☆ Robert E. Finucane, USAAF ☆ George Fischer, USA ☆ John A. Fisher Jr., USA ☆ John Winfield Fisher, USN ☆ Richard C. Fisher, USA ☆ J.P. Fitzgerald Jr., USAAF ☆ Bartholomew A. Flanagan, USMC ☆ Harry H. Flatau, USMC ☆ Clair Fleck, USMC ☆ C. Russell Fleming, USA ☆ John Joseph Fleming, USA ☆ Arnold Fletcher, USA ☆ Francis G. Flood Jr., USMM ☆ William C. Flood, USN ☆ Thomas Foley, USN ☆ Thomas H. Fooks, USA ☆ Arthur J. Ford, USN ☆ Walter W. Ford, USA ☆ Fred A. Formichella, USN ☆ G. Lee Jameson Forster, USAAF ☆ David E. Fox, USA ☆ Leon "Frenchie" Francia, USN ☆ Gordon Summerell Fraser, USN ☆ John A. French, USA ☆ Henry Aaron Frese, USN ☆ Alice A. Fry, Women's Army Corps (WAC) ☆ Roy Fuller, USMC ☆ Paul Fullerton, USA ☆ Oliver H. Furniss, USA

THE SECOND WORLD WAR FACT AND QUIZ BOOK

☆ Oscar H. Furr, USN ☆ Charles Fuscsick, USN ☆ Milton H. Fussell, USMC ☆ **John D. Gaffney, USAAF** ☆ Clifford Gaines, USMM ☆ William D. Gaines, USAAF ☆ Archie A. Galanaugh, USA ☆ Anthony Galantino Sr., USA ☆ George Lindsay Galbraith Jr., USAAF ☆ Anthony J. Gallagher, USAAF ☆ Francis Bernard Gallagher, USN ☆ Andrew B. Galligan, USA ☆ Raymond Gallo, USN ☆ Charles Garabedian, USMC ☆ Francis Xavier Gardner, USMC ☆ John E. Garecht, USA ☆ Laurence Garnett, USA ☆ James Donald Gartland Jr., USAAF ☆ Ralph A Garzia, USA ☆ Philip Reade Gaughens, USMC ☆ Albert J. Gavetti, USA ☆ Lawrence H. Gelbach, USA ☆ Alfred C. George, USA ☆ Joseph J. George, USMC ☆ Margaret M. George, USA ☆ John F. Geraghty, USN ☆ Frank Hight Gerard, USN ☆ Frank J. Gerone, USA ☆ David J. Gerrits, USAAF ☆ William Giampalmi, USN ☆ Martin Gibbons, USN ☆ Edwin R. Gieger, USMC ☆ Harry A. Gilbert, USAAF ☆ Thomas Gillan, Sr., United States Army Signal Corps (USASC) ☆ John Robert Gilligan, USN ☆ James J. Gilronan, USA ☆ Michael Gladish, USA ☆ Alfred F. Glass, USMC ☆ Harry Goff, USA ☆ Samuel Edward Goldhahn, USA ☆ Albert P. Goldsborough, USMC ☆ Cornelius Goldsborough Jr., USMC ☆ Edward C. Goodley, USA ☆ William M. Goodley, USA ☆ Warren Atlee Goodwin, USN ☆ James R. Googe, USA ☆ Jacques Gordon, USAAF ☆ Victor L. Gorga, USA ☆ James W. Gorrel, USAAF ☆ Robert A. Goslee, USN ☆ Charles A. Gours Jr., USAAF ☆ John R. Gownley, USA ☆ Leonard P. Grabuski, USAAF ☆ Joseph A. Grace, USAAF ☆ Durwood L. Grady, USMC ☆ Charles F. Graul, USA ☆ William M. Gravell, USN ☆ Edmund K. Grayson, USA ☆ Bernard W. Green, USMC ☆ Joseph F. Green, USN ☆ Joseph F. Greenhalgh, USN ☆ Robert C. Greenhalgh, USA ☆ James T. Gregg Sr., USAAF ☆ John F. Gregg, USA ☆ Arthur W. Greims Jr., USA ☆ Helen M. Griendling, USN ☆ David H. Griffith, USMC ☆ George T. Griffiths, USAAF ☆ Donald Reeves Groetzinger, USN ☆ William E. Grogan, USA ☆ William O. Grubb, USN ☆ Carlo Guglielmo, USN ☆ Gabriele V. Guglielmo, USA ☆ Joseph P. Guild, USMC ☆ James H. Gullborg, USN ☆ Robert A. Gum, USAAF ☆ Benjamin L. Guzek, USA ☆ Felix Guzzetti, USA ☆ John E. Guzzy, USA ☆ **Robert Haas II, USCG** ☆ Alfred Emil Haid, USN ☆ Morton E. Haim, USA ☆ Edward Stephen Haley, USA ☆ George C. Hall, USMC ☆ Joseph G. Hall Jr., USA ☆ William J. Hallissey, USA ☆ Albert Hallman III, USN ☆ Mary S. Hallowell, WAC ☆ Charles Halvorsen, USMM ☆ George H. Hamby

Jr., USAAF ✯ Gene Hamill, USA ✯ Charles Ward Hamilton Jr., USN ✯ John H. "Jack" Hamilton, USMC ✯ Vincent J. Hanahan, USA ✯ Perry Pitt Hand, USA ✯ Robert H. Handy, USA ✯ John Carl Haner III, USMC ✯ John H. Haney, USA ✯ Andres A. Hanson, USA ✯ Howard Wilson Happersett, USA ✯ Harry D. Hardcastle, USMC ✯ Francis C. Harley, USA ✯ Stoy Otis Harman, USAAF ✯ Frederick T. Harmer, USA ✯ E. Blair Harper, USN ✯ Frederick A. Harris, USA ✯ Joseph Frederick Harrison Jr., USN ✯ Leonard Francis Harsch, USN ✯ Leroy Hartman, USMC ✯ Kenneth W. Hartmann, USAAF ✯ Donald E. Harvey, USMC ✯ John E. Haskin, USMC ✯ Paul E. Hastie, USMC ✯ Thomas Phillip Hastings Sr., USA ✯ Herbert R. Hatton, USMC ✯ William M. Hawkins, USA ✯ Edward Haywood, USA ✯ John J. "Jack" Healey, USN ✯ James T. Heffernan, USA ✯ N. Richard "Dick" Heisner, USN ✯ Vernon Henderson, USA ✯ William James Henderson Sr., USMC ✯ John C. Hendren, USA ✯ Harold Hengst, USAAF ✯ James J. Hennessy, USA ✯ Maurice L. Hennessy, USA ✯ Harry A. Henrich Jr., USA ✯ John "Jack" Herbert, USN ✯ Harold R. Herman, USMC ✯ Stanley L. Hershey, USA ✯ Carl D. Hertzog, USMC ✯ Richard Hertzog, USMC ✯ Robert Edward Hessler, USN ✯ Walter Lanes Hewes, USN ✯ Eric O. Hildenbrand, USMC ✯ Hugh Anthony Hilferty, USA ✯ Ralph T. Hill, USN ✯ Albert P. Hinderhofer, USA ✯ James L. Hinderhofer, USAAF ✯ Joseph L. Hinderhofer, USMC ✯ Peter Hladish, USN ✯ Lorraine Hoagland, USMC ✯ William C. Hoath, USN ✯ John M. Hodge, USA ✯ Robert V. Hoffecker, USA ✯ John L. Hoffman, USA ✯ Joseph Holobovich, USN ✯ Albert W. Holstein, USMC ✯ Howard Honicker Jr., USAA ✯ Nicholas Hook, USA ✯ Robert P. Hoopes, USMC ✯ Henry Robert Hopkins, USA ✯ Thomas W. Horinka, USA ✯ Edward S. Horodynski, USN ✯ F. Horace Hosbach, USAAF ✯ John W. Hosking, USMC ✯ John Hospordar Jr., USA ✯ Joseph F. Hough, USN ✯ John William Howanski, USN ✯ John M. Howard, USN ✯ Kenneth E. Howard, USN ✯ George R. Howell, USA ✯ David MacIntyre Howie Jr., USN ✯ Mary Holmes Howson, Women Airforce Service Pilots (WASP) ✯ Robert M. Hoyt, USA ✯ William H. Hoyt, USMC ✯ Ralph F. Hudelson, USA ✯ John J. Hudyma, USA ✯ John Leroy Hugg, USAAF ✯ Edward N. Hunter, USA ✯ Hilburn A. Hunter, USA ✯ John Hunter, USA ✯ Irving N. Hurley, USA ✯ James McCready Huston Jr., USN ✯ John William Hylan Jr., USMC ✯ John J. "Jack" Hyland, USA ✯ **Ormondo M. Iacono, USA** ✯ Theresa R. (Bielicki) Iacono, WAC ✯ Domenic

Iannone, USAAF ✫ Carmine "Charlie" Innamorato, USN ✫ Joseph Charles Istak, USN ✫ **Harry B. Jackson, USA** ✫ Robert E. Jackson, USAAF ✫ Robert W. Jackson, USN ✫ Errol M. Jacobs, USA ✫ Robert L. James, USA ✫ Gordon Jamison, USN ✫ Raymond Jarman, USA ✫ James P. Jennings, USA ✫ William Marsh Jerdon, USA ✫ William Jocik, USN ✫ Edward F. Jodlowski, USA ✫ John Jodlowski, USA ✫ George J. Johnsen, USN ✫ Daniel P. Johnson, USN ✫ George M. Johnson, USA ✫ James Kent Johnson, USA ✫ John Johnson, USA ✫ Alan Dougal Jones, USA ✫ Desmond David Jones, USA ✫ Harry Peter Jones, USA ✫ Harry Rees Jones, USA ✫ Robert V. Jones, USA ✫ Robert William Jones, USN ✫ Stewart J. Jones, USAAF ✫ James F. Judge Sr., USN ✫ **Nicholas R. Kalynch, USN** ✫ Julian Kaminski, USN ✫ John James Kane, USA ✫ Raymond Karpin, USA ✫ Robert L. Kaufman, USCG ✫ Thomas Joseph Keane, USAAF ✫ James P. Kearney, USMC ✫ Richard L. Kearney Sr., USN ✫ Joseph Kellerman, USA ✫ Robert B. Kelley, USA ✫ Erval W. Kellogg Jr., USAAF ✫ John L. "Wucky" Kelly, USA ✫ William E. Kelly Sr., USA ✫ Clarence R. Kennedy, USA ✫ Joseph G. Kennedy, USN ✫ John Becker Kerner, USN ✫ Raymond W. Kerr, USMC ✫ Elmer Clarence Kerstetter, USMC ✫ Bernard Michael Kida Sr., USA ✫ George E. Kille, USA ✫ James J. King Sr., USA ✫ Joseph F. King, USAAF ✫ Harry L. Kirby, USA ✫ William J. Kirby Sr., USAAF ✫ Harlan Kirkpatrick, USN ✫ Eugene H. Kissinger, USA ✫ Russell Kissinger Jr., USN ✫ John Adam Kiszonas, USA ✫ Henry A. Klem, USMC ✫ Edward Joseph Klodarska, USA ✫ Henry Kloepfer, USA ✫ Paul T. Knight, USMC ✫ William Knight Sr., USA ✫ Clement V. Knowles, USAAF ✫ Joseph S. Knutson, USN ✫ Louis J. Koch Jr., USA ✫ Michael Kocopy, USMC ✫ Manuel Koff, USAAF ✫ Peter J. Kooistra, USN ✫ Herbert P. Korenko, USAAF ✫ Richard W. Kowal, USAAF ✫ Myron Steven Kowall, USN ✫ Edward Kozlowski, USAAF ✫ Harold W. Kramer, USAAF ✫ Charles Krause, USA ✫ Charles Edward Krauss, USAAF ✫ Robert Henry Kreiser, USMC ✫ Roy N. Kriens, USA ✫ Alexander Krowzow, USA ✫ Charles S. Kuester, USA ✫ Anton "Tony" Kuhlberg, USA ✫ Felix G. Kuncas, USA ✫ John Kupsick, USA ✫ Daniel Kuryea, USAAF ✫ **John H. Lacoboulos, USN** ✫ John C. Lafferty, USMC ✫ Salvatore Laganelli, USA ✫ Carmen "Nooch" Laino, USMC ✫ Edward J. Lamberson, USMC ✫ Robert H. Landon, USA ✫ John F. "Franny" Landrum Sr., USN ✫ Raymond Langton, USN ✫ James A. Larkin, USA ✫ Alfred W. Larson, USAAF ✫ John H. Lathbury,

USN ✯ Michael C. LaVerghetta, USMC ✯ Carl D. Lawley, USN ✯ James P. Lawson, USA ✯ Robert F. Lawson, USA ✯ James Lawton, USMC ✯ Daniel J. Leary Jr., USN ✯ Jane Leary, Women Accepted for Volunteer Emergency Service (WAVES) ✯ Joseph R. Leary, USA ✯ Francis B. Lee, USAAF ✯ George David Lee Sr., USN ✯ Irvin H. Leech, USA ✯ George A. Leeper, USA ✯ William A. Lehndorff, USA ✯ Charles Frederick Leinhauser, USN ✯ William J. Lenton, USAAF ✯ John J. Leonard, USMC ✯ Robert E. "Scrapple" Leonard, USMC ✯ William James Leonard, USMC ✯ George Leopold, USA ✯ Stanley Levi, USA ✯ James Robert Lewin, USN ✯ Edward A. Lewis, USA ✯ Ralph C. Lewis, USA ✯ Anthony A. Liguori, USA ✯ Ralph Linaweaver, USMC ✯ Harry L. Linker, USA ✯ Wallace J. Lippincott, USA ✯ Aaron Lipson, USAAF ✯ Robert G. Liston, USA ✯ John P. Livezey, USA ✯ Charles Philip Logan, USN ✯ James Canfield Logan, USN ✯ Charles Peter Lord, USN ✯ Louis J. Louberta, USA ✯ Vernon Henry Lounsberry Jr., USMC ✯ Robert R. Love, USA ✯ Jack Lowe, USA ✯ Frederick S. Loyle, USA ✯ Hilliard Leonard Lubin, USN ✯ Benjamin J. Luglio, USAAF ✯ Louis Luoma, USN ✯ Charles Max Lyle, USA ✯ Martin E. Lyons, USN ✯ Thomas P. Lyons, USN ✯ Wayne G. Lyster, USMC ✯ Robert T. Lythgoe Sr., USA ✯ **Roy MacElwee Jr., USA** ✯ John Calvin MacIntyre, USN ✯ John F. Mack, USA ✯ John E. Mackenzie, USA ✯ Harold Mackin Jr., USMC ✯ David A. MacQueen, USN ✯ Richard O. Maculley, USAAF ✯ Paul V. Madsen, USA ✯ John J. Maginnis, USA ✯ John Carmen Maher, USMC ✯ Daniel Malatesta, USN ✯ Anthony M. Mancini, USA ✯ ✯ Frank Paul Mantegna, USMC ✯ Michael A. Marabito, USMC ✯ William Marinelli, USN ✯ John S. Maroonik, USA ✯ Peter T. Marrone, USA ✯ Angelo Marsella, USN ✯ Joseph L. Marshall Jr., USA ✯ William Warner Marshall Jr., USMC ✯ Alfred F. Martin, USN ✯ Francis James Martin, USN ✯ George Francis Martin, USN ✯ Gladys Mae Martin, WAVES ✯ Henry J. Martin, USA ✯ Joseph F. Martin, USN ✯ Richard Martin, USN ✯ Andrew L. Martischang, USAAF ✯ Joseph Matlock, USA ✯ Salvatore Mattacotti, USA ✯ Anthony "Tony" Mattero, USN ✯ Thaddeus John Matthews, USA ✯ Howard O. Mattice, USA ✯ Rolfe Strickland Mayer, USN ✯ Floyd H. Maynard, USA ✯ Miron Mazepink, USA ✯ Michael Peter Mazza, USN ✯ Francis J. X. McArdle, USN ✯ Joseph P. McCaffrey, USMC ✯ James E. McCambridge, USN ✯ John R. McCarty, USA ✯ John Bernard McCleary Jr., USN ✯ Edward "Reds" McClintock, USN ✯ James McClintock

Sr., USA ☆ John D. McClintock Sr., USA ☆ Richard B. McClintock, USA ☆ Robert W. McClintock, USN ☆ Thomas Brooks McClintock, USN ☆ Emmett W. McCloskey, USN ☆ Isaac C. McConnell, USA ☆ James H. McConnell, USA ☆ Kenneth W. McConnell, USN ☆ William Walter McConnell, USMC ☆ Francis J. McCormick, USA ☆ Frank H. McCracken, USMC ☆ Howard McCreesh, USMC ☆ Leo Thomas McCue, USA ☆ James J. McCullough, USA ☆ John J. McCullough Sr., USA ☆ Joseph H. McDermott, USMC ☆ Charles L. McDevitt, USA ☆ Michael J. McDevitt, USA ☆ Donald James McDonough, USMC ☆ William J. McDowell, Jr., USMC ☆ William H. McElvenny, USMC ☆ William McElwee Jr., USN ☆ Robert McGarry, USA ☆ Francis Xavier McGee, USN ☆ James F. McGillen, USA ☆ Joseph A. McGinnis, USA ☆ John H. McGlynn, USA ☆ Robert V. McGoldrick, USA ☆ William Thomas McGonigle Jr., USMC ☆ James McGuigan, USMC ☆ John J. McGuigan, USN ☆ Donald A. McIlvane, USA ☆ Alan McIntyre, USA ☆ Howard McIntyre Jr., USN ☆ Frederick E. McKanna Jr., USAAF ☆ Francis McKay, USA ☆ James J. McKenna, USMM ☆ Walter McKenna, USN ☆ William F. McKenna, USAAF ☆ Edward "Ted" McKeon, USA ☆ John J. McKeown Jr., USAAF ☆ Warren F. McLaughlin, USAAF ☆ William J. McLung, USMC ☆ Edward J. McMenamin, USN ☆ Gabriel B. McNair, USA ☆ Henry L. McNair, USMC ☆ Thomas J. McNally, USA ☆ Edward Bernard McNamara, USA ☆ James Irvin McNeill, USMC ☆ William John McQuiston, USN ☆ John McRea, USN ☆ George V. McVay, USA ☆ John McWilliams, USA ☆ Robert C. Mealing, USA ☆ Leo J. Meehan Jr., USN ☆ Roland Mehaffey, USA ☆ Louis Sandy Meliori, USMC ☆ Louis Joseph Meredith, USMC ☆ Albert Merlino, USMM ☆ John Joseph Middleton, USA ☆ Louis Joseph Middleton, USMC ☆ Charles W. Miller, USN ☆ Edward M. Miller, USAAF ☆ Irving A. Miller Jr., USMC ☆ John W. Miller Jr., USMC ☆ Robert Miller, USMC ☆ William C. Mills, USA ☆ John H. Minassian, USAAF ☆ William Michael Mirenda Sr., USA ☆ Frank B. Mitch, USMC ☆ Joseph F. "Scoop" Mitchell, USA ☆ G. Modesti, USA ☆ Primo John Modesti, USA ☆ Harold T. Molton, USA ☆ Tony Mondello, USN ☆ Rudolph J. Mongrandi, USA ☆ Albert N. Montella, USN ☆ Charles A. Montgomery, USN ☆ Paul Emerson Montgomery, USN ☆ Louis G. Monville, USMC ☆ John R. Mooney Jr., USMC ☆ Harold V. Moore, USN ☆ John P. Morley, USN ☆ Isaac L. Morrell Jr., USA ☆ Harry G. Morris, USN ☆ Joseph A. Morris, USN ☆ Harmon Morrison, USA

☆ Winsor A. Mowry III, USAAF ☆ James J. Moyes, USA ☆ Anthony M. Muccigrosso, USN ☆ Frederick W. Mueller Jr., USN ☆ Richard E. Muldoon, USA ☆ Edward Murphy, USA ☆ Michael J. Murphy, USN ☆ Donald J. Murray, USAAF ☆ George R. Murray, USAAF ☆ William J. Murray, USA ☆ William H. Myers Jr., USA ☆ **Frederick F. Naab, USA** ☆ Henry D. Nacrelli, USMC ☆ William J. Naimoli Sr., USA ☆ George Nannos, USN ☆ James Joseph Nash Jr., USA ☆ Tony Nazigian, USA ☆ Tom C. Neal, USA ☆ Vram "Ned" Nedurian, USA ☆ John L. Nemeth, USAAF ☆ Frank Nessel, USMC ☆ Gene C. Neubauer, USMM ☆ Leonard J. Newcomb, USA ☆ George H. Newman, USAAF ☆ Samuel Taylor News, USN ☆ James J. Nicholas, USA ☆ John Nicholls, USA ☆ Thomas J. Noonan, USA ☆ Loyal G. Norman, USA ☆ Albert F. Novino, USA ☆ Alfred T. Novino, USA ☆ **John L. Oberdorf, USMC** ☆ Leon J. Ochrymowicz, USN ☆ Gerald F. O'Connell, USA ☆ James O'Connor, USA ☆ Joseph T. O'Connor, USN ☆ Raymond Oden, USA ☆ Charles T. O'Donnell, USA ☆ Francis A. O'Hanlon, USCG ☆ Paul Carney Oliver, USN ☆ Harry M. O'Neill, USMC ☆ Thomas Joseph Opdenaker, USMC ☆ George Edward Orton, USCG ☆ Calvin B. Osborn, USAAF ☆ Joseph J. Ostrander, USAAF ☆ **Eugene J. Pacanowsky, USN** ☆ Ledlie R. Pace, USA ☆ Louis Pace Sr., USA ☆ John A. Paddock, USN ☆ Frank Palecko, USA ☆ Dominic "Rick" Palladino, USN ☆ Paul A. Palladino, USA ☆ Francis W. Palmer, USA ☆ Harman R. Palmer, USMC ☆ Wilford Palmore, USCG ☆ Albert R. Panebianco, USA ☆ Joseph H. Paolantonio, USA ☆ Joseph A. Paolucci, USA ☆ Vincent James Papi, USMC ☆ Thomas J. Parent, USA ☆ Robert V. Parker, USA ☆ Joseph Passaretti, USA ☆ Gene B. Paterson, USA ☆ William Thomas Patton Jr., USN ☆ William J. Paul Jr., USA ☆ Fred Reese Penman, USA ☆ John Penman, USAAF ☆ Stuart Penman Jr., USMC ☆ William S. Pennypacker, USMC ☆ John I. Peoples, USA ☆ Alexander V. Pepe, USA ☆ Michael Perna, USN ☆ Fiore "Chick" Pettica, USA ☆ Albert Pezzella Jr., USAAF ☆ James A. Pfeiffer, USN ☆ Ernest C. Phillips, USAAF ☆ Vaughn R. Pierce, USA ☆ Clarence "Jack" Pilkington, USA ☆ Felix W. Pincurek, USA ☆ Domenic James Pino, USAAF ☆ William G. Piper, USMC ☆ Philip Pisani, USCG ☆ Claudio "Clutch" Pizio, USA ☆ Rudolph N. "Rudy" Pizio, USA ☆ William S. Plattenburg Jr., USAAF ☆ Simon Plennert, USMC ☆ Michael Polenski, USN ☆ Armando A. Pomante, USA ☆ Harold E. Poole Sr.,

USA ☆ Russell A. Poore, USMC ☆ John C. Portner, USA ☆ Samuel Felton Posey, USN ☆ Howard Green Potts, USN ☆ Harry J. Povey, USAAF ☆ Norman Edgar Powell, USA ☆ Robert H. Powell, USN ☆ Gerald Powlus, USMC ☆ Joseph A. Procopio, USA ☆ Samuel D. Puller, USMC ☆ William H. Purcell, USA ☆ Walter F. Puzio, USA ☆ Norman Pysher Sr., USA ☆ **Thomas F. Quinn, USAAF** ☆ **John W. Radell, USMC** ☆ James V. Rafferty Jr., USA ☆ Arthur F. Raimo Sr., USN ☆ Alexander Rapino, USA ☆ Ralph Rapino, USA ☆ Thomas Rapino, USA ☆ Charles G. Rapp, USA ☆ William A. Rappa, USAAF ☆ James E. Rastatter, USMC ☆ Jack Raulerson, USA ☆ Thomas William Rayer, USN ☆ Vincent Anthony Raymondo, USA ☆ Matthew J. Reaney, USA, ☆ James J. Redden, USN ☆ Robert T. Reeves, USA ☆ William W. Reid, USMC ☆ John E. Reilly, USAAF ☆ William Herman Reinbold, USN ☆ Carlisle H. Reville, USA ☆ Kenneth H. Reynolds, USMC ☆ Egidio N. Ricci, USAAF ☆ William J. Ricci, USN ☆ William Rice, USAAF ☆ Nicholas M. Rich, USA ☆ Stuart Paddock Rich, USN ☆ Harry William Ricketts, USN ☆ Robert L. Ricks, USN ☆ Morris T. Risko, USAAF ☆ George J. Ristine Jr., USA ☆ Donald C. Ritschy, USA ☆ Edward B. Ritter, USN ☆ Herman E. Rixstine, USMC ☆ Joseph P. Rizol, USAAF ☆ James Rizzolo, USAAF ☆ James Bonnyman Roak, USN ☆ Thomas J. Roberts, USN ☆ Donald C. Robinson, USA ☆ James K. Robinson, USA ☆ John A. Robinson, USAAF ☆ Louis A. Robinson, USMC ☆ Arthur S. Roche, USA ☆ Alan Wesson Rockwell, USN ☆ Thomas H. Rodgers, USA ☆ William F. "Bud" Rogers Sr., USN ☆ William E. Rollison, USN ☆ Harry J. Rollmar Sr., USA ☆ Arthur Rosato, USA ☆ John Roselli, USAAF ☆ Charles W. Ross, Jr., USA ☆ John Ulysses Rosselet, USA ☆ Bernadino Rossi, USN ☆ Eli Roth, USN ☆ Harry G. Roth, USA ☆ William J. Rowe, USMC ☆ Horace M. Rowland, USMC ☆ Albert Natale Ruggieri, USN ☆ Anthony F. Ruggiero, USA ☆ Stephen C. Rullo, USN ☆ Harry E. Rupertus, USN ☆ Earl G. Russell, USAAF ☆ Albert Rutman, USA ☆ Joseph A. Ryan, USN ☆ Louis A Rydzewski, USMC ☆ **Robert Mario Sablian, USA** ☆ Edward J. Saggese, USA ☆ Harold P. Saks, USA ☆ Edwin R. Salmons Jr., USA ☆ Thomas G. Salvucci, USMC ☆ David P. J. Sanderson, USMC ☆ David R. Sanderson, USMM ☆ Benjamin E. Sarafin, USA ☆ Morton R. Savage, USAAF ☆ Warren J. Savini, USMC ☆ Michael Savinski, USN ☆ Dorothy M. Sayen, USN ☆ Leo Scanlan, USAAF ☆ Arthur Joseph

Schatz, USN ☆ Robert P. Schatz, USMC ☆ Bernard A. Scheib, USA ☆ John W. Schiefer, USMC ☆ Herbert L. Schleicher, USMC ☆ Walter A. Schlott, USMC ☆ Andrew Schmidt, USAAF ☆ Robert R. Schnatz, USA ☆ Charles V. Schneider, USMC ☆ Joseph L. Schnell, USN ☆ Philip M. Schoch, USAAF ☆ Thomas Francis Schoening, USA ☆ Harry Schrader Jr., USAAF ☆ Lewis E. Schulz, USA ☆ Charles Schwartz, USA ☆ Rudolph V. Sciubba, USN ☆ Arthur G. Scott Sr., USA ☆ Frederick A. Scott, USA ☆ George "Buddy" Scully, USN ☆ Francis B. Seals, USMC ☆ Eugene Seeley, USA ☆ Lester Segich Sr., USA ☆ William F. Seiverling Jr., USMC ☆ George E. Sension, USN ☆ Noel R. Servan, USA ☆ Charles E. Sevier, USA ☆ Clarence D. Sewell, USN ☆ John Herman Shade Jr., USA ☆ Frederick Shahadi, USN ☆ Thomas Shahadi, USMC ☆ Michael J. Shaika, USAAF ☆ Joseph E. Shanahan, USN ☆ Donald J. Shannon, USN ☆ William Shepard, USN ☆ William B. Sheridan, USA ☆ Joseph J. Shields, USAAF ☆ William T. Shields, USA ☆ Joseph Edward Shillingsburg, USN ☆ James B. Shimel, USMC ☆ Howard Shourds, USMM ☆ David J. Shumaker, USA ☆ Leon Joseph Sikora, USN, ☆ Leonard H. Simcox, USA ☆ Jay W. Simmons, USA ☆ Paul A. Simon, USAAF ☆ Edward P. Singer, USA ☆ Anthony W. Sisak, USMC ☆ Paul Joseph Skinner, USN ☆ Charles Slackway, USA ☆ Robert John Sladek Sr., USAAF ☆ George Slata, USN ☆ Walter J. Slowik, USA ☆ Russell R. Smeal, USCG ☆ Edmund L. Smith Jr., USN ☆ George F. Smith, USMC ☆ James H. Smith, USA ☆ John T. Smith, USA ☆ Leonard H. Smith, USA ☆ Osborn E. Smith Jr., USA ☆ Ralph Stanley Smith, USAAF ☆ Raymond W. Smith, USA ☆ Stanley S. Smith, USA ☆ Stewart F. Smith, USMC ☆ William Edward Smith, USA ☆ Thomas D. Smyth Jr., USA ☆ Vincent DePaul Smythe, USA ☆ Peter S. Snoich, USA ☆ Samuel Alex Sokolik Sr., USA ☆ Albert J. Solitro, USA ☆ Anthony J. Soprano, USA ☆ Frank A. Soscia, USN ☆ Raymond C. Spencer, USAAF ☆ John Anthony Spera, USN ☆ Nicholas Snowden Stabler Jr., USN ☆ Anthony E. Stalloni, USMC ☆ James Stanton, USN ☆ Jerome J. Stark, USMC ☆ Henry Clay Statzell Jr., USMM ☆ Robert B. Steele, USMC ☆ Joseph A. Stenta, USA ☆ John B. Stetson III, USA ☆ Francis R. Stewart, USAAF ☆ Ian Stewart, USN ☆ Maureen "Stu" Stewart, USA ☆ Robert S. Stinsman, USAAF, ☆ Robert W. S. Stinson, USMC ☆ John Hague Stockman, USMC ☆ John H. Stokes Jr., USN ☆ Leonard Stout, USA ☆ William H. Stover, USMC ☆ Everett

THE SECOND WORLD WAR FACT AND QUIZ BOOK

Thomas Stowe, USA ☆ Harry Edward Strailey, USAAF ☆ Frederick Edward Strang Jr., USMC ☆ Paul Hilton Stull Jr., USAAF ☆ Joseph Suhanick, USAAF ☆ John J. Sullivan, USA ☆ Nicholas S. Sullivan, USAAF ☆ Charles D. Summers, USAAF ☆ Milton B. Suplee, USA ☆ Joseph A. Swanick, USAAF ☆ Edmund Paul Sweeney, USMC ☆ John Joseph Sweeney Jr., USA ☆ Frederic L. Swierczek, USMC ☆ Anthony "Tony" Sylvester, USA ☆ **John "Jack" Taggart, USA** ☆ George L. Tallman, USN ☆ Herbert Henry Taylor, USN ☆ Raymond William Taylor, USMM ☆ Walter L. Tershowski, USN ☆ John James Teuchert, USMC ☆ Roland Paul Therrien, USN ☆ Alfred P. Theurer, USA ☆ Edward R. Thomas Jr., USMC ☆ James F. Thomas, USMC ☆ Joseph L. Thomas, USN ☆ Percy William Thomas Jr., USA ☆ Luther O. Thompson, USAAF ☆ Vernon C. Thompson, USN ☆ William L. Thorpe, USAAF ☆ Harry Tidmarsh, USMC ☆ Merrill Howard Tilghman III, USA ☆ William J. Tini Sr., USA ☆ William Joseph Tobin, USN ☆ Thomas H. Tomarelli, USAAF ☆ Lewis A. Tomasco, USA ☆ Julius J. Tomaszewski, USA ☆ George A. Toms, USMC ☆ Albert A. Torelli, USN ☆ Verne Townsend Jr., USMC ☆ William "Bill" Traband, USA ☆ Frank L. Trasatti, USA ☆ Robert C. Travis, USA ☆ Michael Trovatore, USN ☆ Edmund A. Trudeau, USN ☆ Christie D. Truitt, USAAF ☆ John J. Tucker, USA ☆ Kemble Tucker, USA ☆ Emlen L. Tunnel, USCG ☆ Francis Stanton Tuohey, USN ☆ Lloyd O. Turcuit, USAAF ☆ Howard Frank Turner, USA ☆ James F. "Jiggs" Turner, USMC ☆ John J. Turner, USAAF ☆ Thomas Strickland Turner Sr., USMC ☆ William C. Turner, USA ☆ Walter J. Tyson, USN ☆ **Samuel Lable Uditsky, USN** ☆ Howard G. Umberger, USA ☆ Matthew Ungerleider, USA ☆ William "Bill" Upton, USN ☆ Edward A. Urban, USA ☆ **Vincent C. Vail Sr., USA** ☆ Kenneth R. Vandemark, USA ☆ Francis C. Vanderulis, USAAF ☆ James L. Vauclain, USA ☆ William E. Vauclain, USA ☆ Pasquale C. Vecchio, USA ☆ Walter R. Veth, USN ☆ Henry Eugene Vickers, USN ☆ Robert P. Vickery, USN ☆ Donald E. Virtue, USN ☆ Pasquale J. Vivaldi, USA ☆ Frank D. Vizzarri, USN ☆ Perry Vlahos, USA ☆ Alexander Vogelsohn, USA ☆ Peter F. Vottima, USA ☆ **Albert J. Wallace, USA** ☆ Carl H. Walling Sr., USN ☆ Bernard S. Walmsley, USA ☆ Joseph V. Walmsley, USN ☆ Edward "Bud" Walsh Sr., USMC ☆ Albert Benjamin Walters Jr., USMM ☆ Stanley W. Walz, USA ☆ Charles W. Ward, USMC ☆ John B. Ward, USMC ☆ Thomas A. Ward Sr., USN ☆ Hiram R.

Warder, USMC ✫ John Edward Warhola, USA ✫ John Michael Robert Washlick, USMC ✫ Charles P. Wassell, USAAF ✫ Frank Wassell, USAAF ✫ Harry A. Wassell, USAAF ✫ Donald Watkins, USN ✫ Robert S. Watkins, USN ✫ Albert Joseph Watson, USN ✫ Charles R. Watson, USMC ✫ Malcolm L. Watson, USA ✫ George T. Watts, USN ✫ Harmer H. Way Jr., USAAF ✫ Donald Weightman, USAAF ✫ Arthur R. Weinisch, USMC ✫ Frank L. Welc, USN ✫ Henry Wells, USA ✫ Charles J. Welsh Jr., USN ✫ Henry Emil Wendeler, USN ✫ James L. Wenrich, USN ✫ John L. Werner, USMC ✫ Walter A. Wernher, USA ✫ Keith P. West Sr., USA ✫ William Charles West Sr., USN ✫ Charles W. Westcott, USA ✫ William Charles L. Wetherill, USA ✫ Robert Wetten II, USMC ✫ Robert Lawrence Whaley, USN ✫ Harry E. Whartnaby, USA ✫ James C. Whelan, USN ✫ Francis A. White, USA ✫ Joseph E. Whitehead, USMC ✫ James Montgomery Whiteman, USA ✫ John T. Whitting Jr., USA ✫ Alfred Baxter Whittington Sr., USMC ✫ Joseph Roger Whittington, USN ✫ Norman K. Wiggins, USAAF ✫ Richard A. Wiley, USN ✫ John Wilkers, USA ✫ James W. Wilkinson, USAAF ✫ Robert M. Willauer Sr., USN ✫ George Bennett Williams, USA ✫ James R. Williams, USAAF ✫ Richard Williams, USN ✫ Samuel E. Williams Sr, USAAF ✫ Benjamin O. Wilmer, USMM ✫ Albert V. Wilson, USAAF ✫ Alfred D. Wilson, USN ✫ Donald H. Wilson, USMC ✫ Harry S. Wilson, USA ✫ Grover F. Winfield, USA ✫ Harrie A. Winham, USAAF ✫ William C. Winkler, USA ✫ Warren Donald Wise, USN ✫ John W. Woestman, USASC ✫ Edward A. Wolenski, USMC ✫ Charles R. Wolf, USMC ✫ Eric Fisher Wood Jr., USA ✫ George J. Woodland, USN ✫ Lawrence E. Woodward, USA ✫ Isaac L. Worrell Jr., USA ✫ William Thomas Worrilow, USN ✫ Austin M. Wortley Jr., USMC ✫ Llewelyn Wright, USA ✫ Thomas C. Wright, USMC ✫ Winfield E. Wright Jr., USA ✫ Jack Wyatt, USN ✫ **Arthur J. Yacola, USN** ✫ Edward J. Yancoskie, USCG ✫ William E. Yerger, USA ✫ Stephen P. Yorden, USN ✫ Joseph MacArthur Youmans Sr., USA ✫ Alan R. Young, USN ✫ Robert L. Young Jr., USAAF ✫ **Zigmond Zamlynsky, USMC** ✫ Nicholas L. Zarrilli, USN ✫ Joseph Edward Zdun, USAAF ✫ Frank F. Zebley, USMC ✫ Morris Zeitzeff Jr., USA ✫ Jack Zelen, USAAF ✫ William H. Zeuner, USAAF ✫ Robert Zultowski, USN ✫ Charles "Chuck" Zurman, USN ✫ William Henry Zwaan, USA ✫ Joseph Zygmunt, USAAF

I would like to express my appreciation to the following individuals for helping me compile the above list: Lynn Becker, Jim McCans, Christina Saunders, and Shannon Strigle. To those that I have failed to mention, please accept my apologies and my gratitude.

William E. Scott
Springfield, PA
August 2024

Endnotes

Introduction

1. Robert Lehrman, "Rhetoric Revisited: FDR's 'Infamy' Speech," *American Experience*, December 6, 2016, https://www.pbs.org/wgbh/americanexperience/features/rhetoric-revisited-fdrs-infamy-speech.
2. Douglas MacArthur, "General Douglas MacArthur: Opening and Closing Statements at the Japanese Surrender Ceremony," American Rhetoric, September 2, 1945, https://www.americanrhetoric.com/speeches/douglasmacarthurussmissourispeech.htm.
3. James Grossman, "AHA Today: James Baldwin on History," *Perspectives on History*, August 3, 2016, https://www.historians.org/research-and-publications/perspectives-on-history/summer-2016/james-baldwin-on-history.

Chapter One: Adolf Hitler & The Holocaust

4. Brendan Simms, *Hitler: A Global Biography*, (New York: Basic Books, 2019), 9.
5. Simms, *Hitler*, 10.
6. Ian Kershaw, *Hitler: A Biography*, (New York: W. W. Norton & Company, 2008), 60.
7. William L. Shirer, *The Rise and Fall of the Third Reich: A History of Nazi Germany*, (New York: Simon & Schuster, 2011), 32.
8. Kathleen Haley, "100 Years After WWI: The Lasting Impacts of the Great War," *Syracuse University News*, July 28, 2014, https://news.syr.edu/blog/2014/07/28/100-years-after-wwi-the-lasting-impacts-of-the-great-war.
9. Robert Ley, ed., "Modern History Sourcebook: The 25 Points 1920: An Early Nazi Program," https://sourcebooks.fordham.edu/mod/25points.asp.
10. Adolf Hitler, *Mein Kampf*, (New York: Houghton Mifflin, 1969), 293–96.
11. Erin Blakemore, "A Ship of Jewish Refugees Was Refused US Landing in 1939. This Was Their Fate," History.com, June 4, 2019, https://www.history.com/news/wwii-jewish-refugee-ship-St-louis-1939.

12 Katrin Bennhold, "80 Years Ago the Nazis Planned the 'Final Solution.' It Took 90 Minutes." *The New York Times,* January 20, 2022, https://www.nytimes.com/2022/01/20/world/europe/lake-wanssee-conference-final-solution-holocaust.

Chapter Two: Generals and Admirals

13 Orvelin Valle, "Patton Earned the Nickname 'Old Blood and Guts,'" *We Are the Mighty,* April 2, 2018, https://www.wearethemighty.com/articles/how-general-patton-earned-the-fearless-name-old-blood-guts.
14 Dwight D. Eisenhower, *Crusade in Europe,* (New York: Doubleday, 1948), 56.
15 Henry Probert, *Bomber Harris: His Life and Times,* (London: Greenhill Books, 2001), 413.
16 Thomas Alexander Hughes, *Admiral Bill Halsey: A Naval Life,* (Cambridge, Massachusetts: Harvard University Press, 2016), front cover.
17 Hank H. Cox, "Meet John C. H. Lee: The Forgotten Logistical Mastermind Behind the Allied Invasion of France," Military History Now, April 26, 2018, https://militaryhistorynow.com/2018/04/26 meet-john-c-h-lee-the-forgotten-logistical-mastermind-behind-the-allied-invasion-of-europe.
18 George Forty, *The Reich's Last Gamble: The Ardennes Offensive, December 1944,* (London: Cassell & Company, 2000), 216.
19 Mike Polston, "Brehon Burke Somervell (1895–1955)," *Encyclopedia of Arkansas,* February 28, 2022, https://encyclopediaofarkansas.net/entries/brehon-burke-somervell-2817.

Chapter Three: Battles and Campaigns

20 John Keegan, *The Second World War,* (New York: Penguin Books, 2005), 275.
21 David Bianculli, "In Many Ways, Author Says, Spanish Civil War Was 'The First Battle of WWII,'" *NPR,* March 10, 2017, https://www.npr.org/2017/03/10/519462137/in-many-ways-author-says-spanish-civil- war-was-the-first-battle-of-wwii.
22 Stephen L. Moore, *The Battle for Hell's Island,* (New York: New American Library, 2015), 112.
23 Harold J. Goldberg, *D-Day in the Pacific: The Battle of Saipan,* (Bloomington, Indiana: Indiana University Press, 2007), front cover.
24 Andrew Roberts, *Churchill: Walking With Destiny,* (New York: Viking, 2018), 563.

25 Nick Hollkamp, "8 Things to Know About the Battle of the Bulge on Its 75th Anniversary," *Louisville Courier Journal*, December 16, 2019, https://www.courier-journal.com/story/news/history/2019/12/16/battle-bulge-8-things-know-the-greatest-american-battle-wwii/4311758002.

CHAPTER FOUR: WEAPONS

26 Dr. Carolyn Apple, "World War II: America's Heavy Hitter-The B-17 Flying Fortress," Delaware Historical and Cultural Affairs, https://history.delaware.com/word-war-ii-americas-heavy-hitter-the b-17-flying-fortress.

27 T. Logan Metesh, "Patton & the Garand: 'Greatest Battle Implement Ever Devised,'" *The Armory Life*, December 28, 2020, https://www.thearmorylife.com/patton-and-the-garand-greatest-battle-implement-ever-devised.

28 Katie Sanders and Mara Storey, "Andrew Higgins Designed Landing Boats That Eisenhower Said Won the War," *Business Insider*, March 19, 2023, https://www.businessinsider.com/andrew-higgins-designed-landing-boats-that-eisenhower-said-won-the-wwii-2023-3.

29 Steven J. Zaloga, *US Half-Tracks of World War II*, (London: Osprey Publishing, 1983), 6.

30 Will Burchfield, "Go Inside A C-47 Skytrain, the Plane That Helped Win WWII," CBS Video, May 25, 2017, https://www.cbsnews.com/detroit/news/go-inside-a-c-47-skytrain-the-plane-that-helped-win-wwii-videos.

31 Mark Nash, "WW2 British Funnies: Churchill Crocodile, A22F," May 12, 2017, https://tanks-encyclopedia.com/ww2/gb/churchill-crocodile.

32 Mark R. Peattie, *Sunburst: The Rise of Japanese Naval Air Power, 1909–1941*, (Annapolis, Maryland: Naval Institute Press, 2001), 91.

33 Ryleigh Salmon, "How the Jeep Was Invented for World War II," February 11, 2021, https://www.landerscountry.com/how-the-jeep-was-invented-for-world-war-ii.

34 David Stahel, *Operation Barbarossa and Germany's Defeat in the East*, (New York: Cambridge University Press, 2009), 169.

35 *Hero Ships: USS Laffey*, 45 minutes, produced by Sammy Jackson and Liz Reph (A&E Home Video, 2011), DVD.

CHAPTER FIVE: CONFERENCES AND CODE NAMES

36 Elmer Bendiner, *A Time For Angels: The Tragicomic History of the League of Nations*, (New York: Alfred Knopf, 1975), 82.

37 Andrew Roberts, *Churchill:Walking With Destiny*, (New York: Viking, 2018), 434.
38 Harm Venhuizen, "Hitler Released His Failed Plan to Invade England 80 Years Ago Today," *Army Times*, July 16, 2020, https://www.armytimes.com/veterans/military-history/2020/07/16/hitler-released-his-failed-plan-to-invade-england-80-years-ago-today.
39 Thomas A. Bailey, *A Diplomatic History of the American People*, (Englewood Cliffs, New Jersey: Prentice Hall, Inc, 1980), 781.
40 Bailey, *A Diplomatic History*, 757.
41 Herman S. Wolk, "Decision at Casablanca," *Air & Space Forces Magazine*, January 1, 2003, https://www.airandspaceforces.com/article/0103casa.
42 Joseph N. Mueller, *Guadalcanal 1942: The Marines Strike Back*, (Westport, Connecticut: Praeger Publishing, 2004), 7.

Chapter Six: Complete the Quotation

43 Omar N. Bradley, *A General's Life*, (New York: Simon & Schuster, 1983), 139.
44 David Fraser, *Knight's Cross: A Life of Field Marshal Erwin Rommel*, (New York: HarperCollins, 1993), 382.
45 Roger Parkinson, *Attack on Pearl Harbor*, (New York: G. P. Putnam's Sons, 1973), 117.
46 Jean Edward Smith, *FDR*, (New York: Random House, 2007), 532.
47 Smith, *FDR*, 538.
48 Winston S. Churchill, *Never Give In!: The Best of Winston Churchill's Speeches*, (New York: Hyperion, 2003), 206.
49 Bradley, *A General's Life*, 218.
50 Gordon W. Prange, *At Dawn We Slept: The Untold Story of Pearl Harbor*, (New York: Penguin Books, 2001), 11.
51 Smith, *FDR*, 537.
52 Carlos D'Este, *Eisenhower: A Soldier's Life*, (New York: Henry Holt & Company, 2002), 559.
53 D'Este, *Eisenhower*, 391.
54 Robert G. Kaiser, *Russia: The People and the Power*, (New York: Atheneum, 1967), 207.
55 General James H. "Jimmy," Doolittle, and Carroll V. Glines, *I Could Never Be So Lucky Again*, (New York: Bantam Books, 1991), 392.
56 Gerald Fleming, *Hitler and the Final Solution*, (Berkeley, California: University of California Press, 1984), 17.
57 Audie Murphy, *To Hell and Back: The Classic Memoir of World War II by America's Most Decorated Soldier*, (New York: Owl Books, 2002), 203.

58 Ronald H. Spector, *Eagle Against the* Sun, (New York: The Free Press, 1985), 347.
59 Petty Officer Rachel A. Treon, "Marine Corps Commemorates 75th Anniversary of Iwo Jima," USMC, February 19, 2020, https://www.marines.mil/News/News Display/Article/2088180/marine-corps-commemorates-75th-anniversary-of-iwo-jima.
60 D'Este, *Eisenhower*, 583.
61 Henry H. Adams, *The Life of Fleet Admiral William D. Leahy*, (Annapolis, Maryland: Naval Institute Press, 1985), 246.
62 Claudia Koontz, *The Nazis Conscience*, (Cambridge, Massachusetts: Belknap Press, 2003), 13.
63 Ed Cray, *General of the Army: George C. Marshall, Soldier and Statesman*, (New York: Simon & Schuster, 1991), 591.
64 Wilhelm Canaris, "Wilhelm Canaris (1887–1945)," Jewish Virtual Library, https://jewishvirtual Library.org.
65 Bradley, *A General's Life*, 341.
66 Major General Mungo Melvin, *Manstein: Hitler's Greatest General*, (New York: St. Martin's Press, 2010), 274.
67 D'Este, *Eisenhower*, 337.
68 William Manchester, *American Caesar: Douglas MacArthur, 1885–1964*, (Boston, Massachusetts: Little, Brown & Company, 1978), 195.
69 Marc D. Bernstein, "Joseph Stilwell's Escape From Burma During World War II," HistoryNet, June 12, 2006, https://www.historynet.com/joseph-stilwell-escape-from-burma-during-world-war-ii.
70 Melvin, *Manstein*, 274.
71 B.J. Pollock, "'Air Raid Pearl Harbor! This is No Drill!'" *Fort Bend Herald*, December 5, 2003,https://www.fbherald.com/air-raid-pearl-harbor-this-is-no-drill/article_Ocfc82b7-78c15dO3-b3f6-21758845133e.html.
72 D'Este, *Eisenhower*, 405.
73 Charlie Dunlap, J.D., "Thinking About President Roosevelt's Prayer on D-Day, June 6, 1944,"Lawfire, June 6, 2022, https://sites.duke.edu/lawfire/2022/06/06/thinking-about-president-roosevelts-prayer-on-d-day-june-6-1944.
74 Melvin, *Manstein*, 328.
75 Senator Arthur H. Vandenberg, "Classic Senate Speeches." US Senate, January 10, 1945, https://www.senate.gov/artandhistory/history/common/generic/Speeches_Vandenberg.htm.
76 Thomas Sheppard, "'I Have No Expectation of Success': The War in the Pacific Before and After Midway," *Providence Magazine*, August 29, 2017, https://providencemag.com/2017/08/i-have-no-expectation-of-success-the-war-in-the-pacific-after-midway.

77 Smith, *FDR*, 572.
78 Albert Speer, *Inside the Third Reich: Memoirs by Albert Speer*, (New York: Macmillan, 1970), 363.
79 Eugene Kinkead, "The Pilot Who Dropped the Atomic Bomb on Hiroshima," *The New Yorker*, December 28, 1945, https://www.newyorker.com/magazine/1946/01/05/usher.
80 John Toland, *The Rising Sun: The Decline and Fall of the Japanese Empire*, (New York: Modern Library, 2003), 216.
81 Spector, *Eagle Against*, 503.
82 Winston Churchill, *The Second World War, Volume II: Their Finest Hour*, (Boston, Massachusetts: Houghton Mifflin, 1949), 105.
83 Frazier Hunt, *MacArthur and the War Against Japan*, (New York: C. Scribner's Sons, 1944), 71.
84 Allan Bullock, *Hitler and Stalin: Parallel Lives*, (New York: Vintage Books, 1993), 715.
85 Samuel Eliot Morison, *The Two Ocean War: A Short History of the United States Navy in the Second World War*, (Boston, Massachusetts: Little, Brown & Company, 1963), 70.
86 Richard P. Hallion, "Airpower From the Ground Up," *Air and Space Forces Magazine*, November 1, 2000, https://www.airandspaceforces.com/article/1100airpower.
87 Mark W. Clark, *Calculated Risk*, (New York: Harper & Brothers, 1950), 6.
88 Walter Gorlitz, ed., *The Memoirs of Field Marshal Wilhelm Keitel*, (New York: Stein and Day, 1966), 52.
89 Gar Alperovitz, *The Decision to Use the Atomic Bomb and the Architecture of an American Myth* (New York: Alfred A. Knopf, 1995), 321.
90 Winston S. Churchill, *Never Give In!: The Best of Winston Churchill's Speeches*, (New York: Hyperion, 2003), 229.
91 D'Este, *Eisenhower*, 526.
92 Fraser, *Knight's Cross*, 390.
93 Commander Robert McFarlin, "Hit Hard, Hit Fast, Hit Often!" *Proceedings*, July 2021, https://www.usni.org/magazines/proceedings/2021/july/hit-hard-hit-fast-hit-often.
94 C.N. Trueman, "General Percy Hobart," The History Learning Site, April 21, 2015, https://www.history/learningsite.co.uk/world-war-two-in-western-europe/d-day-index/general-percy-hobart.
95 C. Peter Chen, "Robert Taft," World War II Database, February 2008, https://ww2db.com/person_bio.php?person_id=442.
96 Hallion, "Airpower."
97 President Ronald Reagan, "The History Place: Great Speeches Collection: Ronald Reagan on the 40th Anniversary of D-Day," The History Place, June 6, 1984, https://www.historyplace.com/Speeches/Reagan-d-day.htm.

98   Alperovitz, *The Decision to Use*, 261.
99   Kai Bird and Martin J. Sherwin, *American Prometheus: The Triumph and Tragedy of J. Robert Oppenheimer*, (New York: Vintage Books, 2006), 185–86.
100 Leon Goldensohn, *The Nuremberg Interviews*, (New York: Alfred A. Knopf, 2004), 190.
101 John C. McManus, "The Man Who Took Omaha Beach," *Politico Magazine*, June 5, 2014, https://politico.com/magazine/story/2014/06/the-man-who-took-omaha-beach-107509.
102 John Simkin, "Alan Brooke, Baron Alanbrooke of Brookeborough," Spartacus Educational, April 20022, https://spartacus-educational.com/2WWbrookeA.htm.
103 Smith, *FDR*, 576.
104 Spector, *Eagle Against*, 123.
105 Alperovitz, *The Decision to Use*, 350.
106 Alperovitz, *The Decision to Use*, 117.
107 D'Este, *Eisenhower*, 400.
108 Fleming, *Hitler*, 171.
109 Ernie Pyle, "Reporting America at War: Ernie Pyle: The Death of Captain Waskow," PBS, 2003, https://www.pbs.org/weta/reportingamericaatwar/reporters/pyle/waskow.html.
110 Robin Cross, *Fallen Eagle: The Last Days of the Third Reich*, (New York: John Wiley & Sons, 1995), 21.
111 President Barack Obama, "Remarks by President Obama at the 70th Anniversary of D-Day-Omaha Beach, Normandy," White House Press Office, June 6, 2014, https://obamawhitehouse.Archives.gov/the-press-office/2014/06/06/remarks-president-obama-70th-anniversary-d-day-omaha-beach-normandy.
112 Alperovitz, *The Decision*, 28.
113 President George W. Bush, "President Bush, President Chirac Mark 60th Anniversary of D-Day," White House Press Office, June 6, 2004, https://georgewbush-whitehouse.archives.gov/news/Releases/2004/06/20040606.html.
114 Dudley Seward, *Bomber Harris: The Story of Marshal of the Royal Air Force Sir Arthur Harris*, (New York: Doubleday, 1985), 24.
115 Henry C. Clausen and Bruce Lee, *Pearl Harbor: Final Judgement*, (New York: Crown Publishers, Inc, 1992), 166.
116 Keith Feiling, *The Life of Neville Chamberlain*, (London: Macmillan, 1970), 427–28.
117 Alperovitz, *The Decision*, 33.
118 Toland, *The Rising Sun*, 754.
119 Senator Daniel K. Inouye, "Quotes," Daniel K. Inouye Institute, June 26, 2023, https//dkii.org/quotes.
120 Edward Crankshaw, *Gestapo: Instrument of Tyranny*, (New York: Viking Press, 1956), 103.

121 Doolittle and Glines, *I Could Never*, 392.
122 Larry Slawson, "Claus von Stauffenberg's Plot to Kill Adolf Hitler," Owlocation, January 2, 2023, https://owlocation.com/humanities/Claus-von-Stauffenberg-The-Plot-Tto-Kill-Adolf- Hitler.
123 John Norris, "Harold Raynesford Stark," Pennsylvania Center for the Book, Summer 2008, https://pabook.libraries.psu.edu/literary-cultural-heritage-map-pa/bios/Stark_Harold.
124 William L. Shirer, *The Rise and Fall of the Third Reich: A History of Nazi Germany*, (New York: Simon & Schuster, 2011), 568.
125 Alperovitz, *The Decision*, 334.
126 Spector, *Eagle Against*, 503.
127 Spector, *Eagle Against*, 556
128 Bill Yenne, *The Imperial Japanese Army: The Invincible Years, 1941–1942*. (Oxford, United Kingdom: Osprey Publishing, 2014), 337.
129 Logan Nye, "11 of the Craziest Lines Ever Spoken In Battle," We Are The Mighty, January 5, 2022, https://www.wearethemighty.com/popular/11-of-the-craziest-lines-ever-spoken-battle.
130 Heinz Guderian, *Panzer Leader*, (New York: E.P. Dutton, 1952), 427.
131 Alperovitz, *The Decision*, 62.
132 Aubrey Saint Kenworthy, *The Tiger of Malaya: The Story of General Tomoyuki Yamashita*, (New York: Exposition Press, 1953), 38.
133 Obama, "Remarks."
134 Cornelius Ryan, *The Longest Day: June 6, 1944*, (New York: Simon & Schuster, 1959), 8.
135 Clausen and Lee, *Pearl Harbor*, 229.
136 Churchill, *Never Give In!*, 395.
137 Alperovitz, *The Decision*, 165.
138 Benno Müller-Hill, *Murderous Science: Elimination by Scientific Selection of Jews, Gypsies, and Others, Germany 1933–1945*, (Oxford, United Kingdom: Oxford University Press, 1998), 48.
139 General James M. Gavin, "The Jump Into Sicily," *American Heritage*, April/May 1978, https://www.americanheritage.com/jump-sicily.
140 Christopher C. Harmon, "Alanbrooke and Churchill: Finest," International Churchill Society, Autumn 2001, https://winstonchurchill.org/publications/finest-hour/finest-hour-112/alanbrooke-and-churchill.
141 Thomas B. Buell, *Master of Seapower: A Biography of Fleet Admiral Ernest J. King*, (Boston, Massachusetts, Little, Brown, & Company, 1980), 498.
142 Chester Wilmot, *The Struggle for Europe*, (Westport, Connecticut: Greenwood Press, 1972), 20.

Chapter Eight: Hollywood Goes to War

143 *Hacksaw Ridge,* 139 minutes, directed by Mel Gibson (Lionsgate Home Entertainment, 2017), DVD, https://www.imdb.com.
144 *When Trumpets Fade,* 92 minutes, produced by David R. Ginsburg, et al. (HBO Studios, 2006), DVD, https://www. imdb.com.
145 *The Longest Day*, 178 minutes, directed by Andrew Marton, et al. (20th Century Fox Home Entertainment, 2006), DVD.
146 Chris Fujiwara, "*The Cranes Are Flying: A Free Camera,*" The Criterion Collection, March 27, 2020, https://www.criterion.com/current/posts/200-the-cranes-are-flying-a-free-camera.
147 *In Harm's Way*, 165 minutes, directed by Otto Preminger, (Paramount Home Entertainment, 2001), DVD.
148 Cornelius Ryan, *A Bridge Too Far*, (New York: Simon & Schuster), 461.

Chapter Nine: The Living Room War

149 *The Pacific*, 530 minutes, produced by Steven Spielberg, et al. (HBO Studios, 2010), DVD, https://www.imdb.com.
150 *McHale's Navy*, 3,660 minutes, produced by Edward J. Montagne (Shout! Factory, 2018), DVD.
151 *The Rat Patrol*, 1,440 minutes, produced by Jon Epstein, et al., (Shout! Factory, 2017), DVD.
152 *Hogan's Heroes*, 4,275 minutes, produced by Edward H. Feldman (Paramount Home Media, 2016), DVD.
153 *Colditz*, 184 minutes, produced by Justin Bodle, et al. (Shout! Factory, 1984), DVD. https://www.imdb.com.

Chapter Ten: The Way We Were: 1939–1945

154 "Yes, It's the Most Famous Understatement in America," *Life*, November 10, 1941, 147.
155 "Most Popular Cup in My Trophy Room!" *Life*, November 10, 1941, 117.
156 "Speed the Materials of War in Victory Bound Convoys." *Time*, April 6, 1942, 61.

Bibliography

BOOKS

Adams, Henry H. *The Life of Fleet Admiral William D. Leahy*. Annapolis, Maryland: Naval Institute Press, 1985.

Alperovitz, Gar. *The Decision to Use the Atomic Bomb and the Architecture of an American Myth*. New York: Alfred A. Knopf, 1995.

Atkinson, Rick. *An Army at Dawn: The War in North Africa, 1942–1943*. New York: Henry Holt & Company, 2002.

Atkinson, Rick. *The Day of Battle: The War in Sicily and Italy, 1943–1944*. New York: Henry Holt & Company, 2008.

Atkinson, Rick. *The Guns at Last Light: The War in Western Europe, 1944–1945*. New York: Henry Holt & Company, 2013.

Bailey, Thomas A. *A Diplomatic History of the American People*. Englewood Cliffs, New Jersey: Prentice Hall, Inc., 1980.

Baime, A.J. *The Arsenal of Democracy: FDR, Detroit, and an Epic Quest to Arm an America at War*. Boston, Massachusetts: Mariner Books, 2015.

Bendiner, Elmer. *A Time For Angels: The Tragicomic History of the League of Nations*. New York: Alfred A. Knopf, 1975.

Bird, Kai, and Martin J. Sherwin. *American Prometheus: The Triumph and Tragedy of J. Robert Oppenheimer*. New York: Vintage Books, 2006.

Bradley, Omar N. *A General's Life*. New York: Simon & Schuster, 1983.

Bradley, Omar N. *A Soldier's Story*. Westport, Connecticut: Greenwood Press, 1975.

Buell, Thomas B. *Master of Seapower: A Biography of Fleet Admiral Ernest J. King*. Boston, Massachusetts: Little, Brown, & Company, 1980.

Buell, Thomas B. *The Quiet Warrior: A Biography of Admiral Raymond A. Spruance.* Annapolis, Maryland: Naval Institute Press, 2009.

Bullock, Allan. *Hitler and Stalin: Parallel Lives.* New York: Vintage Books, 1993.

Churchill, Winston S. *Never Give In!: The Best of Winston Churchill's Speeches.* New York: Hyperion, 2003.

Churchill, Winston S. *The Second World War, Volume II: Their Finest Hour.* Boston, Massachusetts: Houghton Mifflin, 1949.

Clark, Mark W. *Calculated Risk.* New York: Harper & Brothers, 1950.

Clausen, Henry C., and Bruce Lee. *Pearl Harbor: Final Judgement.* New York: Crown Publishers, Inc, 1992.

Crankshaw, Edward. *Gestapo: Instrument of Tyranny.* New York: Viking Press, 1956.

Cray, Ed. *General of the Army: George C. Marshall, Soldier and Statesman.* New York: Simon & Schuster, 1991.

Cross, Robin. *Fallen Eagle: The Last Days of the Third Reich.* New York: John Wiley & Sons, 1995.

Davis, Kenneth S. *FDR: The War President, 1941–1943.* New York: Random House, 2000.

D'Este, Carlos. *Eisenhower: A Soldier's Life.* New York: Henry Holt & Company, 2002.

Doolittle, General James H. "Jimmy," and Carroll V. Glines. *I Could Never Be So Lucky Again.* New York: Bantam Books, 1991.

Eisenhower, Dwight D. *Crusade in Europe.* New York: Doubleday, 1948.

Feiling, Keith. *The Life of Neville Chamberlain.* London: Macmillan, 1970.

Ferrell, Robert H. *Harry Truman: A Life.* Columbia, Missouri: University of Missouri, 1994.

Fleming, Gerald. *Hitler and the Final Solution.* Berkeley, California: University of California Press, 1984.

Fleming, Nicholas. *August 1939: The Last Days of Peace.* London: Davies, 1979.

Forty, George. *The Reich's Last Gamble: The Ardennes Offensive, December 1944.* London: Cassell & Company, 2000.

Fraser, David. *Knight's Cross: A Life of Field Marshal Erwin Rommel.* New York: HarperCollins, 1993.

Gavin, James M. *On to Berlin: Battles of an Airborne Commander, 1943–1946.* New York: Viking Press, 1978.

Giangreco, D.M. *Hell to Pay: Operation Downfall and the Invasion of Japan, 1945–1947*. Annapolis, Maryland: Naval Institute Press, 2009.

Goldberg, Harold J. *D-Day in the Pacific: The Battle of Saipan*. Bloomington, Indiana: Indiana University Press, 2007.

Goldensohn, Leon. *The Nuremberg Interviews*. New York: Alfred A. Knopf, 2004.

Gorlitz, Walter, ed. *The Memoirs of Field Marshal Wilhelm Keitel*. New York: Stein and Day, 1966.

Guderian, Heinz. *Panzer Leader*. New York: E. P. Dutton, 1952.

Hitler, Adolf. *Mein Kampf*. New York: Houghton Mifflin, 1969.

Hughes, Thomas Alexander. *Admiral Bill Halsey: A Naval Life*. Cambridge, Massachusetts: Harvard University Press, 2016.

Hunt, Frazier. *MacArthur and the War Against Japan*. New York: C. Scribner's Sons, 1944.

Kaiser, Robert G. *Russia: The People and the Power*. New York: Atheneum, 1967.

Keegan, John. *The Second World War*. New York: Penguin Books, 2005.

Kenworthy, Aubrey Saint. *The Tiger of Malaya: The Story of General Tomoyuki Yamashita*. New York: Exposition Press, 1953.

Kershaw, Ian. *Hitler: A Biography*. New York: W. W. Norton & Company, 2008.

Koontz, Claudia. *The Nazis Conscience*. Cambridge, Massachusetts: Belknap Press, 2003.

Leckie, Robert. *Helmet for My Pillow: From Parris Island to the Pacific*. New York: Bantam Books, 2010.

Liddell Hart, B. H., ed. *The Rommel Papers*. New York: Harcourt, Brace and Company, 1953.

Manchester, William. *American Caesar: Douglas MacArthur, 1885–1964*. Boston, Massachusetts: Little, Brown & Company, 1978.

McManus, John C. *September Hope: The American Side of a Bridge Too Far*. New York: New American Library, 2012.

Melvin, Major General Mungo. *Manstein: Hitler's Greatest General*. New York: St. Martin's Press, 2010.'

Moore, Stephen L. *The Battle for Hell's Island*. New York: New American Library, 2015.

Morison, Samuel Eliot. *The Two Ocean War: A Short History of the United States Navy in the Second World War*. Boston, Massachusetts: Little, Brown & Company, 1963.

Mueller, Joseph N. *Guadalcanal 1942: The Marines Strike Back*. Westport, Connecticut: Praeger Publishing, 2004.

Müller-Hill, Benno. *Murderous Science: Elimination by Scientific Selection of Jews, Gypsies, and Others, Germany 1933–1945*. Oxford, United Kingdom: Oxford University Press, 1998.

Murphy, Audie. *To Hell and Back: The Classic Memoir of World War II by America's Most Decorated Soldier*. New York: Owl Books, 2002.

Nelson, Craig. *The First Heroes: The Extraordinary Story of the Doolittle Raid: America's First World War II Victory*. New York: Viking Penguin, 2002.

Parkinson, Roger. *Attack on Pearl Harbor*. New York: G.P. Putnam's Sons, 1973.

Peattie, Mark A. *Sunburst: The Rise of Japanese Naval Air Power, 1909–1941*. Annapolis, Maryland: Naval Institute Press, 2001.

Prange, Gordon W. *At Dawn We Slept: The Untold Story of Pearl Harbor*. New York: Penguin Books, 2001.

Probert, Herbert. *Bomber Harris: His Life and Times*. London: Greenhill Books, 2001.

Roberts, Andrew. *Churchill: Walking With Destiny*. New York: Viking, 2018.

Rommel, Erwin. *Infantry Attacks*. Novato, California: Presidio Press, 1990.

Ryan, Cornelius. *A Bridge Too Far*. New York: Simon & Schuster, 1974.

Ryan, Cornelius. *The Longest Day: June 6, 1944*. New York: Simon & Schuster, 1959.

Seward, Dudley. *Bomber Harris: The Story of Marshal of the Royal Air Force Sir Arthur Harris*. New York: Doubleday, 1985.

Shirer, William L. *The Rise and Fall of the Third Reich: A History of Nazi Germany*. New York: Simon & Schuster, 2011.

Simms, Bernard. *Hitler: A Global Biography*. New York: Basic Books, 2019.

Sledge, E.B. *With the Old Breed: At Peleliu and Okinawa*. New York: Random House, 2007.

Smith, Jean Edward. *FDR*. New York: Random House, 2007.

Spector, Ronald H. *Eagle Against the Sun*. New York: The Free Press, 1985.

Speer, Albert. *Inside the Third Reich: Memoirs by Albert Speer*. New York: Macmillan, 1970.

Stahel, David. *Operation Barbarossa and Germany's Defeat in the East*. New York: Cambridge University Press, 2009.

Stanton, Shelby L. *World War II Order of Battle: U.S. Army Ground Units.* Mechanicsburg, Pennsylvania: Stackpole Books, 2006.

Stimson, Henry L. *On Active Service in Peace and War.* New York: Octagon Books, 1971.

Tatum, Charles W. *Red Blood, Black Sand: Fighting Alongside John Basilone From Boot Camp to Iwo Jima.* New York: Berkley Caliber, 2012.

Toland, John. *The Rising Sun: The Decline and Fall of the Japanese Empire.* New York: Modern Library, 2003.

Wilmot, Chester. *The Struggle for Europe.* Westport, Connecticut: Greenwood Press, 1972.

Yenne, Bill. *The Imperial Japanese Army: The Invincible Years, 1941–1942.* Oxford, United Kingdom: Osprey Publishing, 2014.

Zaloga, Steven J. *US Half-Tracks of World War II.* London: Osprey Publishing, 1983.

PERIODICALS

"Most Popular Cup in My Trophy Room!" *Life.* November 10, 1941, 117.

"Speed the Materials of War in Victory Bound Convoys." *Time.* April 6, 1942, 61.

"Yes, It's the Most Famous Understatement in America." *Life.* November 10, 1941, 147.

DOCUMENTARIES

The Cold Blue. 73 minutes, DVD. Produced by Erik Nelson and Peter Hankoff, Kino Lorber, 2022.

Hero Ships: USS Laffey. 45 minutes, DVD. Produced by Sammy Jackson and Liz Reph, A&E Home Video, 2011.

Pearl Harbor: 24 Hours After. 80 minutes, DVD. Produced by Anthony Giacchino, Lionsgate, 2012.

Tales of the Gun: US Guns of WWII. 50 minutes, DVD. Produced by Wayne Weiss, A&E Home Video, 2009.

The US and the Holocaust. 300 minutes, DVD. Produced by Ken Burns, PBS, 2022.

Victory at Sea. 936 minutes. (DVD: Complete Series). Produced by Henry Salomon, Mill Creek, 2012.

The World at War. 1,357 minutes. (DVD: Complete Series). Produced by Jeremy Issacs, Lionsgate, 2013.

FILMS

1941. 146 minutes. DVD. Directed by Steven Spielberg. Universal Pictures Home Entertainment, 2010.

Above and Beyond. 122 minutes. DVD. Directed by Melvin Frank and Norman Panama. Warner Home Video, 2009.

A Bridge Too Far. 176 minutes. DVD. Directed by Richard Attenborough. MGM Home Entertainment, 2013.

The Americanization of Emily. 115 minutes. DVD. Directed by Arthur Hiller. Warner Home Video, 2014.

Anzio. 125 minutes. DVD. Directed by Duilio Coletti and Edward Dmytryk. Sony Pictures Home Entertainment, 2001.

Attack! 107 minutes. DVD. Directed by Robert Aldrich. MGM Home Entertainment, 2003.

A Walk in the Sun. 117 minutes. DVD. Directed by Lewis Milestone. Kit Parker Films, 2022.

Bad Day at Black Rock. 81 minutes. DVD. Directed by John Sturges. Warner Home Video, 2012.

Battleground. 118 minutes. DVD. Directed by William Wellman. Warner Home Video, 2006.

Battle of Britain. 132 minutes. DVD. Directed by Guy Hamilton. MGM Home Entertainment, 2003.

Battle of the Bulge. 170 minutes. DVD. Directed by Ken Annakin. Warner Home Video, 2007.

The Best Years of Our Lives. 168 minutes. DVD. Directed by William Wyler. MGM Home Entertainment, 2000.

Between Heaven and Hell. 94 Minutes. DVD. Directed by Richard Fleischer. 20th Century Fox Home Entertainment, 2008.

Brass Target. 111 minutes. DVD. Directed by John Hough. Warner Home Video, 2012.
The Bridge at Remagen. 115 minutes. DVD. Directed by John Guillermin. MGM Home Entertainment, 2006.
The Bridge on the River Kwai. 162 minutes. DVD. Directed by David Lean. Columbia TriStar Home Video, 2000.
The Caine Mutiny. 125 minutes. DVD. Directed by Edward Dmytryk. Sony Pictures Home Entertainment, 2007.
Casablanca. 103 minutes. DVD. Directed by Michael Curtz. Warner Home Video, 2010.
Catch-22. 121 minutes. DVD. Directed by Mike Nichols. Paramount Home Entertainment, 2001.
The Dam Busters. 124 minutes. DVD. Directed by Michael Anderson. Film Movement, 2021.
Darkest Hour. 125 minutes. DVD. Directed by Joe Wright. Universal Pictures Home Entertainment, 2018.
Das Boot. 209 minutes. DVD. Directed by Wolfgang Petersen. Columbia TriStar Home Video, 1997.
The Desert Fox. 88 minutes. DVD. Directed by Henry Hathaway. 20th Century Fox Home Entertainment, 2003.
The Devil's Brigade. 131 minutes. DVD. Directed by Andrew V. McLaglen. MGM Home Entertainment, 2002.
The Dirty Dozen. 149 minutes. DVD. Directed by Robert Aldrich. Warner Home Video, 2006.
Downfall. 155 minutes. DVD. Directed by Oliver Hirschbiegel. Sony Pictures Home Entertainment, 2005.
Dunkirk. 102 minutes. DVD. Directed by Christopher Nolan. Warner Brothers Home Entertainment, 2020.
The Eagle Has Landed. 118 minutes. DVD. Directed by John Sturges. ITV Studios Home Entertainment, 2007.
Enemy at the Gates. 131 minutes. DVD. Directed by Jean-Jacques Annaud. Paramount Home Entertainment, 2001.
The Enemy Below. 98 minutes. DVD. Directed by Dick Powell. 20th Century Fox Home Entertainment, 2004.

Eye of the Needle. 112 minutes. DVD. Directed by Richard Marquand. MGM Home Entertainment, 2006.

Fat Man and Little Boy. 126 minutes. DVD. Directed by Roland Joffé. Paramount Home Media, 2019.

The Fighting Seabees. 100 minutes. DVD. Directed by Edward Ludwig. Artisan Entertainment, 2000.

Flags of Our Fathers. 132 minutes. DVD. Directed by Clint Eastwood. DreamWorks Home Entertainment, 2007.

Flying Leathernecks. 102 minutes. DVD. Directed by Nicholas Ray. Warner Home Video, 2007.

From Here to Eternity. 118 minutes. DVD. Directed by Fred Zinnemann. Columbia TriStar Home Entertainment, 2001.

Fury. 135 minutes. DVD. Directed by David Ayer. Sony Pictures Home Entertainment, 2015.

The Gallant Hours. 116 minutes. DVD. Directed by Robert Montgomery. MGM Home Entertainment, 2010.

The Great Dictator. 125 minutes. DVD. Directed by Charlie Chaplin. Criterion Collection, 2011.

The Great Escape. 172 minutes. DVD. Directed by John Sturges. MGM Home Entertainment, 1998.

The Guns of Navarone. 157 minutes. DVD. Directed by J. Lee Thompson. Columbia TriStar Home Video, 2000.

Hacksaw Ridge. 139 minutes. DVD. Directed by Mel Gibson. Lionsgate Home Entertainment, 2017.

The Halls of Montezuma. 113 minutes. DVD. Directed by Lewis Milestone. 20th Century Fox Home Entertainment, 2002.

Heaven Knows Mr. Allison. 108 minutes. DVD. Directed by John Huston. 20th Century Fox Home Entertainment, 2003.

Hell in the Pacific. 103 minutes. DVD. Directed by John Boorman. KL Studio Classics, 2017.

Hell Is for Heroes. 89 minutes. DVD. Directed by Donald Siegel. Paramount Home Entertainment, 2001.

The Heroes of Telemark. 130 minutes. DVD. Directed by Anthony Mann. Sony Pictures Home Entertainment, 2011.

Indiana Jones and the Last Crusade. 127 minutes. DVD. Directed by Steven Spielberg. Paramount Home Entertainment, 2008.

Inglorious Basterds. 153 minutes. DVD. Directed by Quentin Tarantino. Universal Pictures Home Entertainment, 2011.

In Harm's Way. 165 minutes. DVD. Directed by Otto Preminger. Paramount Home Entertainment, 2001.

Is Paris Burning? 172 minutes. DVD. Directed by Rene Clement. Paramount Home Entertainment, 2003.

Jaws. 124 minutes. DVD. Directed by Steven Spielberg. Universal Pictures Home Entertainment, 2012.

Judgment at Nuremberg. 186 minutes. DVD. Directed by Stanley Kramer. MGM Home Entertainment, 2004.

Kelly's Heroes. 143 minutes. DVD. Directed by Brian G. Hutton. Warner Home Video, 2010.

Letters from Iwo Jima. 140 minutes. DVD. Directed by Clint Eastwood. Warner Home Video, 2006

The Longest Day. 178 minutes. DVD. Directed by Andrew Marton, et al. 20th Century Fox Home Entertainment, 2006.

The Man Who Never Was. 103 minutes. DVD. Directed by Ronald Neame. 20th Century Fox Home Entertainment, 2005.

McHale's Navy. 93 minutes. DVD. Directed by Edward J. Montagne. Universal Pictures Home Entertainment, 2017.

McHale's Navy Joins the Air Force. 90 minutes. DVD. Directed by Edward J. Montagne. Universal Pictures Home Entertainment, 2007.

Memphis Belle. 107 minutes. DVD. Directed by Michael Caton-Jones. Warner Home Video, 1998.

Merrill's Marauders. 98 minutes. DVD. Directed by Samuel Fuller. Warner Home Video, 2008.

Merry Christmas, Mr. Lawrence. 124 minutes. DVD. Directed by Nagisa Oshima. Criterion Collection, 2010.

Midway. 132 minutes. DVD. Directed by Jack Smight. Universal Pictures Home Entertainment, 2003.

Midway. 138 minutes. DVD. Directed by Roland Emmerich. Lionsgate Home Entertainment, 2020.

The Monuments Men. 118 minutes. DVD. Directed by George Clooney. 20th Century Fox Home Entertainment, 2014.

Mr. Roberts. 123 minutes. DVD. Directed by John Ford and Mervyn LeRoy. Warner Home Video, 2006.

Mrs. Miniver. 134 minutes. DVD. Directed by William Wyler. Warner Home Video, 2010.

The Night of the Generals. 138 minutes. DVD. Directed by Anatole Litvak. Columbia TriStar Home Entertainment, 2004.

Objective, Burma! 142 minutes. DVD. Directed by Raoul Walsh. Warner Home Video, 2016.

The Outsider. 108 minutes. DVD. Directed by Delbert Mann. Hollywood Gold Series, 2021.

Patton. 171 minutes. DVD. Directed by Franklin J. Schaffner. 20th Century Fox Home Entertainment, 2006.

Pearl Harbor. 180 minutes. DVD. Directed by Michael Bay. Walt Disney Studios Home Entertainment, 2007.

The Pianist. 150 minutes. DVD. Directed by Roman Polanski. Universal Studios Home Entertainment, 2003.

PT-109. 140 minutes. DVD. Directed by Leslie H. Martinson. Warner Home Video, 2011.

Raid on Rommel. 98 minutes. DVD. Directed by Henry Hathaway. Universal Studios Home Entertainment, 2011.

Reach for the Sky. 136 minutes. DVD. Directed by Lewis Gilbert. VCI Entertainment, 2011.

Redtails. 125 minutes. DVD. Directed by Anthony Hemingway. 20th Century Fox Home Entertainment, 2012.

Run Silent Run Deep. 93 minutes. DVD. Directed by Robert Wise. MGM Home Entertainment, 1999.

Sahara. 98 minutes. DVD. Directed by Zoltan Korda. Sony Pictures Home Entertainment, 2001.

The Sands of Iwo Jima. 108 minutes. DVD. Directed by Allan Dwan. Universal Pictures Home Entertainment, 2005.

Saving Private Ryan. 169 minutes. DVD. Directed by Steven Spielberg. DreamWorks Home Entertainment, 1999.

Schindler's List. 196 minutes. DVD. Directed by Steven Spielberg. Universal Pictures Home Entertainment, 2018.
Sink the Bismarck! 97 minutes. DVD. Directed by Lewis Gilbert. 20th Century Fox Home Entertainment, 2003.
Stalag 17. 120 minutes. DVD. Directed by Billy Wilder. Paramount Home Entertainment, 2006.
The Story of G. I. Joe. 108 minutes. DVD. Directed by William Wellman. Image Entertainment, 2000.
The Thin Red Line. 170 minutes. DVD. Directed by Terrence Malick. 20th Century Fox Home Entertainment, 2001.
36 Hours. 115 minutes. DVD. Directed by George Seaton. Warner Home Video, 2017.
To Hell and Back. 107 minutes. DVD. Directed by Jesse Hibbs. Universal Pictures Home Entertainment, 2004.
Tora! Tora! Tora! 144 minutes. DVD. Directed by Kinji Fukasaku, et al., 20th Century Fox Home Entertainment, 2006.
The Train. 133 minutes, DVD. Directed by John Frankenheimer. KL Studio Classics, 2015.
Twelve O'Clock High. 132 minutes. DVD. Directed by Henry King. 20th Century Fox Home Entertainment, 2001.
Up Periscope! 111 minutes. DVD. Directed by Gordon Douglas. Warner Home Video, 2006.
Valkyrie. 120 minutes. DVD. Directed by Bryan Singer. MGM Home Entertainment, 2009.
Von Ryan's Express. 117 minutes. DVD. Directed by Mark Robson. 20th Century Fox Home Entertainment, 2007.
War Time Comedies: Buck Privates. 84 minutes. DVD. Directed by Arthur Lubin. Universal Pictures Home Entertainment, 2015.
Where Eagles Dare. 155 minutes. DVD. Directed by Brian G. Hutton. Warner Home Video, 2010.
The Young Lions. 167 minutes. DVD. Directed by Edward Dmytryk. 20th Century Fox Home Entertainment, 2002.

TV PROGRAMS, TELEMOVIES, & MINISERIES

A Family at War. 2,563 minutes. (DVD: The Complete Series). Produced by Richard Doubleday. Acorn, 2006.

Baa Baa Black Sheep. 1,822 minutes. (DVD: The Complete Series). Produced by Stephen J. Cannell. Fabulous Films Limited, 2016.

Band of Brothers. 705 minutes. (DVD: The Complete Series). Produced by Steven Spielberg, et al. HBO Studios, 2014.

Colditz. 184 minutes. DVD. Produced by Justin Bodle, et al. Shout! Factory, 1984.

Combat! 7,269 minutes. (DVD: The Complete Series). Produced by Selig J. Seligman. Image Entertainment, 2013.

Conspiracy. 95 minutes. DVD. Produced by Nick Gillot and Frank Pierson. HBO Studios, 2005.

Danger UXB. 650 minutes. (DVD: The Complete Series). Produced by John Hawkesworth. A&E Home Video, 2012.

Escape From Sobibor. 119 minutes. DVD. Produced by Dennis Doty, et al. Alpha Video, 2008.

Foyle's War. 2,760 minutes. (DVD: The Complete Series). Produced by Jill Green, et al. Acorn, 2015.

The Gallant Men. 1,300 minutes. (DVD: The Complete Series). Produced by William T. Orr. Warner Home Video, 2012.

Gilligan's Island. 2,507 minutes. (DVD: Complete series). Produced by Sherwood Schwarz. Turner Home Entertainment, 2007.

Hogan's Heroes. 4,275 minutes. (DVD: The Complete Series). Produced by Edward H. Feldman. Paramount Home Media, 2016.

Holocaust. 475 minutes. DVD. Produced by Herbert Brodkin. Paramount Home Entertainment, 2008.

Home Fires. 720 minutes. DVD. Produced by Francis Hopkinson, et al. PBS, 2015.

Ike: Countdown to D-Day. 89 minutes. DVD. Produced by Dennis A. Brown. Columbia TriStar Home Entertainment, 2004.

The Last Days of Patton. 147 minutes. DVD. Produced by Alfred R. Kelman and William F. Storke. Gemstone Entertainment, 2001.

McHale's Navy. 3,660 minutes. (DVD: The Complete Series). Produced by Edward J. Montagne. Shout! Factory, 2018.

Mission of the Shark: The Saga of the USS Indianapolis. 93 minutes. DVD. Produced by Richard Maynard. 20th Century Fox Home Entertainment, 2014.

Mussolini: The Untold Story. 330 minutes, DVD. Produced by Bernard Sofronski. Arrow Video, 2020.

The Pacific. 530 minutes. (DVD: The Complete Series). Produced by Steven Spielberg, et al. HBO Studios, 2010.

Pearl. 278 minutes. DVD. Produced by Frank Konigsberg and Stirling Silliphant. Warner Home Video, 2011.

The Rat Patrol. 1,440 minutes. (DVD: The Complete Series). Produced by Jon Epstein, et al. Shout! Factory, 2017.

The Scarlet and the Black. 138 minutes. DVD. Produced by Bill McCutchen. Timeless Media, 2014.

The Tuskegee Airmen. 114 minutes. DVD. Produced by Frank Price and Robert Wayland Williams. HBO Studios, 2010.

The Twilight Zone. 4,475 minutes. (DVD: The Complete Series). Produced by Rod Serling. Paramount Home Entertainment, 2020.

War and Remembrance. 1,338 minutes. (DVD: The Complete Series). Produced by Dan Curtis. Fabulous Film Limited, 2016.

When Trumpets Fade. DVD. Produced by David R. Ginsburg et al. HBO Studios, 2006.

The Winds of War. 879 minutes. (DVD: The Complete Series). Produced by Dan Curtis. Paramount Home Entertainment, 2004.

WEB ARTICLES

Apple, Dr. Carolyn. World War II: "America's Heavy Hitter-The B-17 Flying Fortress." Delaware Historical and Cultural Affairs. https://history.delaware.com/world-war-ii-americas-heavy-hitter-the-b-17-flying-fortress.

Bennhold, Katrin. "80 Years Ago the Nazis Planned the 'Final Solution.' It Took 90 Minutes." *The New York Times.* January 20, 2022, https://www.nytimes.com/2022/01/20/world/europe/lake-wanssee-conference-final-solution-holocaust.

Bernstein, Marc D. "Joseph Stilwell's Escape From Burma During World

War II." HistoryNet. June 12, 2006, https://www.historynet.com/joseph-stilwell-escape-from-burma-during-world-war-ii.

Bianculli, David. "In Many Ways, Author Says, Spanish Civil War Was 'The First Battle of WWII.'" NPR. March 10, 2017, https://www.npr.org/2017/03/10/519462137/in-many-ways-author-says-spanish-civil-war-was-the-first-battle-of-wwii.

Blakemore Erin. "A Ship of Jewish Refugees Was Refused US Landing in 1939. This Was Their Fate." History.com. June 4, 2019, https://www.history.com/news/wwii-jewish-refugee-ship-st-louis-1939.

Burchfield, Will. "Go Inside A C-47 Skytrain, The Plane That Helped Win WWII." CBS Video. May 25, 2017, https://www.cbsnews.com/detroit/news/go-inside-a-c-47-skytrain-the-plane-that-helped-win-wwii-videos.

Bush, President George W. "President Bush, President Chirac Mark 60th Anniversary of D-Day." White House Press Office. June 6, 2004, https://georgewbush-whitehouse.archives.gov/news/releases/2004/06/20040606.html.

Canaris, Wilhelm. "Wilhelm Canaris (1887-1945)." Jewish Virtual Library. https://jewishvirtualLibrary.org.

Chen, C. Peter. "Robert Taft." World War II Database. February 2008, https://ww2db.com/person_bio.php?person_id=442.

Cox, Hank H. "Meet John C. H. Lee: The Forgotten Logistical Mastermind Behind the Allied Invasion of France," Military History Now. April 26, 2018, https://militaryhistorynow.com/2018/04/26/meet-john-c-h-lee-the-forgotten-logistical-mastermind-behind-the-allied-invasion-of-europe.

Dunlap, J.D., Charlie. "Thinking About President Roosevelt's Prayer on D-Day, June 6, 1944." Lawfire. June 6, 2022, https://sites.duke.edu/lawfire/2022/06/06/thinking-about-president-roosevelts-prayer-on-d-day-june-6-1944.

Fujiwara, Chris. "*The Cranes Are Flying: A Free Camera*." The Criterion Collection. March 27, 2020, https://www.criterion.com/current/posts/200-the-cranes-are-flying-a-free-camera.

Gavin, General James M. "The Jump Into Sicily." *American Heritage*. April/May 1978, https://www.americanheritage.com/jump-sicily.

Grossman, James. "AHA Today: James Baldwin on History." *Perspectives on History*.

August 3, 2016, https://www.historians.org/research-and-publications/perspectives-on-history/summer-2016/james-baldwin-on-history.

Hallion, Richard P. "Airpower From the Ground Up." *Air and Space Forces Magazine.* November 1, 2000, https://www.airandspaceforces.com/article/1100airpower.

Harmon, Christopher C. "Alanbrooke and Churchill: Finest." International Churchill Society. Autumn 2001, https://winstonchurchill.org/publications/finest-hour/finest-hour-112/alanbrooke-and-churchill.

Hollkamp, Nick. "8 Things to Know About the Battle of the Bulge on Its 75th Anniversary." *Louisville Courier Journal.* December 16, 2019, https://www.courier-journal.com/story/news/history/2019/12/16/battle-bulge-8-things-know-the-greatest-american-battle-wwii/4311758002.

Inouye, Senator Daniel K. "Quotes." Daniel K. Inouye Institute. June 26, 2023, https//dkii.org/quotes.

Kinkead, Eugene. "The Pilot Who Dropped the Atomic Bomb on Hiroshima." *The New Yorker.* December 28, 1945, https://www.newyorker.com/magazine/1946/01/05/usher.

Lehrman, Robert. "Rhetoric Revisited: FDR's 'Infamy' Speech." American Experience. December 6, 2016, https://www.pbs.org/wgbh/americanexperience/features/rhetoric-revisited-fdrs-infamy-speech.

Ley, Robert, ed. "Modern History Sourcebook: The 25 Points 1920: An Early Nazi Program." https://sourcebooks.fordham.edu/mod/25points.asp.

MacArthur, Douglas. "General Douglas MacArthur: Opening and Closing Statements at the Japanese Surrender Ceremony." American Rhetoric. September 2, 1945, https://www.american rhetoric.com/speeches/douglasmacarthurussmissourispeech.htm.

McFarlin, Commander Robert. "Hit Hard, Hit Fast, Hit Often!" *Proceedings.* July 2021, https://www.usni.org/magazines/proceedings/2021/july/hit-hard-hit-fast-hit-often.

McManus, John C. "The Man Who Took Omaha Beach." *Politico Magazine.* June 5, 2014, https://politico.com/magazine/story/2014/06/the-man-who-took-omaha-beach-107509.

Metesh, T. Logan. "Patton & the Garand: 'Greatest Battle Implement Ever

Devised.'" *The Armory Life.* December 28, 2020, https://www.thearmorylife.com/patton-and-the-garand-greatest-battle-implement-ever-devised.

Nash, Mark. "WW2 British Funnies: Churchill Crocodile, A22F." May 12, 2017, https//www.tanks-encyclopedia.com/ww2/gb/churchill-crocodile.

Norris, John. "Harold Raynesford Stark." Pennsylvania Center for the Book. Summer 2008, https://pabook.libraries.psu.edu/literary-cultural-heritage-map-pa/bios/Stark_Harold.

Nye, Logan. "11 of the Craziest Lines Ever Spoken In Battle." *We Are The Mighty*. January 5, 2022, https://www.wearethemighty.com/popular/11-of-the-craziest-lines-ever-spoken-battle.

Obama, President Barack. "Remarks by President Obama at the 70th Anniversary of D-Day-Omaha Beach, Normandy." White House Press Office. June 6, 2014, https://obamawhitehouse.Archives.gov/the-press-office/2014/06/06/remarks-president-obama-70th-anniversary-d-day-omaha-beach-normandy.

Pollock, B.J. "'Air Raid Pearl Harbor! This is No Drill!'" *Fort Bend Herald.* December 5, 2003, https://www.fbherald.com/air-raid-pearl-harbor-this-is-no-drill.

Polston, Mike. "Brehon Burke Somervell (1895-1955)." *Encyclopedia of Arkansas.* February 28, 2022, https://encyclopediaofarkansas.net/entries/brehon-burke-somervell-2817.

Pyle, Ernie. "Reporting America at War: Ernie Pyle: The Death of Captain Waskow." PBS. 2003, https://www.pbs.org/weta/reportingamericaatwar/reporters/pyle/waskow.html.

Reagan, President Ronald. "The History Place: Great Speeches Collection: Ronald Reagan on the 40th Anniversary of D-Day." The History Place. June 6, 1984, https://www.historyplace.com/speeches/reagan-d-day.htm.

Salmon, Ryleigh. "How the Jeep Was Invented for World War II." February 11, 2021, https://www.landerscountry.com/how-the-jeep-was-invented-for-world-war-ii.

Sanders, Katie, and Mara Storey. "Andrew Higgins Designed Landing Boats That Eisenhower Said Won the War." *Business Insider*. March 19, 2023, https://www.businessinsider.com/andrew-higgins-designed-landing-boatsthst-eisenhower-said-won-the-wwii-2023-3.

Sheppard, Thomas. "'I Have No Expectation of Success': The War in the Pacific Before and After Midway." *Providence Magazine.* August 29, 2017, https://

providencemag.com/2017/08/i-have-no-expectation-of-success-the-war-in-the-pacific-after-midway.

Simkin, John. "Alan Brooke, Baron Alanbrooke of Brookeborough." Spartacus Educational. April 2022, https://spartacus-educational.com/2WWbrookeA.htm.

Slawson, Larry. "Claus von Stauffenberg's Plot to Kill Adolf Hitler." Owlocation. January 2, 2023, https://owlocation.com/humanities/Claus-von-Stauffenberg-The-Plot-to-Kill-Adolf-Hitler.

Treon, Petty Officer Rachel A. "Marine Corps Commemorates 75th Anniversary of Iwo Jima." USMC. February 19, 2020, https://www.marines.mil/News/NewsDisplay/Article/2088180/marine-corps-commemorates-75th-anniversary-of-iwo-jima.

Trueman, C.N. "General Percy Hobart." The History Learning Site. April 21, 2015, https://www.history/learningsite.co.uk/world-war-two-in-western-europe/d-day-index/general-percy-hobart.

Valle, Orvelin. "Patton Earned the Nickname 'Old Blood and Guts.'" *We Are the Mighty.* April 2, 2018, https://www.wearethemighty.com/articles/how-general-patton-earned-the-name-old-blood-and-guts.

Vandenberg, Senator Arthur H. "Classic Senate Speeches." US Senate. January 10, 1945, https://www.senate.gov/artandhistory/history/common/generic/Speeches_Vandenberg.htm.

Venhuizen, Harm. "Hitler Released His Failed Plan to Invade England 80 Years Ago Today." *Army Times.* July 16, 2020, https://www.armytimes.com/veterans/military-history/2020/07/16/hitler-released-his-failed-plan-to-invade-england-80-years-ago-today.

Waxman, Olivia B. "How the Battle of the Bulge Got Its Name." *Time.* December 16, 2019, https://time.com/5748498/battle-of-the-bulge-history.

Wolk, Herman S. "Decision at Casablanca." *Air & Space Forces Magazine.* January 1, 2003, https://www.airandspaceforces.com/article/0103casa.

WEBSITES

IMDB (Internet Movie Database), https://www.imdb.com.

About The Author

William E. Scott, an award-winning educator who earned his BA in American History from West Chester University and graduate degrees from Villanova University and American Military University, is the author of *November 22, 1963: A Reference Guide to the JFK Assassination*, and *The Kennedy Assassination: The Ultimate Quiz Book*, which renowned forensic pathologist Dr. Cyril Wecht called "intellectually stimulating and informative." He currently resides in Springfield, Pennsylvania with his wife, Diane.

www.ingramcontent.com/pod-product-compliance
Lightning Source LLC
Chambersburg PA
CBHW050735010526
44107CB00010B/855